Tactics for TOEIC®
Speaking and Writing Tests

Grant Trew

Contents

IIBC

OXFORD
UNIVERSITY PRESS

Introduction

The TOEIC® Test

The TOEIC® (Test of English for International Communication) test is an English language proficiency test for non-native speakers of English. It measures the everyday English listening and reading skills of people working in an international environment. More than 5,000 corporations and institutions in over 60 countries use the TOEIC test, with nearly 5 million people registering to take it each year.

The TOEIC® test has recently been redesigned, with some question types remaining the same and some replaced with authentic tasks that test a broader range of sub-skills. The score scale and the range of difficulty tested have not changed, so scores on both forms of the test are comparable. The redesigned test provides useful information for test users and test takers, allowing them to make informed decisions regarding job recruitment, placement, promotion, and further training.

The TOEIC® Speaking and Writing Tests

Developed in response to market demand for reliable assessments of productive English language skills, the TOEIC® Speaking and Writing components are Internet-delivered tests that complement the TOEIC Listening and Reading test sections. The TOEIC Speaking and Writing tests are designed to measure the test-taker's ability to communicate clearly in spoken and written English with tasks that are set in general and workplace contexts.

Both the TOEIC Speaking and Writing tests are made up of a number of tasks that provide evidence of test-taker performance across a broad range of proficiency. Responses to the tasks are scored online by trained and calibrated human raters using task-specific scoring guides. Scores on different tasks are weighted according to their level of difficulty, and the total score on each test is converted to a scaled score. Descriptions of the skills typical of test takers at different points on the score range provide test users and test takers with information that can help them make well-informed decisions.

TOEIC® Test Preparation

English learners who are preparing to take any of the TOEIC® test components (Listening and Reading; Speaking, or Writing) generally do best when they are very familiar with the test format. A thorough understanding of test directions and task requirements allows the test taker to focus fully on demonstrating his or her language proficiency. Because TOEIC tests are proficiency tests that assess a wide range of language, test takers who have become familiar with the TOEIC test format should concentrate on improving their overall language skills.

This book is designed to help you prepare for the TOEIC® Speaking and Writing tests.

Tactics for TOEIC® Speaking and Writing Tests

About this course

The course was designed to help you develop the test-taking and linguistic skills that you will need to do well on the TOEIC Speaking and Writing tests. It is endorsed by ETS (Educational Testing Service) and contains authentic ETS test questions and examiner comments.

Sample Speaking and Writing Tests
In both the Speaking and Writing sections of the course, there is a sample test with official questions provided by the developers of the TOEIC Speaking and Writing tests. You can see just how the test questions or tasks will be presented on the computer screen when you take the actual test.

Authentic sample responses to test tasks
Along with the sample tests, there are authentic student responses for each score level of each test task, with sample Speaking test and responses included on audio CD.

Examiner's comments on sample responses
Authentic responses to sample test tasks are accompanied by scores, examiners' comments and scoring guidelines for each question.

Scoring information
Useful information on how to interpret test scores is included in both the Speaking and Writing sections of the book.

Test-taking strategies
Each unit of the book provides information and strategies that will help you to maximize your success when you take the test. You will become very familiar with test directions and test tasks. Tips on how to manage your time will help you to demonstrate your proficiency efficiently and effectively.

Strategies for improving language proficiency
Each unit includes a variety of strategies to build and reinforce your natural use of English and to improve your overall language proficiency in the skill areas tested.

How the book is organized

The book is divided into two sections, the first section focusing on preparation for the TOEIC Speaking Test and the second section on the TOEIC Writing Test. The complete course includes 20 units with each unit covering one part of one test. In a cyclical approach to test preparation, each part is covered at least twice in the book.

Every unit follows a consistent and easy-to-follow format. The main focus of each unit, and the key test-taking and linguistic skills developed in the unit, are shown below.

A. Focus
This part of each unit features a number of "test tips" that provide important information about the test along with advice on how to use the tips. The key points fall into two areas:

1. **Language building** – This includes a variety of different tasks aimed at building vocabulary and grammatical knowledge relevant to specific parts of the test and to the test as a whole.
2. **Test tactics** – These activities give immediate practice and reinforcement of test-taking skills such as time management and help you to approach test tasks effectively and efficiently.

B. Tactic practice
This part of the unit aims to further contextualize and reinforce the language building and/or test tactics points that have been introduced. Tactic practice activities feature tasks that follow the same format as those on the actual test.

C. Mini-test
The Mini-tests aim to give practice for each test part, with timings similar to those in the actual TOEIC Speaking and Writing tests. All the items in the Mini-tests are official TOEIC Speaking and Writing Test items.

Using natural English
This feature appears just before the Mini-tests in each unit of the speaking section and focuses on the development of native-like intonation, stress, and patterns of connected speech – features that give English its rhythmic characteristics and contribute significantly to perceived fluency.

Word list and accompanying quizzes
Building an extensive vocabulary is a key way to improve your communication skills. To help you accomplish this, the most challenging vocabulary from each unit is listed, defined and exemplified at the back of the book. These words are organized by unit to allow for easy after-class review, or they may be studied in advance to prepare for a lesson. To help ensure that these words are understood and remembered, the word list for each unit includes quiz exercises for students to test themselves.

Key and tapescripts
The Key and tapescripts for Units 1–20 are in a separate booklet at the back of the Student's Book.

How to approach the course

The teacher or test taker using this book can choose to work through each unit from the beginning or tailor the material to suit individual needs. The text was specifically written to suit a variety of course lengths and styles.

Approach 1: Fixed courses
For fixed courses of 30 to 40 hours, Units 1–20 can all be covered in the order presented.

Approach 2: Shorter/Non-fixed courses
Courses may be custom-designed for shorter/non-fixed study durations, or ones which aim to only target a specific test or specific test part.

Those wishing to prepare for only one of the tests can turn directly to the appropriate section of the book.

To isolate specific test parts you can use the quick find design feature on the side of each page.

unit
1

Speaking Test

The TOEIC Speaking Test: An Overview

The TOEIC Speaking Test is designed to measure the ability to communicate in spoken English in the context of the international workplace. The test is composed of eleven tasks and takes approximately twenty minutes to complete. The range of ability among English learners who will take the TOEIC Speaking Test is expected to be broad; that is, both very capable speakers and speakers of limited ability can take the test. The test is designed to provide information about the language ability of speakers across a range of language proficiency levels. To this end, the tasks are organized to support the following three claims:

1. *The test taker can generate language intelligible to native and proficient non-native English speakers.*
2. *The test taker can select appropriate language to carry out routine social and occupational interactions (such as giving and receiving directions, asking for and giving information, asking for and giving clarification, making purchases, greetings and introductions, etc.)*
3. *The test taker can create connected, sustained discourse appropriate to the typical workplace.*

These claims are meant to be hierarchical. A test taker who can successfully complete the tasks that support the third claim will probably be very successful at carrying out the tasks that support the first and second claims. Conversely, the tasks that support the third claim will distinguish between moderately high-level speakers and very high-level speakers.

The following chart shows how the tasks in the TOEIC Speaking Test are organized:

Question	Task	Evaluation Criteria
1–2	Read a text aloud	• pronunciation • intonation and stress
3	Describe a picture	all of the above, plus • grammar • vocabulary • cohesion
4–6	Respond to questions	all of the above, plus • relevance of content • completeness of content
7–9	Respond to questions using information provided	all of the above
10	Propose a solution	all of the above
11	Express an opinion	all of the above

How to Improve Your Score on the TOEIC Speaking Test

The TOEIC Speaking Test features a variety of timed tasks appropriate for test takers across a broad range of proficiency. There are several areas on which you can focus in order to improve your performance on this test.

Key test-taking strategies

- Familiarity with the test format, instructions and question types – Although all the instructions are printed at the start of each test part, knowing these beforehand will save you time and energy on the day of the test.
- Time management – The tasks in the Speaking Test are timed. Understanding how much time you have to complete each of the various tasks and maintaining an appropriate pace as you prepare and produce your responses will help you to improve your overall performance.

Linguistic skills

- Phonological skills – Your pronunciation, intonation, and stress will be directly evaluated in the Speaking Test. Developing these areas will improve your ability to score well on the test and will make your speech more comprehensible in everyday conversation.
- Grammar knowledge – The Speaking Test will require you to speak in longer sentences and to produce paragraph-length speech. An understanding of grammatical form, meaning, and use will help you express yourself clearly. Maintaining a consistent level of accuracy will improve your overall performance on the Speaking Test and will also help you communicate in everyday situations.
- Knowledge of key vocabulary and useful phrases – Vocabulary, both in single words and in phrases, is a key area contributing to scores in each part of the test. This course provides a selection of high-frequency vocabulary and phrases that are appropriate to the tasks in the test.
- Listening comprehension skills – Some tasks in the Speaking Test will require you to listen and respond appropriately. Good listening comprehension skills are important in completing these tasks successfully.
- Understanding of organizational conventions – Some of the language tasks in the Speaking Test, such as responding to a voice mail or giving an opinion, can be more easily completed if you can follow standardized organizational patterns in English. An understanding of the ways ideas are organized, and of the words and phrases that are often used to join ideas together, will also help you to be understood in English in the real world.

TOEIC Speaking Claims

The tasks in the TOEIC Speaking Test are designed to capture evidence of a test taker's speaking abilities as defined in the TOEIC Speaking Claims.

General Claim: The test taker can communicate in spoken English to function effectively in an international workplace context.

Claims and specific tasks

Claim 1: The test taker can generate language intelligible to native and proficient non-native English speakers.

This claim is supported by two tasks:

Questions 1–2: Read a text aloud

The test taker reads aloud two short passages. The passages are texts that would naturally be spoken aloud in a real-world context; e.g., an announcement or advertisement

> **For this task, the test taker will be measured on these criteria:**
> *Pronunciation*
> *Intonation and stress*

Question 3: Describe a picture

The test taker describes a photograph. The subjects of the photograph are people involved in a familiar activity.

> **For this task, the test taker will receive an overall score based on these criteria:**
> *Pronunciation*
> *Intonation and stress*
> *Grammar*
> *Vocabulary*
> *Cohesion*

Claim 2: The test taker can select appropriate language to carry out routine social and occupational interactions (such as giving and receiving directions, asking for information, asking for clarification, making purchases, greetings and introductions, etc.)

This claim is supported by two sets of tasks:

Questions 4–6: Respond to questions

The test taker is asked three questions about a topic.

> **For these tasks, the test taker will receive an overall score based on these criteria:**
> *Pronunciation*
> *Intonation and stress*
> *Grammar*
> *Vocabulary*
> *Cohesion*
> *Relevance of content*
> *Completeness of content*

Questions 7–9: Respond to questions using information provided

The test taker responds immediately to three questions about a written agenda.

For these tasks, the test taker will receive an overall score based on these criteria:
Pronunciation
Intonation and stress
Grammar
Vocabulary
Cohesion
Relevance of content
Completeness of content

Claim 3: The test taker can create connected, sustained discourse appropriate to the typical workplace.

This claim is supported by two tasks:

Question 10: Propose a solution

The test taker responds to a voice mail message.

For this task, the test taker will receive an overall score based on these criteria:
Pronunciation
Intonation and stress
Grammar
Vocabulary
Cohesion
Relevance of content
Completeness of content

Question 11: Express an opinion

The test taker states a personal opinion or position on an issue and gives reasons or examples for the opinion.

For this task, the test taker will receive an overall score based on these criteria:
Pronunciation
Intonation and stress
Grammar
Vocabulary
Cohesion
Relevance of content
Completeness of content

TOEIC® Pre-test Screens

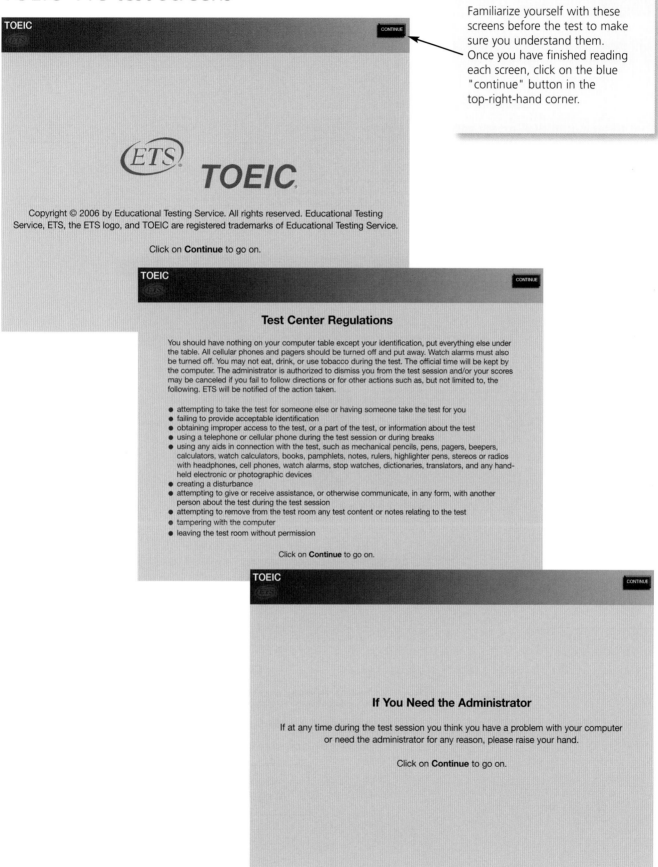

Familiarize yourself with these screens before the test to make sure you understand them. Once you have finished reading each screen, click on the blue "continue" button in the top-right-hand corner.

TOEIC   CONTINUE

TOEIC

Copyright © 2006 by Educational Testing Service. All rights reserved. Educational Testing Service, ETS, the ETS logo, and TOEIC are registered trademarks of Educational Testing Service.

Click on **Continue** to go on.

TOEIC   CONTINUE

Test Center Regulations

You should have nothing on your computer table except your identification, put everything else under the table. All cellular phones and pagers should be turned off and put away. Watch alarms must also be turned off. You may not eat, drink, or use tobacco during the test. The official time will be kept by the computer. The administrator is authorized to dismiss you from the test session and/or your scores may be canceled if you fail to follow directions or for other actions such as, but not limited to, the following. ETS will be notified of the action taken.

- attempting to take the test for someone else or having someone take the test for you
- failing to provide acceptable identification
- obtaining improper access to the test, or a part of the test, or information about the test
- using a telephone or cellular phone during the test session or during breaks
- using any aids in connection with the test, such as mechanical pencils, pens, pagers, beepers, calculators, watch calculators, books, pamphlets, notes, rulers, highlighter pens, stereos or radios with headphones, cell phones, watch alarms, stop watches, dictionaries, translators, and any hand-held electronic or photographic devices
- creating a disturbance
- attempting to give or receive assistance, or otherwise communicate, in any form, with another person about the test during the test session
- attempting to remove from the test room any test content or notes relating to the test
- tampering with the computer
- leaving the test room without permission

Click on **Continue** to go on.

TOEIC   CONTINUE

If You Need the Administrator

If at any time during the test session you think you have a problem with your computer or need the administrator for any reason, please raise your hand.

Click on **Continue** to go on.

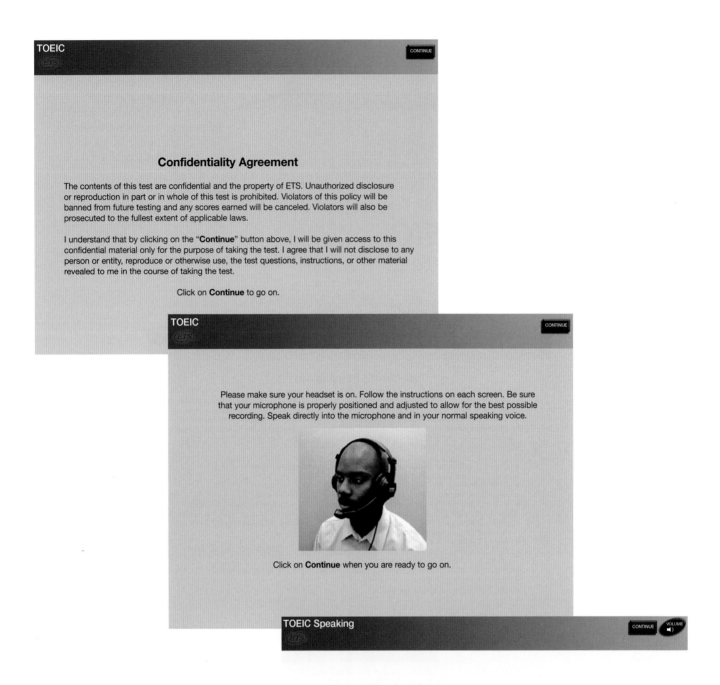

Confidentiality Agreement

The contents of this test are confidential and the property of ETS. Unauthorized disclosure or reproduction in part or in whole of this test is prohibited. Violators of this policy will be banned from future testing and any scores earned will be canceled. Violators will also be prosecuted to the fullest extent of applicable laws.

I understand that by clicking on the "**Continue**" button above, I will be given access to this confidential material only for the purpose of taking the test. I agree that I will not disclose to any person or entity, reproduce or otherwise use, the test questions, instructions, or other material revealed to me in the course of taking the test.

Click on **Continue** to go on.

Please make sure your headset is on. Follow the instructions on each screen. Be sure that your microphone is properly positioned and adjusted to allow for the best possible recording. Speak directly into the microphone and in your normal speaking voice.

Click on **Continue** when you are ready to go on.

Changing the Volume

To change the **volume**, click on the Volume icon at the top of the screen. The volume control will appear. Move the volume indicator to the left or to the right to change the volume.

To close the volume control, click on the volume icon again.

You will be able to change the volume during the test if you need to.

> *You may now change the volume.*
> *When you are finished, click on Continue.*

Adjusting the Microphone

In order to adjust your **microphone volume**, please answer the practice question below, using your normal tone and volume. The microphone volume will be automatically adjusted as you speak.

Begin speaking after the beep. Continue speaking until a message appears.

"Describe the city you live in".

TOEIC Speaking

In order to adjust you... ...e question below, using your normal tor... ...tomatically adjusted as you speak.

Begin speaking after ...ears.

Success

Your microphone volume has been successfully adjusted.

Click on Continue to go on.

CONTINUE

TOEIC Speaking

In order to adjust you... ...e question below, using your normal tor... ...tomatically adjusted as you speak.

Begin speaking after ...ears.

Unsuccessful

The microphone check was unsuccessful.

Please raise your hand for assistance from the administrator.

TRY AGAIN   STOP TEST

Sample TOEIC® Speaking Test

TOEIC Speaking Test Directions

Speaking Test Directions

This is the TOEIC Speaking Test. This test includes eleven questions that measure different aspects of your speaking ability. The test lasts approximately 20 minutes.

Question	Task	Evaluation Criteria
1–2	Read a text aloud	• pronunciation • intonation and stress
3	Describe a picture	all of the above, plus • grammar • vocabulary • cohesion
4–6	Respond to questions	all of the above, plus • relevance of content • completeness of content
7–9	Respond to questions using information provided	all of the above
10	Propose a solution	all of the above
11	Express an opinion	all of the above

For each type of question, you will be given specific directions, including the time allowed for preparation and speaking.

It is to your advantage to say as much as you can in the time allowed. It is also important that you speak clearly and that you answer each question according to the directions.

Click on **Continue** to go on.

Question 1: Read a text aloud

Questions 1–2: Read a text aloud

Directions: In this part of the test, you will read aloud the text on the screen. You will have 45 seconds to prepare. Then you will have 45 seconds to read the text aloud.

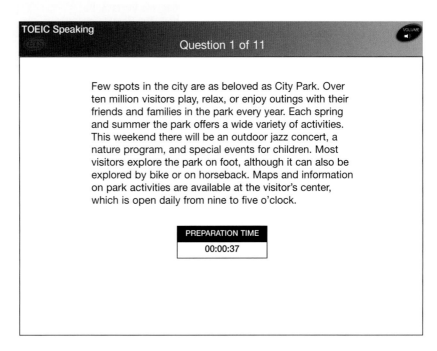

Few spots in the city are as beloved as City Park. Over ten million visitors play, relax, or enjoy outings with their friends and families in the park every year. Each spring and summer the park offers a wide variety of activities. This weekend there will be an outdoor jazz concert, a nature program, and special events for children. Most visitors explore the park on foot, although it can also be explored by bike or on horseback. Maps and information on park activities are available at the visitor's center, which is open daily from nine to five o'clock.

PREPARATION TIME
00:00:37

🎧 Listen to Speaker 1–3 responses.

Pronunciation

	Score	Examiner's comments
Speaker 1	03	The speaker's pronunciation is always intelligible. The speaker delivers the passage fluently.
Speaker 2	02	Pronunciation is generally intelligible, with some lapses ("park", "visitors").
Speaker 3	01	The speaker's pronunciation is often unintelligible.

Intonation & Stress

	Score	Examiner's comments
Speaker 1	03	The speaker's use of emphases, pauses, and rising and falling pitch is appropriate to the text.
Speaker 2	03	The speaker's intonation and stress are appropriate to the text.
Speaker 3	02	The speaker's use of emphases, pauses, and rising and falling pitch is generally appropriate; the response includes other language influence.

Question 2: Read a text aloud

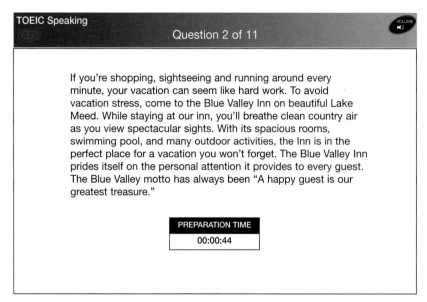

If you're shopping, sightseeing and running around every minute, your vacation can seem like hard work. To avoid vacation stress, come to the Blue Valley Inn on beautiful Lake Meed. While staying at our inn, you'll breathe clean country air as you view spectacular sights. With its spacious rooms, swimming pool, and many outdoor activities, the Inn is in the perfect place for a vacation you won't forget. The Blue Valley Inn prides itself on the personal attention it provides to every guest. The Blue Valley motto has always been "A happy guest is our greatest treasure."

PREPARATION TIME
00:00:44

🎧 Listen to Speaker 1–3 responses.

Pronunciation

	Score	Examiner's comments
Speaker 1	03	Although she makes occasional phonemic errors, the speaker can be understood without listener effort.
Speaker 2	02	The speaker's pronunciation is uneven with some self-correction and inaccuracy that impedes comprehension, so that listener effort is required.
Speaker 3	01	After the first sentence, which is quite comprehensible, pronunciation deteriorates and only occasional words can be easily understood.

Intonation & Stress

	Score	Examiner's comments
Speaker 1	03	The speaker's stress and intonation create an accurate oral interpretation of the text.
Speaker 2	03	The speaker's stress and intonation are appropriate at times, but delivery is often flat and rhythm is choppy.
Speaker 3	01	The speaker stumbles over self-correction and multi-syllabic words and while he tries to maintain a breathless pace, his innacurate stress and flat delivery impede comprehension.

Questions 1–2: Read a text aloud
Analytical Scoring Guidelines

Intonation & Stress

3 Speaker's use of emphases, pauses, and rising and falling pitch is appropriate to the text.

2 Speaker's use of emphases, pauses, and rising and falling pitch is generally appropriate to the text, though the response includes some lapses and/or moderate other language influence.

1 Speaker's use of emphases, pauses, and rising and falling pitch is not appropriate and the response includes significant other language influence.

0 No response OR response is completely unconnected to the stimulus.

Pronunciation

3 Pronunciation is highly intelligible, though the response may include minor lapses and/or other language influence.

2 Pronunciation is generally intelligible, though it includes some lapses and/or other language influence.

1 Pronunciation may be intelligible at times, but significant other language influence interferes with appropriate delivery of the text.

0 No response OR response is completely unconnected to the stimulus.

Question 3: Describe a picture

Question 3: Describe a picture

Directions: In this part of the test, you will describe the picture on your screen in as much detail as you can. You will have 30 seconds to prepare your response. Then you will have 45 seconds to speak about the picture.

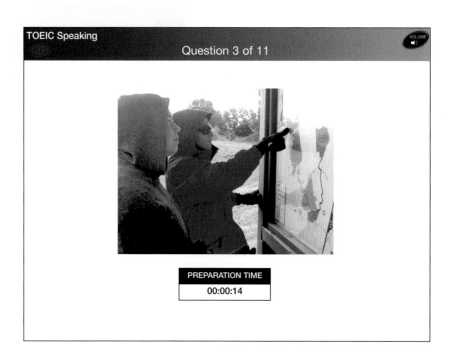

🎧 Listen to Speaker 1 response.

	Score	Examiner's comments
Speaker 1	02	Some listener effort is required. The use of structures occasionally interferes with overall comprehensibility.

Question 3: Describe a picture Scoring Guidelines

3   The response is relevant to the picture and includes appropriate details.

- Speaker's delivery is almost always smooth and consistent with almost no listener effort required.

- Speaker's vocabulary is accurate and relevant to the picture.

- Speaker's use of structures allows coherent expression of ideas.

2   The response is relevant to the picture, but may leave out important content or may dwell on minor details.

- Speaker's delivery is generally smooth, but some listener effort is required.

- Speaker's vocabulary may be limited or inaccurate at times.

- Speaker's use of structures may be limited and may interfere with overall comprehensibility.

1   The response may be connected to the picture, but ideas conveyed are severely limited.

- Speaker's delivery is marked by long pauses and frequent hesitations and requires significant listener effort.

- Speaker's choice of vocabulary may interfere with meaning and word choice may be highly repetitive.

- Speaker's use of structures significantly interferes with comprehensibility.

0   No response OR response is completely unconnected to the stimulus.

Question 4: Respond to questions

Questions 4–6: Respond to questions

Directions: In this part of the test, you will answer three questions. For each question, begin responding immediately after you hear a beep. No preparation time is provided. You will have 15 seconds to respond to Questions 4 and 5 and 30 seconds to respond to Question 6.

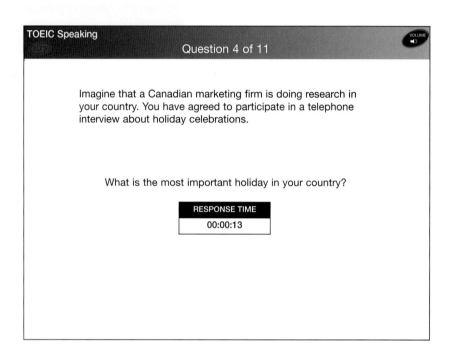

🎧 Listen to Speaker 1–3 responses.

	Score	Examiner's comments
Speaker 1	03	The delivery is almost always smooth and consistent. The speaker's use of grammar fulfills the demands of the task.
Speaker 2	02	The content is relevant but significant listening effort is required.
Speaker 3	01	The response is largely unintelligible.

Question 5: Respond to questions

Imagine that a Canadian marketing firm is doing research in your country. You have agreed to participate in a telephone interview about holiday celebrations.

Why do you think this holiday is so important?

RESPONSE TIME
00:00:13

🎧 Listen to Speaker 1–2 responses.

	Score	Examiner's comments
Speaker 1	03	Very smooth delivery and complete content. Word choice is accurate. Control of grammar fulfills the demands of the task.
Speaker 2	02	Delivery is smooth, but content is very limited, and the use of grammar requires some interpretation.

Question 6: Respond to questions

TOEIC Speaking

Imagine that a Canadian marketing firm is doing research in your country. You have agreed to participate in a telephone interview about holiday celebrations.

How do people in your country celebrate this holiday?

RESPONSE TIME
00:00:29

Listen to Speaker 1–3 responses.

	Score	Examiner's comments
Speaker 1	03	The delivery is almost always smooth and consistent. Control of grammar is good though there are minor errors.
Speaker 2	02	The delivery is not smooth. Use of structure requires some listener effort for interpretation.
Speaker 3	01	Grammar and content very limited and weak. One sentence is repeated. The delivery is halting.

Questions 4–6: Respond to questions
Scoring Guidelines

3   Response addresses the task appropriately.

- Speaker's delivery is almost always smooth and consistent with almost no listener effort required.

- Speaker's vocabulary is appropriate to the question and word choice is accurate.

- Speaker's use of structures fulfills the demands of the task.

2   Response connected to the task, though meaning may be obscured at times.

- Speaker's delivery requires some listener effort, but is generally intelligible.

- Speaker's vocabulary may be limited or somewhat inaccurate, although overall meaning is clear.

- Speaker's use of structures requires some listener effort for interpretation.

1   Response does not address the task appropriately.

- Speaker's delivery requires significant listener effort.

- Speaker's vocabulary is inaccurate, or relies on repetition of the prompt.

- Speaker's use of structures interferes with comprehensibility.

0   No response OR response is completely unconnected to the stimulus.

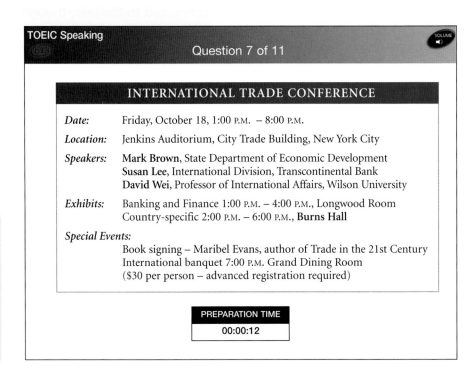

Questions 7–9: Respond to questions using information provided

Directions: In this part of the test, you will answer three questions based on the information provided. You will have 30 seconds to read the information before the questions begin. For each question, begin responding immediately after you hear a beep. No additional preparation time is provided. You will have 15 seconds to respond to Questions 7 and 8 and 30 seconds to respond to Question 9.

In the test, you only hear Questions 7–9. You will not be able to read them too.

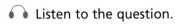 Listen to the question.

This is Carlos Gonzalez. I am planning to attend the International Trade Conference, but I've lost the original invitation, so I need some information.

When is the conference exactly?

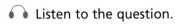 Listen to Speaker 1–4 responses.

	Score	Examiner's comments
Speaker 1	03	The delivery is smooth and consistent; information is relevant and accurate.
Speaker 2	03	The delivery is smooth and consistent; information is relevant and accurate.
Speaker 3	02	The delivery requires some listener effort but is generally intelligible. Information is incomplete.
Speaker 4	01	Significant hesitation in delivery renders the response incomplete.

Question 8: Respond to questions using information provided

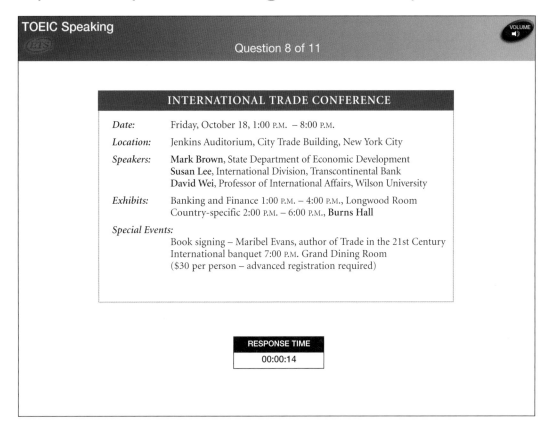

INTERNATIONAL TRADE CONFERENCE

Date: Friday, October 18, 1:00 P.M. – 8:00 P.M.

Location: Jenkins Auditorium, City Trade Building, New York City

Speakers: **Mark Brown**, State Department of Economic Development
Susan Lee, International Division, Transcontinental Bank
David Wei, Professor of International Affairs, Wilson University

Exhibits: Banking and Finance 1:00 P.M. – 4:00 P.M., Longwood Room
Country-specific 2:00 P.M. – 6:00 P.M., **Burns Hall**

Special Events:
Book signing – Maribel Evans, author of Trade in the 21st Century
International banquet 7:00 P.M. Grand Dining Room
($30 per person – advanced registration required)

RESPONSE TIME
00:00:14

🎧 Listen to the question.

I don't know what the exhibits are or where they are. Can you help me?

🎧 Listen to Speaker 1–3 responses.

	Score	Examiner's comments
Speaker 1	03	The delivery is smooth and consistent. Content is thoroughly covered. Good control of grammar.
Speaker 2	02	The speaker's delivery requires some listener effort. Overall meaning is clear.
Speaker 3	01	Halting delivery requires significant listener effort. The task is not addressed appropriately.

Question 9: Respond to questions using information provided

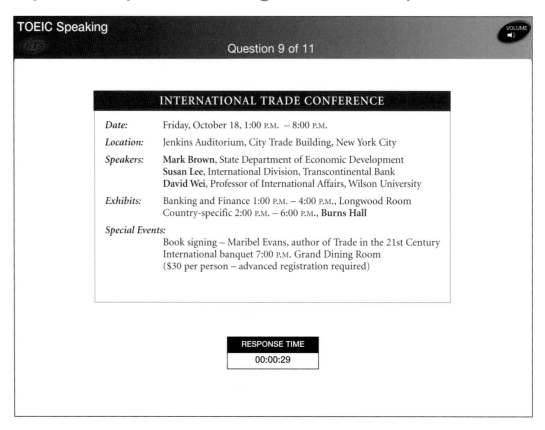

INTERNATIONAL TRADE CONFERENCE

Date: Friday, October 18, 1:00 P.M. – 8:00 P.M.

Location: Jenkins Auditorium, City Trade Building, New York City

Speakers: **Mark Brown**, State Department of Economic Development
Susan Lee, International Division, Transcontinental Bank
David Wei, Professor of International Affairs, Wilson University

Exhibits: Banking and Finance 1:00 P.M. – 4:00 P.M., Longwood Room
Country-specific 2:00 P.M. – 6:00 P.M., **Burns Hall**

Special Events:
Book signing – Maribel Evans, author of Trade in the 21st Century
International banquet 7:00 P.M. Grand Dining Room
($30 per person – advanced registration required)

RESPONSE TIME
00:00:29

🎧 Listen to the question.

Other than talks from the main speakers, what else is going on?

🎧 Listen to Speaker 1–3 responses.

	Score	Examiner's comments
Speaker 1	03	The delivery is smooth. Vocabulary used is appropriate and information given is relevant and thoroughly covered. Generally good control of grammar.
Speaker 2	02	Information is incomplete. Good delivery, but grammar is limited by fragmentary answer.
Speaker 3	01	The answer is given as a list, so control of grammar is not demonstrated. Information is ignored.

Questions 7–9: Respond to questions using information provided Scoring Guidelines

3   The response addresses the task appropriately and information from the schedule is accurate.

- Speaker's delivery is almost always smooth and consistent with almost no listener effort required.

- Speaker's vocabulary is appropriate to the question.

- Speaker's use of structures addresses the task.

2   The response is generally appropriate, though information from the schedule may be incomplete or inaccurate in part.

- Speaker's delivery may require some listener effort, but is generally intelligible.

- Speaker's vocabulary may be limited or somewhat inaccurate, although overall meaning is clear.

- Speaker's use of structures requires some listener effort for interpretation.

1   The response does not address the task appropriately. Information from the schedule is ignored or inaccurate.

- Speaker's delivery requires significant listener effort.

- Speaker's use of vocabulary is inaccurate, or relies on repetition of the prompt.

- Speaker's use of structures interferes with comprehensibility.

0   No response OR response is completely unconnected to the stimulus.

Question 10: Propose a solution

Question 10: Propose a solution

Directions: In this part of the test, you will be presented with a problem and asked to propose a solution.

You will have 30 seconds to prepare. Then you will have 60 seconds to speak.

In your response, be sure to

- show that you recognize the problem, and
- propose a way of dealing with the problem.

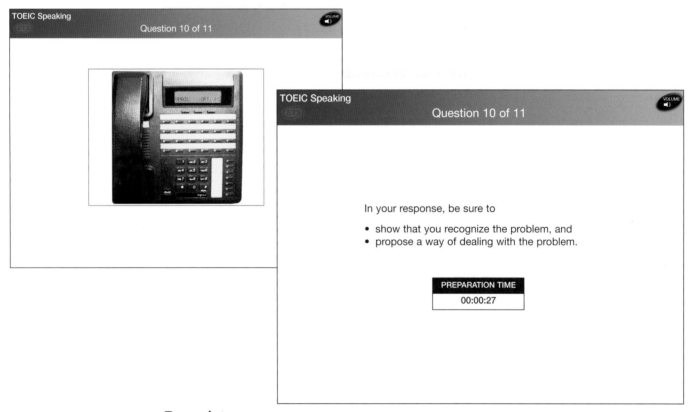

Transcript:

Hi, this is Marsha Syms. Um, I'm calling about my bank card. I went to the bank machine early this morning, you know – the ATM ... because the bank was closed so only the machine was open. Anyway, I put my card in the machine and got my money out ... but then my card didn't come out of the machine. I got my receipt and my money but then my bank card just didn't come out. And I'm leaving for my vacation tonight so I'm really going to need it. ... I had to get to work early this morning, and couldn't wait around for the bank to open ... . Could you call me here at work, and let me know how to get my bank card back? I'm really busy today, and really need you to call me soon. I can't go on vacation without my bank card. This is Marsha Syms at 555-1234. Thanks.

🎧 Listen to Speaker 1–6 responses.

	Score	Examiner's comments
Speaker 1	05	The speaker apologizes and promises to investigate and call back with an explanation; she also promises speedy delivery of a new bank card. Her progression of ideas is clear, the delivery is well paced, and she exhibits good control of grammatical structures.
Speaker 2	04	The speaker begins with a clear summary of the problem and tells what will be done about it. She begins to falter and hesitate as she proposes a solution. This lapse in expression of ideas affects overall fluency, but does not seriously interfere with the message.
Speaker 3	04	The response is sustained and provides information relevant to both tasks. It recognizes the problem and proposes a solution (the bank will recover the card from the machine and then telephone her, presumably to arrange delivery). It is intelligible, coherent, with fluidity of expression. There are some noticeable lapses in the expression of ideas, for example, in "we apologize for the inconvenient for the things" and in telling the caller her own name and number.
Speaker 4	03	Delivery is choppy, characterized by pauses, and restarts throughout. The speaker seems to have problems finding content as well as vocabulary to complete the task adequately.
Speaker 5	02	The response is very limited in content and is filled with long pauses. The three utterances are minimally connected to the task.
Speaker 6	01	The speaker makes two statements about the usefulness of an ATM machine, and attempts to restate the problem from the stimulus, including the phone number. Even though the speaker uses sentences, the response does not address the task.

Question 10: Propose a solution Scoring Guidelines

5   Response is effective and consists of highly intelligible, sustained, coherent discourse. Characterized by all of the following:

- Response presents a clear progression of ideas and conveys the relevant information required by the tasks. It includes appropriate detail, though it may have minor omissions.

- Speech is clear with generally well-paced flow and fluid expression. Response may include minor lapses or minor difficulties with pronunciation or intonation patterns which do not affect overall intelligibility.

- Response exhibits a fairly high degree of automaticity with good control of basic and complex structures (as appropriate). Some minor errors may be noticeable but do not obscure meaning.

- Use of vocabulary is accurate and precise.

4   Response addresses the prompt appropriately, but may fall short of being fully developed. It is generally intelligible and coherent, with some fluidity of expression though it exhibits some noticeable lapses in the expression of ideas.

- Response is sustained and conveys relevant information required by the tasks. However, it exhibits some incompleteness, inaccuracy or lack of specificity.

- Speech is generally clear with some fluidity of expression, though minor difficulties with pronunciation, intonation, or pacing may be noticeable and may require listener effort at times (though overall intelligibility is not significantly affected).

- Response demonstrates fairly automatic and effective use of grammar. Response may be somewhat limited in the range of structures used. This may affect overall fluency, but it does not seriously interfere with the communication of the message.

- Use of vocabulary is fairly effective. Some vocabulary may be inaccurate or imprecise.

3   Response attempts to address the prompt, but tasks or parts of tasks are neglected. It contains intelligible speech, although problems with delivery and/or overall coherence occur; meaning is obscured in places.

- Response conveys some relevant information, but is clearly incomplete or inaccurate.

- Speech is basically intelligible, though listener effort is needed because of unclear articulation, awkward intonation, or choppy rhythm/pace; meaning may be obscured in places.

- Response demonstrates limited control of grammar. These limitations often prevent full expression of ideas. For the most part, only basic sentence structures are used successfully and spoken with fluidity. Structures may express mainly simple (short) and/or general propositions, with simple or unclear connections made among them (listing, conjunction, juxtaposition).

- Response demonstrates a limited range of vocabulary.

2   Response is very limited in content and/or coherence or speech is largely unintelligible.

- Limited relevant content is expressed. May be inaccurate, vague, or repetitious. There is minimal or no audience awareness.

- Attempts at sentence-level speech are evident, but consistent pronunciation, stress, and intonation difficulties may cause considerable listener effort; delivery is fragmented, or telegraphic; there are long pauses and frequent hesitations.

- Some control of grammar at the sentence level may be evident, but expression of ideas and connections are severely limited. The response may rely heavily on practiced or formulaic expressions.

- Use of vocabulary is severely limited.

1   Response is a minimal reaction to the prompt or a misunderstanding of the prompt.

- Response may be completely unintelligible.

- Response may consist of isolated words or phrases, or mixtures of the first language and English.

- Response may show no awareness of the tasks in the prompt.

0   No response OR response is completely unconnected to the stimulus.

Question 11: Express an opinion

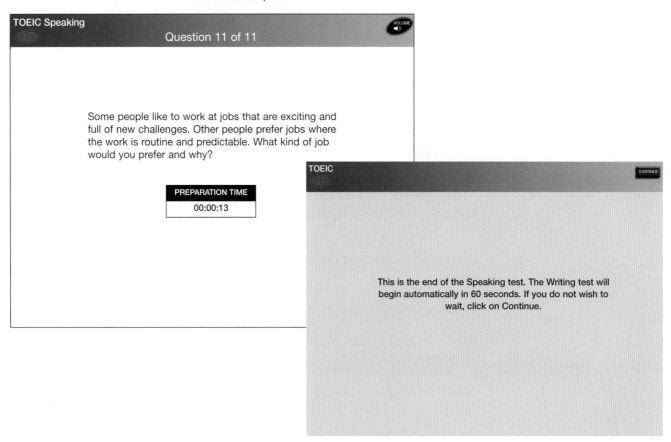

Question 11: Express an opinion

Directions: In this part of the test, you will give your opinion about a specific topic. Be sure to say as much as you can in the time allowed. You will have 15 seconds to prepare. Then you will have 60 seconds to speak.

TOEIC Speaking

Question 11 of 11

Some people like to work at jobs that are exciting and full of new challenges. Other people prefer jobs where the work is routine and predictable. What kind of job would you prefer and why?

PREPARATION TIME
00:00:13

TOEIC

This is the end of the Speaking test. The Writing test will begin automatically in 60 seconds. If you do not wish to wait, click on Continue.

🎧 Listen to Speaker 1–4 responses.

	Score	Examiner's response
Speaker 1	04	The response addresses the task appropriately, with choices supported. Relationships between ideas are not always clear. Speech is generally well-placed but minor difficulties with pronunciation are noticeable, sometimes requiring listener effort.
Speaker 2	04	Speech is generally coherent and fluid in delivery. The speaker demonstrates good use of idioms such as "sick and tired." There is relevant content and effective use of grammar.
Speaker 3	03	The response is relevant and mostly intelligible, but delivery is somewhat hesitant and choppy. The response is limited in content.
Speaker 4	01	The response mostly repeats the prompt.

Question 11: Express an opinion Scoring Guidelines

5   Communication is effective. It is highly intelligible and exhibits sustained, coherent discourse. Characterized by all of the following:

- Response is sustained and sufficient to the task. It is generally well developed and coherent; relationships between ideas are clear.

- Speech is clear with generally well-paced flow. It may include minor lapses or minor difficulties with pronunciation or intonation patterns which do not affect overall intelligibility.

- Response exhibits good control of basic and complex structures (as appropriate). Some minor errors may be noticeable but do not obscure meaning.

- Use of vocabulary is accurate and precise.

4   Response addresses the task appropriately but may fall short of being fully developed. It is generally intelligible and coherent, with some fluidity of expression.

- Response clearly indicates the speaker's choice or opinion and supports the choice or opinion with more than one reason or with one reason and elaboration.

- Minor difficulties with pronunciation, intonation, or pacing are noticeable and may require listener effort at times, although overall intelligibility is not significantly affected.

- Response demonstrates fairly automatic and effective use of grammar, but may be somewhat limited in the range of structures used.

- Use of vocabulary is fairly effective. Some vocabulary may be inaccurate or imprecise.

3   Response addresses the task, but development of the topic is limited. It contains intelligible speech, although problems with delivery and/or overall coherence may occur; meaning may be obscured in places.

- Response expresses a choice, preference or opinion and provides at least one reason supporting the choice, preference or opinion. However, it provides little or no elaboration of the reason, repeats itself with no new information, is vague, or is unclear.

- Speech is basically intelligible, though listener effort may be needed because of unclear articulation, awkward intonation, or choppy rhythm/pace; meaning may be obscured in places.

- Response demonstrates limited control of grammar; for the most part, only basic sentence structures are used successfully.

- Use of vocabulary is limited.

2   Response is very limited in content and/or coherence or is only minimally connected to the task, or speech is largely unintelligible.

- Limited relevant content is expressed. The response successfully states a choice, preference, or opinion, but the speaker is unable to successfully give a reason for the choice or opinion.

- Consistent difficulties with pronunciation, stress, and intonation cause considerable listener effort; delivery is choppy, fragmented, or telegraphic; there may be long pauses and frequent hesitations.

- Control of grammar severely limits expression of ideas and clarity of connections among ideas.

- Use of vocabulary is severely limited or highly repetitious.

1   Response does not address the task.

- Response fails to state a choice, preference, or opinion as required by the prompt.

- Response is unintelligible. It may consist primarily of isolated words and phrases, or it may be entirely borrowed from the prompt.

0   No response OR response is completely unconnected to the stimulus.

Speaking Scores

How your responses are rated

Responses to all TOEIC Speaking tasks are sent to ETS's Online Scoring Network. Overall, the responses from each test taker are scored by at least three different human raters. In addition, some of the individual tasks are each scored by two raters to ensure the reliability of the scores.

Interpreting your scores

Scaled scores

After you have taken the TOEIC Speaking Test, you will receive a scaled score indicating your overall performance on the test. The scaled scores range from 0 to 200 in increments of 10. Your scores indicate the general proficiency in speaking that you have demonstrated by your performance on the test.

Raw scores

Before your scaled score can be calculated, your performance on each task must be considered. The Speaking Test is made up of tasks of different levels of difficulty that are rated on individual scales. The *Read a text aloud* tasks are the only tasks that receive separate ratings for pronunciation and for intonation and stress, each on a scale of 0–3 according to the scoring guidelines on page 17. The *Describe a picture* tasks receive an overall rating on a scale of 0–3 in accordance with the scoring guidelines on page 19. The *Respond to questions* and the *Respond to questions using information provided* tasks are each rated on a scale of 0–3, according to the scoring guidelines on pages 23 and 27. The *Propose a solution* tasks are scored on a scale of 0–5 according to the scoring guidelines on pages 30–31, and the *Express an opinion* task is scored on a scale of 0–5 according to the scoring guidelines on pages 33–34.

Converting raw scores to scaled scores

The test is designed so that the earlier tasks require less proficiency in spoken English than the later tasks do; in fact, the test progresses in a series of steps. Your performance on the higher-level tasks contributes more to your overall score than does your performance on the lower-level tasks.

Although the formulas that ETS uses to calculate your scaled score are complicated, the basics of how your performance is converted into the score are quite simple. If you have someone who can give you accurate ratings of your responses, look at the table on the following page to get an approximate estimate of your score and level. Begin by looking at your performance on the last tasks on the TOEIC Speaking Test, the *Propose a solution* and *Express an opinion* tasks.

In this table you can see some frequently observed patterns of scores. Not all possible patterns are represented here. Note that, across different forms of the TOEIC Speaking test, the same raw scores will not always translate exactly to the same scaled scores.

SPEAKING LEVEL	SPEAKING SCALED SCORE	Opinion and Voice-Mail Tasks	Question Tasks	Describe a Picture and Read Aloud Tasks
1	0–30	no response or off topic	no response or off topic	no response or off topic
2	40–50	1, 1	mostly 1 or no response	mostly 1
		2, 1	mostly 1 or no response	mostly 1
3	60–70	2, 1	mostly 1	some 2, some 1
		2, 2	mostly 1	some 2, some 1
4	80–100	2, 2	some 2, some 1	some 2, some 1
		3, 2	some 2, some 1	some 2, some 1
5	110–120	3, 2	mostly 2, some 3	mostly 2
		3, 3	mostly 2, some 1	mostly 2
6	130–150	3, 3 or 3, 4	all 2 or better	mostly 3
7	160–180	4, 4 or 4, 5	more than half 3	all or nearly all 3
8	190–200	5, 5	all or nearly all 3	all or nearly all 3

Official scores on the test are given by trained ETS raters. These raters complete a rigorous training program and are required to pass a certification test before they can score the test. Keep in mind that people who are not authorized/certified by ETS to assign scores may not be able to give you a completely accurate rating of your response.

Proficiency Levels

Depending on where your total score falls on the scaled score range of 0 to 200, you will be provided with a description of your level of speaking proficiency. Additionally, Intonation and Stress and Pronunciation performance descriptors will be included. There are 8 proficiency levels covering the 0–200 total score range for the Speaking Test. The proficiency level descriptors outline the types of general skills and abilities in speaking English that are common for most people who have achieved a score similar to yours. The descriptor associated with the level that you have achieved will help you understand the strengths and weaknesses of your spoken English.

SPEAKING Scaled Score	SPEAKING Proficiency Level
0–30	1
40–50	2
60–70	3
80–100	4
110–120	5
130–150	6
160–180	7
190–200	8

These descriptors will appear on individual score reports. For further information go to www.ets.org/toeic

Speaking Proficiency Level Descriptors

Level 8 Scale score 190–200
Typically, test takers at level 8 can create connected, sustained discourse appropriate to the typical workplace. When they express opinions or respond to complicated requests, their speech is highly intelligible. Their use of basic and complex grammar is good and their use of vocabulary is accurate and precise.

Test takers at level 8 can also use spoken language to answer questions and give basic information.

Their pronunciation and intonation and stress are at all times highly intelligible.

Level 7 Scale score 160–180
Typically, test takers at level 7 can create connected, sustained discourse appropriate to the typical workplace. They can express opinions or respond to complicated requests effectively. In extended responses, some of the following weaknesses may sometimes occur, but they do not interfere with the message:

- minor difficulties with pronunciation, intonation, or hesitation when creating language
- some errors when using complex grammatical structures
- some imprecise vocabulary

Test takers at level 7 can also use spoken language to answer questions and give basic information.

When reading aloud, test takers at level 7 are highly intelligible.

Level 6 Scale score 130–150
Typically, test takers at level 6 are able to create a relevant response when asked to express an opinion or respond to a complicated request. However, at least part of the time, the reasons for, or explanations of, the opinion are unclear to a listener. This may be because of the following:

- unclear pronunciation or inappropriate intonation or stress when the speaker must create language
- mistakes in grammar
- a limited range of vocabulary

Most of the time, test takers at level 6 can answer questions and give basic information. However, sometimes their responses are difficult to understand or interpret.

When reading aloud, test takers at Level 6 are intelligible.

Level 5 Scale score 110–120
Typically, test takers at level 5 have limited success at expressing an opinion or responding to a complicated request. Responses include problems such as:

- language that is inaccurate, vague, or repetitive
- minimal or no awareness of audience
- long pauses and frequent hesitations
- limited expression of ideas and connections between ideas
- limited vocabulary

Most of the time, test takers at level 5 can answer questions and give basic information. However, sometimes their responses are difficult to understand or interpret.

When reading aloud, test takers at Level 5 are generally intelligible. However, when creating language, their pronunciation, intonation and stress may be inconsistent.

Level 4 Scale score 80–100
Typically, test takers at level 4 are unsuccessful when attempting to explain an opinion or respond to a complicated request. The response may be limited to a single sentence or part of a sentence. Other problems may include:

- severely limited language use
- minimal or no audience awareness

- consistent pronunciation, stress, and intonation difficulties
- long pauses and frequent hesitations
- severely limited vocabulary

Most of the time, test takers at level 4 can not answer questions or give basic information.

When reading aloud, test takers at Level 4 vary in intelligibility. However, when they are creating language, speakers at level 4 usually have problems with pronunciation, and intonation and stress. For more information, check the "Read Aloud Pronunciation and Intonation and Stress ratings."

Level 3 Scale score 60–70
Typically, test takers at level 3 can, with some difficulty, state an opinion, but they can not support the opinion. Any response to a complicated request is severely limited.

Most of the time, test takers at level 3 can not answer questions and give basic information.

Typically, test takers at level 3 have insufficient vocabulary or grammar to create simple descriptions.

When reading aloud, speakers at level 3 may be difficult to understand. For more information, check the "Read Aloud Pronunciation and Intonation and Stress ratings."

Level 2 Scale Score 40–50
Typically, test takers at level 2 can not state an opinion or support it. They either do not respond to complicated requests or the response is not at all relevant.

In routine social and occupational interactions such as answering questions and giving basic information, test takers at level 2 are difficult to understand.

When reading aloud, speakers at level 2 may be difficult to understand. For more information, check the "Read Aloud Pronunciation and Intonation and Stress ratings."

Level 1 Scale score 0–30
Test takers at level 1 left a significant part of the TOEIC Speaking Test unanswered. Test takers at level 1 may not have the listening or reading skills in English necessary to understand the test directions or the content of the test questions.

Pronunciation Levels

Low 0–1.5
When reading aloud your pronunciation is not generally intelligible.
Medium 1.6–2.5
When reading aloud your pronunciation is generally intelligible with some lapses.
High 3
When reading aloud your pronunciation is highly intelligible.

Intonation and Stress Levels

(Intonation and Stress refer to your ability to use emphases, pauses and rising and falling pitch to convey meaning to a listener.)
Low 0–1.5
When reading aloud your use of intonation and stress is generally not effective.
Medium 1.6–2.5
When reading aloud your use of intonation and stress is generally effective.
High 3
When reading aloud your use of intonation and stress is highly effective.

Speaking Test
Questions 1–2   Read a text aloud

A Focus: Pronunciation and intonation

In the test

← **Sample test pp15–17**
Speaking Test Questions 1–2

- In each of these questions, you will be given a paragraph of 40–60 words to read aloud.
- You will be given 45 seconds to prepare and 45 seconds to read the text aloud.
- You will be scored on your pronunciation, and the intonation and stress of your sentences.
- In this unit, we will focus on pronunciation and stress of individual words and intonation in lists and questions.
- In Unit 7, we will focus on pace, stress and intonation with transition words.

Test tip

Practice the sounds you find difficult in English

In the test, you will be asked to read aloud a paragraph similar to the one in A. There will be some sounds within words that you may find difficult to say. It is a good idea to know what these are and to practice them.

1 Language building: Pronunciation practice

A 🎧 You will hear a native speaker reading the paragraph below. Listen carefully to how the words in **bold** are pronounced.

I'd **like** to ask employees to **see** that all **personal** items are removed from the **floor** when you finish **work** and **leave** the office tonight. During the weekend, the **air conditioning** will be **serviced**, and the carpets, the windows, and the **chairs** in the **lounge** will be **cleaned**. **Please** make **sure** the **lights** are **turned** off and all windows are **closed**. **Thank** you for your **cooperation**.

B 🎧 Listen to one of the words in each pair in 1–9 being read aloud. Mark (✓) the one you hear in each pair.

1. a. see _____   b. she _____   ⇒ p226 s / ʃ practice
2. a. work _____   b. walk _____   ⇒ p226 ɜː / ɔː practice
3. a. fill _____   b. hill _____   ⇒ p226 f / h practice
4. a. live _____   b. leave _____   ⇒ p226 ɪ / iː practice
5. a. hair _____   b. air _____   ⇒ p227 h / no h practice
6. a. chairs _____   b. shares _____   ⇒ p227 tʃ / ʃ practice
7. a. lights _____   b. rights _____   ⇒ p227 l / r practice
8. a. vat _____   b. bat _____   ⇒ p227 v / b practice
9. a. thank _____   b. sank _____   ⇒ p227 θ / s practice

Follow up: Now you will do some practice with the sounds you may have problems with. Turn to pages 226–227.

C 🎧 Listen again to extracts from the paragraph in A. The words in **bold** include sounds that some learners may have problems with. Listen carefully and repeat.

1. I'd **like** to ask employees to **see** that all **personal** items …
2. … are removed from the **floor** when you finish **work** and **leave** the office tonight.
3. During the weekend, the **air conditioning** will be **serviced,** …
4. … and the carpets, the windows, and the **chairs** in the **lounge** will be **cleaned**.
5. **Please** make **sure** the **lights** are turned off …
6. … and all windows are **closed**.
7. **Thank** you for your **cooperation.**

D 🎧 Listen to the words in 1–15. Repeat them. Count the number of syllables.

One syllable
1. asked
2. steak
3. cheap
4. clothes
5. make

Two syllables
6. mo|ney
7. chi|cken
8. o|range
9. ja|cket
10. wan|ted

Three syllables
11. em|ploy|ees
12. per|so|nal
13. ma|na|ger
14. te|le|phone
15. com|ple|ted

E 🎧 In words of two or more syllables, one of the sounds is stronger than the other(s). Listen to the words in 6–15 again and mark which of the syllables is emphasized in some way. The first is done for you.

    ●
6. mo|ney

unit 1

Test tip

Be aware of influences from your own language

Some people add extra sounds to words because of how words are written in English or because of the sounds that exist in their own languages. When you come across new words, learn the meaning, how to pronounce them and how many syllables they have.

Test tip

Be aware of which syllable to stress

In words of two or more syllables, one syllable will be stressed more than the others. Stressing the wrong syllable of a word is very likely to cause problems of misunderstanding, so learn where common words and types of words are usually stressed.

Test tip

Practice pronouncing longer words

In Questions 1–2, there may be one or two longer words with four or five syllables to read aloud. Practice saying these, learn which syllable is stronger than the other ones and how the syllables run together.

Test tip

Word stress can vary depending on accent

In some cases, the stress in a word pronounced in American English will be different than that in Canadian, British, or Australian English. In the TOEIC Speaking Test, any form of English is acceptable, as long as you are consistent.

Test tip

A word can sometimes be different parts of speech

Some words can act like a noun or a verb without changing form. When they are used as a different part of speech, the stress placement will sometimes be different.

F Listen and repeat the words in 1–5. Each one will be read aloud three times.

1.   ●
  co|o|pe|ra|tion

2.   ●
  di|sa|ppoin|ted

3.   ●
  in|con|ve|ni|ence

4.   ●
  pro|fi|ta|bi|li|ty

5.   ●
  un|for|tu|nate|ly

G Listen to the words in F being read in the context of sentences. Repeat each sentence after you have heard it.

1. The main aim of this meeting is to improve the cooperation between us.
2. I am very disappointed in their decision to close the department.
3. We would like to apologize for any inconvenience caused.
4. At this point in time, the company's main concern is its profitability.
5. Unfortunately, this service will be canceled until further notice.

H Read sentences 1–10 and decide what parts of speech the words in **bold** are.

1. I can't find any **record** of your order.
2. I have to **record** your name and number before you can enter.
3. Mr. Basenji **exports** carpets to Europe.
4. **Exports** of car parts have decreased recently.
5. I wanted to get a **refund** on the broken gift.
6. The store refused to **refund** the money.
7. At the end of the year, we **present** achievement awards.
8. It was so very thoughtful of you to buy a **present**.
9. Metals expand and **contract** when the temperature changes.
10. Congratulations! I just heard they've renewed your **contract**.

Follow up: Listen to the sentences in H and mark the stress on the words in **bold**.

2 Test tactic: Intonation in lists and questions

A 🎧 In this part of the test, the text you read aloud will include a list. Make sure you are familiar with the common intonation pattern for lists. Listen to the sentence in sections and repeat each part. Try to imitate the intonation used by the speaker.

        ↗   ↗   ↘

I'd like some **apples**, some **plums**, and a **melon**.

Pronunciation note

Intonation in lists

All texts in Questions 1 & 2 will include a set of things in a list. Learn the common intonation pattern that lists follow.

If there are three or more items in the list, the first ones will have an upward intonation after the main stress to indicate that there is more to come, and the last item in the list will go down after the last stressed syllable to indicate the end of the list. (↗, ↗, ↘)

B 🎧 In pairs, read sentences 1–4 aloud and mark the intonation of the words in **bold**. Then listen, repeat, and check your answers.

1. Appointments may be made on the **third**, **tenth**, and **twenty-first** of each month.

2. Destinations include **Greece**, **Turkey**, and **Egypt**.

3. You will be introduced to the **president**, the **vice president**, and the **senior manager**.

4. You will have to pay for **food**, **accommodation**, and **transportation**.

Follow up: Now tell your partner:
- three things you have bought recently
- three places you have been on holiday
- three foods you have eaten in the last week.

C 🎧 In this part of the test, the text you read aloud may include a question. Make sure you are familiar with the common intonation patterns for questions. Listen to 1 and 2 and repeat each. Try to imitate the intonation used by the speaker.

                    ↗

1. May I interest you in these products?

            ↘

2. Who will volunteer?

Intonation in questions

In Questions 1–2, there may be a question to read aloud. Learn the common intonation patterns that questions follow.

If the question begins with an auxiliary word (*do, did, is, are, was, were*) or a modal word (*may, can, could, would,* etc.), there will be an upward intonation on the last syllable of the last word.

If the question begins with a *wh-* word (*which, where, what, why, when*) or *how,* the intonation will go down on the last syllable of the last word.

D In pairs, read sentences 1–3 out loud and mark the intonation of the words in **bold**. Then listen, repeat, and check your answers in the Key on page 2.

1. Can I make an **announcement**?

2. Where can you go for big **savings**?

3. Does anyone have any **questions**?

Follow up: Now ask your partner:
- three questions about their family.
- three questions about their hobbies.
- three questions about their job.

E Prepare the announcement below by following steps 1–5. Highlight pauses, emphasized words, and intonation patterns on the text itself.

In the 45 seconds you have to prepare, read the paragraph silently and consider the following:

1. Are there any sounds that you may find difficult to pronounce?
2. Practice the numbers of syllables, especially in longer words.
3. Note which words make up the list, and remind yourself of the up, up, down (↗, ↗, ↘) intonation you need to use.
4. Are there any questions? What sort of intonation do they require? Remember auxiliary/model ↗, or *Wh-* word ↘.
5. Relax. Speak slowly and clearly. Make sure that you pause where necessary and that your voice goes up and down appropriately.

May I have your attention for a moment, please? Unfortunately, the lecture originally scheduled for this time, "An introduction to accounting", has been canceled for personal reasons. You may attend this lecture on Monday, Wednesday, or Thursday of next week, however. If those days are inconvenient, we will be pleased to give you a full refund. Thank you for your attention.

☑ Look out for any unknown words, or words that are difficult to pronounce.

☑ Think about where the stress goes in individual words.

☑ Look for the list in each read-aloud task, and remember the **up, up, down** pattern.

☑ Are there any questions? Remember the common intonation patterns in questions.

unit
1

Test tip

Prepare quickly but carefully

You have 45 seconds to prepare the paragraph. If you practice preparing lots of texts, you will soon know what to look out for and be familiar with how to prepare.

B Tactic practice

Prepare texts 1–4 following the steps in the Test technique. After each step compare your answers with your partner. Then choose one text each and read it aloud.

1.

Thank you for calling Union Motorcycles. We have the city's largest selection of sport and cruising bikes, and also a full selection of parts, accessories, and riding wear. Visit between nine a.m. and nine p.m. on weekdays, and let our experienced staff attend to all your riding needs. Where else could you go for better riding advice?

2.

I would like to summarize the initial response to our recent early retirement proposal. It is no secret that this program aims to reduce monthly salary costs, cut our health premiums, and increase our profits. Nevertheless, it has turned out to be very popular, especially among our most senior workers.

3.

And now, the local news. The Bailey Brothers Carnival opens tonight at the city fairground. This thrill-packed show will feature clowns, acrobats, and exotic animals from around the world. Tickets go fast, so be sure to get yours soon. You don't want to miss the most exciting show on the planet!

4.

Before I start our meeting, I would just like to thank all of you who contributed to John's retirement gift. If you didn't make it to his party, we used the money to buy him a set of pens, a new watch, and a season ticket for his favorite baseball team.

🎧 Using natural English

In natural spoken English, sounds are sometimes changed, combined, or dropped. Listen to a native speaker saying the following sentences and write in the words they say.

I _____ record your name and number.

We will be _____ give you a full refund.

You don't _____ miss the most exciting show.

Check your answers in the Key on page 3.

Listen again and practice these sentences with the correct sound and rhythm.

C Mini-test

Now apply the Test tactics to prepare for and read aloud the following text. Use the recommended test time for Questions 1–2.

TOEIC Speaking

Questions 1–2: Read a text aloud

Directions: In this part of the test, you will read aloud the text on the screen. You will have 45 seconds to prepare. Then you will have 45 seconds to read the text aloud.

Question 1

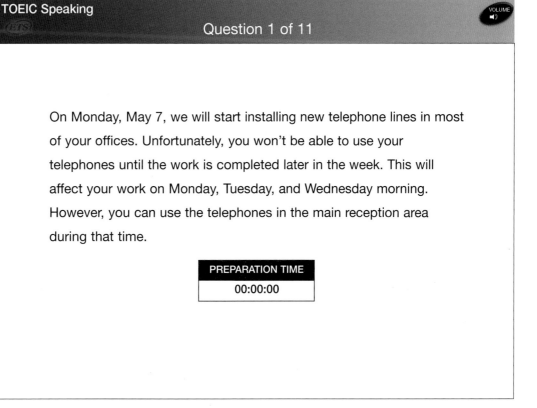

TOEIC Speaking
Question 1 of 11

On Monday, May 7, we will start installing new telephone lines in most of your offices. Unfortunately, you won't be able to use your telephones until the work is completed later in the week. This will affect your work on Monday, Tuesday, and Wednesday morning. However, you can use the telephones in the main reception area during that time.

PREPARATION TIME
00:00:00

Question 2

unit
1

All right everyone, we've come to the end of our tour of the downtown area, and we're about to enter the public gardens, where we'll take a short break. There's a café here, where you can rest, get something to drink, and look over the schedule for the rest of the day. Let me know if you have any questions.

PREPARATION TIME
00:00:00

If you want to do the follow-up unit to this test item now, please go to Unit 7, page 86.

A Focus: Describing the people and the scene; how to plan and organize your response

In the test

← Sample test pp18–19
Speaking Test Question 3

- In this part of the test, you will be given a picture to describe in as much detail as you can.
- You will have 30 seconds to prepare your response.
- You will have 45 seconds to speak about the picture.
- Speak clearly, but say as much as you can in the time allowed.
- The focus of the picture may be of one of the following areas: *free-time activities, eating, drinking, entertainment, health, household tasks, shopping, travel,* or *street scenes.*
- In this unit, we will practice how to describe the scene and the people, and how to plan and organize your response.

unit
2

1 Language building: How to describe the people and the scene

1.

2.

3.

4.

Test tip

**Use the present continuous or
*there is/are + -ing***

Use the present continuous or *there is /there are + -ing* to describe activities you can see in the picture. (e.g. *The dog is walking* down the steps. *There is a woman buying* some vegetables.*)

A Match sentences 1–6 to the pictures 1–4 they are describing.

1. The waiter **is serving** some food. _____

2. People **are shopping** at a street market. _____

3. The dog **is lying** on the grass. _____

4. One of the boys **is leaning** against the railing. _____

5. She **is painting** a landscape picture. _____

6. **There is** a woman **handing** something to another woman. _____

B Take turns making two more sentences each for pictures 1–4 using the present continuous or *there is/are + -ing*. Ask your partner to guess which picture you are describing. Use these words to help you.

| hold | paint | smile | stand | walk | look | buy | give | sit |

unit
2

Test tip

Use prepositions to describe location

Use prepositions to say where the object or person is located, e.g. *I can see a dog next to the woman.*

Test tip

Use the present simple or *there is/are*

Use the present simple of the verb *to be* and *to have* or *there is/there are* to talk about objects and people in the picture, e.g. *The woman on the right is the customer. There are lots of vegetables for sale at the market.*

C Match sentences 1–4 to the pictures 1–4 they describe. Underline the prepositions.

1. There is a bike near the steps. _____
2. She has a paintbrush in her right hand. _____
3. Vegetables are for sale at the market. _____
4. There is some salt and pepper on the table. _____

D Match the prepositions to sentences 1–5 to describe the pictures.

| behind | in | next to | on | at |

1. There **is** a dog _____ the woman.
2. The two women **are** _____ the table.
3. There **are** some flowers _____ the garden.
4. I **can see** two boys and a dog _____ the steps.
5. The vendor **is** _____ the stand.

E Take turns making two more sentences for each picture 1–4 using the present simple of the verb *to be*, *there is/are* and a preposition where appropriate. Use these words to help you.

| dog | skateboard | bicycle | saltshaker | vegetables |
| steps | basket | restaurant | fence | |

| next to | with | at | in | on | in front of | behind |

F Look at the pictures again and brainstorm as many words as you can to add to each category below.

| Adjective | Color | Adverb |
| *sunny* | *green* | *quietly* |

Test tip

Use modifiers to make your description more precise and interesting

Make use of adjectives (e.g. *big, expensive*), colors (e.g. *bright red, gold, dark blue*), and adverbs (e.g. *carefully, slowly*), to add detail to your descriptions.

G Complete sentences 1–5 using the prepositions and the adjectives and adverbs.

| from | fresh | pink | between | yellow | quietly | at | orange |

1. The dog is lying _____ on the grass.
2. I can see some _____, _____, and _____ flowers growing in front of the fence.
3. The dog is walking _____ the two boys.
4. The women are looking _____ the plate of food.
5. The woman is buying some _____ vegetables _____ the vendor.

H Take turns making two more sentences for each picture 1–4 using similar words to describe location and/or distinguishing features.

I Describe picture 5 using the present simple, present continuous, prepositions, and modifiers to describe the scene, the people, and the action.

5.

🎧 *Follow up*: Listen to a sample answer.

2 Test tactic: Planning and organizing your description

A With your partner add as many nouns, verbs, adjectives, and adverbs as you can to the lists for pictures 1 and 2.

1.

Nouns	Verbs	Adjectives/ Adverbs
diagram	*look at*	*closely*

2.

Nouns	Verbs	Adjectives/ Adverbs
money	*insert*	*quickly*

Test tip

Start by brainstorming vocabulary

You will have 30 seconds to study the picture before you speak. Start by quickly picking out all the nouns, verbs, adjectives, and adverbs you can see in the picture.

Think of an introduction that answers the *Wh*-questions

During the preparation time, think of introductory sentences that answer questions such as: *Where is this? Who are these people? What are they doing? Why are they here?* These answers will form the basis of your introduction.

unit
2

B Take turns making sentences using the words from A, e.g. *They are looking closely at the diagram.*

C Look at picture 3 and the sentences that could be used to start your description. What question does each sentence answer? The first one is done for you.

This picture shows a café.
e.g. *Where is this?*

3.

This picture shows a café. We can see a waiter and some customers. The waiter is serving coffee to them.

D Now make similar introductory sentences about pictures 4–6 by answering the three questions you formulated in C.

4.

5.

6.

Be clear about where things are in the picture

It is important to help your listener quickly find the things you are describing. One way to do this is to describe their location in the picture, e.g. *on the left, in the background*, or use a separate phrase to pick out distinguishing features, e.g. *The girl with the red skirt is … The man with the beard is … .*

E Match location words a–g to the arrows 1–7 on the picture.

Location words

a. in the foreground

b. in the background

c. at the left of the picture

d. on the right-hand side of the picture

e. at the bottom right of the picture

f. at the top left of the picture

g. in the middle

F Complete sentences 1–6 describing picture 8. Use the location words in E or the descriptive phrases below.

Descriptive phrases

… in the white shirt …   … sitting on the counter …   … standing up …

1. The man _____ is next to the woman.

2. _____ I can see a bed.

3. The man _____ is talking to the other people.

4. _____ there is a doorway.

5. There is a table with a bowl of fruit _____ .

6. _____ there is a vase of flowers.

G Take turns making sentences about picture 9. Your partner should point as quickly as possible to the thing being described.

9.

🎧 *Follow up*: Listen to a sample answer.

Test technique

B Tactic practice

☑ Brainstorm vocabulary (20 seconds – Preparation).

☑ Plan introductory sentences that answer *Where, Who, What, Why* (10 seconds – Preparation).

☑ After your introduction, focus on details and clearly signal where they are (using location phrases and descriptive clauses).

☑ Add adjectives/ adverbs and prepositions to give more information.

Describe each of the pictures 1–4 following the steps in the Test technique. After each step, compare your answers with your partner.

1.

2.

3.

4.

🎧 **Using natural English**

In natural spoken English, sounds are sometimes changed, combined, or dropped. Listen to a native speaker saying the following sentences and write in the words they say.

_____ shopping at a street market.

The two _____ next to the table.

The _____ sitting on the step.

Check your answers in the Key on page 7.
Listen again and practice these sentences with the correct sound and rhythm.

C Mini-test

Now apply the Test tactics to draft an outline for the following question.
Use the recommended test time for Question 3.

Question 3:
Describe a picture

Question 3: Describe a picture

Directions: In this part of the test, you will describe the picture on your screen in as much detail as you can. You will have 30 seconds to prepare your response. Then you will have 45 seconds to speak about the picture.

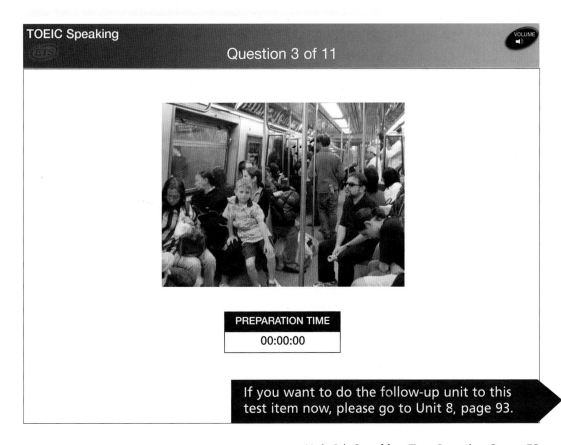

A Focus: Answering experience questions

> ### In the test
>
> ← **Sample test pp20–23**
> **Speaking Test Questions 4–6**
>
> - In Questions 4–6, you will be asked to imagine that you are taking part in a market research telephone interview.
> - You will be asked to respond to three related questions without preparation.
> - The questions will be about familiar topics: entertainment, purchases, dining out, family and friends, health, housing, news, shopping, travel, etc.
> - You will be scored on using relevant vocabulary and structures, and for answering the question appropriately.
> - In Unit 9, we will look at how to answer Question 6, which asks you to give a longer response of 30 seconds.
> - In this unit, we will look at how to answer Questions 4–5, which ask you to give a short response of 15 seconds in answer to one or two questions.
> - In this unit, we will also look at dealing with common question types and how to answer them.

unit
3

Test tip

Know how to answer opinion questions

Many of the questions in this part of the test will ask you about your favorite thing, or about things you prefer or like or think are the best. Do not give one word answers, e.g. "football". Say why you like it, too.

Test tip

Watch out for questions with two parts

Some questions may have two parts to them: make sure you answer both questions. For example, *Where would you like to live, and why?*

1 Language building: Dealing with common question types

A Match questions 1–5 to the answers a–e.

1. What sports do you most enjoy playing or watching? _____
2. What is your favorite national holiday, and why? _____
3. What kinds of movies do you usually watch, and where? _____
4. What do you think is the best way to travel long distances, and why? _____
5. Where do you think is the best place for a summer vacation? _____

a. I usually watch all types of movies, but the ones I enjoy the most are action movies. You know, like martial arts. I really like Jackie Chan.
b. I think the best way to travel long distances is by train. It is very relaxing.
c. I would say the best place for a summer vacation is Yellowstone National Park. I really like canoeing and nature.
d. I really like watching tennis. My favorite competition is the Australian Open.
e. Hmm … . Let me see … . My favorite national holiday is Independence Day. I love the fireworks!

🎧 *Follow up*: Listen to the questions in A followed by the correct answers. Check your answers.

B Look again at the questions and answers in A. Which questions ask two questions? Which answer does not respond to one of the two questions asked? Why do you think the answers are longer than one or two words?

C Take turns asking questions 1–5 in A. This time give your own answers. Make sure you answer all the questions and give as much information as you can.

D 🎧 Complete the answers to *Wh-* questions 1–6 with the correct endings a–g. Then listen and check your answers.

1. Q: Where do you go when you want to be alone?

   A: When I want to be alone, I _____.

2. Q: Why do you want to improve your English?

   A: I want to improve my English _____.

3. Q: Where would you like to go to celebrate your birthday?

   A: For my birthday, I would like to go _____.

4. Q: What is the most famous building in the area where you live?

   A: The most famous building is _____.

5. Q: What is the best season in your country?

   A: I think the best season in my country is _____.

6. Q: What do you usually do in the evenings?

   A: Usually I _____ or sometimes _____.

   a. ... the City Stadium. Our football team plays there
   b. ... watch TV
   c. ... winter, because I really like skiing
   d. ... usually go to my bedroom
   e. ... I take a walk
   f. ... to the Boston Grill. It has the best steaks
   g. ... for my work

E Take turns asking questions 1–6 in D. This time give your own answers.

F 🎧 Listen to someone answering questions 1–6 below. Write down the answers you hear. Repeat the audio in between if necessary.

1. How long have you been living in your current home?

   _____

2. How often do you go to the movies?

   _____

3. How did you come here today?

   _____

4. How many hours a week do you spend watching TV?

   _____

5. How do people in your country usually find a job?

   _____

6. How did you meet your best friend?

   _____

G Read the questions in F again. Which *How* questions ask about method and which about quantity or time? Which ones ask about the present and which ones ask about the past? What extra information could you add to each answer?

H Take turns asking questions 1–6 in F. This time give your own answers.

2 Test tactic: Rephrasing the question

Test tip

Begin your answer by rephrasing the question

Pick out the key words in the question and rephrase these to give the start of your answer. This will give you extra time to think of what you want to say and means you won't have a long pause at the beginning of your talk. (See Unit 9, page 103 for more hesitation devices to use when you need time to think.)

A Answer questions 1–6 by following steps a–c.

1. What is the most expensive thing you have ever bought?
2. How long does it usually take you to clean your room?
3. What is the best book you have ever read, and why?
4. Where and when do you usually get your hair cut?
5. How often do you use computers?
6. What animal do you think makes the best pet, and why?

a. Note the key words in the question, not including question words.
   How often do you go out with friends?

b. Immediately start your answer by rephrasing the question using the key words. This gives you a bit of time to plan your answer. *I go out with friends ...*

c. Complete your answer.
   I go out with friends about once a week.

Test tip

Add extra details to shorter answers

It is important to "answer the question as fully as possible." If your answer is short, always try to think of something else to say, but keep it relevant.

B For question 1, which of the extra details a–e would you add to your answer?

1. What is the most expensive thing you have ever bought?
   The most expensive thing I've ever bought is a car.

Possible extra details:
a. It was a red Ford Escort.
b. My friend recently bought a house.
c. It was $25,000.
d. I bought it three years ago.
e. My sneakers were quite expensive, too.

C With a partner, brainstorm some extra details you could add to your answers for questions 2–6 in A. Then take turns asking and answering the questions, adding in some of the extra ideas you came up with.

🎧 *Follow up*: Listen to a sample answer. Which question does it answer?

unit
3

☑ Listen carefully and pick out the key words in the question.

☑ If you need a few more moments to think, start your answer by rephrasing the words from the question.

☑ Give a full answer. Add extra details or examples.

B Tactic practice

Prepare the answers to questions 1–6 following the Test technique.
Then with a partner, take turns asking and answering the questions.

1. Do you prefer eating at home or eating out, and why?
2. What is the most popular type of "fast food" in your country?
3. What are some of the things you like about your home?
4. Which room in your home is your favorite, and why?
5. What entertainment facilities are there in your area?
6. What is your favorite form of entertainment, and why?

🎧 **Using natural English**

In natural spoken English, sounds are sometimes changed, combined, or dropped. Listen to a native speaker saying the following sentences and write in the words they say.

I usually _____ my bedroom.

I'd like to _____ the Boston Grill.

For my vacations I like to _____ Hawaii.

Check your answers in the Key on page 8.

Listen again and practice these sentences with the correct sound and rhythm.

---

unit
3

C Mini-test

Now apply the Test tactics to answer the following questions. Use the recommended test time for Questions 4–6.

Important

In this part of the test, you will have to answer three questions (4–6).
In this unit, we have practiced question-types 4–5.
See Sample test, page 22 or Unit 9, page 99 for practice on Question 6.

Questions 4–6:
Respond to questions

Questions 4–6: Respond to questions

Directions: In this part of the test, you will answer three questions.

For each question, begin responding immediately after you hear a beep.

No preparation time is provided. You will have 15 seconds to respond to

Questions 4 and 5 and 30 seconds to respond to Question 6.

Question 4

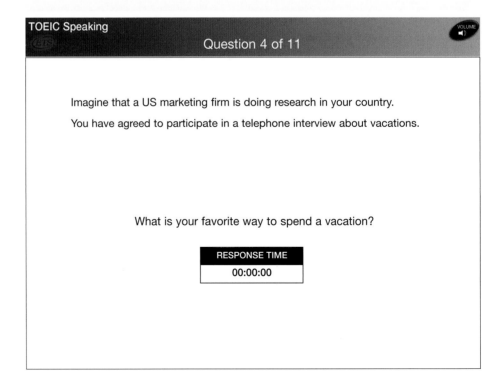

TOEIC Speaking
Question 4 of 11

Imagine that a US marketing firm is doing research in your country.
You have agreed to participate in a telephone interview about vacations.

What is your favorite way to spend a vacation?

RESPONSE TIME
00:00:00

Question 5

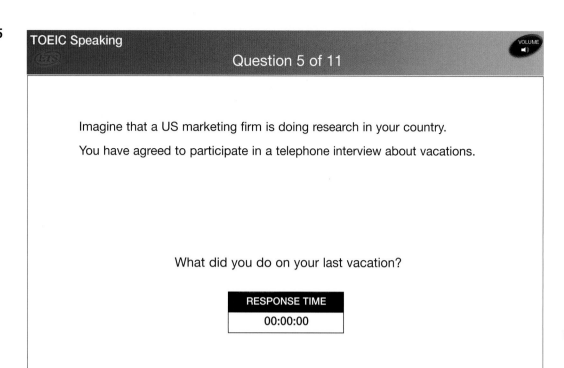

Imagine that a US marketing firm is doing research in your country.

You have agreed to participate in a telephone interview about vacations.

What did you do on your last vacation?

RESPONSE TIME
00:00:00

Question 6

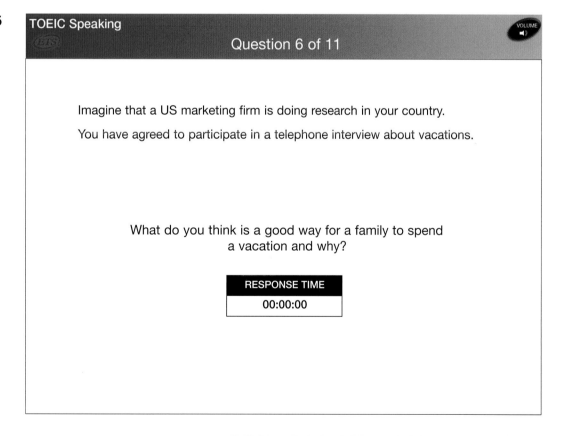

Imagine that a US marketing firm is doing research in your country.

You have agreed to participate in a telephone interview about vacations.

What do you think is a good way for a family to spend
a vacation and why?

RESPONSE TIME
00:00:00

If you want to do the follow-up unit to this
test item now, please go to Unit 9, page 99.

A Focus: Answering specific information / confirmation questions

Important

In the test, Questions 7–9 appear together. In this book, Questions 7–8 are covered here in Unit 4. Question 9 is covered in Unit 10.

In the test

← **Sample test pp24–27**
Speaking Test Questions 7–9

- In Questions 7–9, you will be given 30 seconds preparation time to read a written agenda or schedule.
- You will then be asked three questions by a "caller" who needs information from your written schedule.
- You will only hear the questions once, and they do not appear as text on the screen.
- You will be scored on using relevant vocabulary and structures and giving accurate information. You will need to speak clearly.
- In this unit, we will focus on how to answer Questions 7–8, which allow you 15 seconds to make your response for each question.
- In Unit 10, we will focus on how to answer Question 9, which allow you 30 seconds to make your response.
- In this unit, we will also focus on understanding natural questions, what to do in the preparation time, and how to answer Questions 7–8.

unit
4

1 Language building: Understanding natural questions and forming appropriate answers

Test tip

Learn to understand natural questions

Questions in the test and in real life rarely appear in the simple interrogative form. It is important to learn to recognize the different forms that questions can take in natural English.

Understanding questions asking for specific information

A Sentences 1–3 ask for specific information. Match them to two of the simplified meanings a–f.

1. Could you tell me what time the meeting starts and how long it will last? _____ _____

2. OK, first, I need to know their arrival time, and the flight number. _____ _____

3. Could you let me know the admission price and where the tickets are being sold? _____ _____

a. What time does the plane arrive?
b. How much do the tickets cost?
c. When does the meeting start?
d. Where can we buy tickets?
e. How long is it?
f. What is the flight number?

Understanding *yes/no* questions

B Match the *yes/no* questions 1–4 to the simplified meanings a–d.

1. I'm afraid I can't make it by 8:00. If I can get to the theater by 8:45, will that be OK? ____

2. Dr. Johnson said that the visit would feature a guided tour around the building. Is that still going to take place? ____

3. I'd also like to visit the Asian exhibits. I believe these are included in the cost of the package, right? ____

4. I am looking forward to taking European representatives to the theater. Were you able to reserve orchestra seats as I requested? ____

a. Did you reserve orchestra seats?
b. Can we visit the Asian exhibits at no extra cost?
c. Will there be a guided tour?
d. Is it OK to arrive at 8:45?

C Write simplified questions for 1–5.

1. Would you be able to tell me when the meeting is likely to end?

   _____

2. Do you mind if I ask how long the show will last?

   _____

3. As I understood from Stephen's e-mail, they were planning on voting on the proposal. Is that still going ahead?

   _____

4. Can you tell me the location of the event and what time it starts?

   _____

5. I heard that the train arrives in Barton at 11:00 a.m. Would it be possible to have a taxi waiting there to pick us up at 11:15?

   _____

D Match answers a–e to the questions in C.

a. **Let me see now …** . It starts at 7:30 p.m. and finishes at 10:00 p.m, so that makes it two and a half hours. ____

b. **Let me just check the agenda …** . The event is taking place at the National Theater, and it starts at 7:30 p.m. ____

c. **Looking at the agenda, it shows** the meeting starts at 12:00 p.m. and lasts for two hours, so I guess it should be finished by 2:00 p.m. at the latest. ____

d. **I'm really sorry, but I'm afraid** you'll have to get from the station to the hotel on your own. It isn't very far. ____

e. **I'm sorry, but** we won't be voting on the proposal as planned, as it isn't ready yet. ____

Practice reading times aloud

There are different ways to read times, e.g. *seven thirty* (*p.m*), *half past seven* (*in the evening*). There is no right or wrong way. It's a matter of personal choice.

E   Listen to the questions and answers you matched in C and D and check your answers. Then answer questions 1–3.

1. How did they say the times in a–e?

   a. 12:00 p.m. _____

   b. 2:00 p.m. _____

   c. 7:30 p.m. _____

   d. 11:00 a.m. _____

   e. 11:15 _____

2. Do you know any other ways to say these times?

3. Look at the useful phrases in **bold** at the beginning of sentences a–e in D. Why do you think the speaker uses these phrases?

Referring back to the agenda

F   Match replies a–c to questions 1–3 in A.

   a. **Yes, certainly. I'll just have a look for you.** They will arrive at 3:20 p.m. on flight PA 638. ____

   b. **Let me just check the agenda** … . It starts at 2:00 p.m. and is due to finish at 5:00 p.m. ____

   c. **Of course. Let me see now** … . The price for an adult is US$20. You can buy them at the ticket office or online. ____

    Follow up: Listen to the questions and answers you matched in A and F and check your answers.

Introducing bad news

G   Match replies a–d to questions 1–4 in B. Notice the introductory phrases in **bold**. They are in order from quite casual to very polite.

   a. **No, actually,** we won't have time for the guided tour. ____

   b. **I'm sorry, but** all of the orchestra tickets were sold out. ____

   c. **Sorry, I'm afraid** that will be too late. ____

   d. **I'm terribly sorry, but I'm afraid** there is an extra charge for the Asian exhibits. ____

Test tip

Use appropriate phrases to refer to the agenda

When answering a specific question, you will need to find the answer in your agenda. Learn phrases like *Let me see now, …* or *I'll just have a look for you …* to give you time and to avoid a long pause at the beginning of your response.

Test tip

Use appropriate phrases to introduce bad news

When refusing a request or giving bad news, you should use phrases like *I'm very sorry, but …* or *I'm afraid that … .*

unit
4

Watch for asterisks (*) and related footnotes

Pay attention to asterisks and their related footnotes and any other information in parentheses or a note in small print. There may be a question related to this additional information.

H 🎧 Take 30 seconds to read the agenda. Then listen to questions 1–3 and practice making similar statements to those in F and G. Refer back to the agenda or give bad news based on the information in the agenda.

Portland Investment Seminar

Date: July 12th   **Time:** 10:00–16:00
Venue: Portland West View College. Meet at Main Hall at 9:30.

10:00–11:00	"Basic Investments" – Jeff Molsen, School of Economics
11:00–12:00	"Advanced Equities" – Pamela Kinnear, General Manager Inc.
12:00–1:00	Lunch*
1:00–2:00	~~"Getting the Most out of Mutual Funds" – Peter Mendel, Fund Manager~~
	(Canceled due to sudden illness. Trying to find a replacement.)
2:00–3:00	"Money Management Advice" – Greg Andrews, Personal Financial Adviser
3:00–4:00	"Electronic Investment – Internet-based Trading" – Clyde Swift, IT Expert

* Not included in the seminar price. Vegetarian food available, providing a reservation is made 3 days in advance.

---

2 Test tactic: Using the 30-second preparation time and answering Questions 7–8

A Read the heading and decide which topic 1–4 the agenda is about.

Arrival of the Malaysian Delegation

7:45	Flight CA132 from Kuala Lumpur scheduled to arrive at Terminal 3
9:15	Train to Brighton (first class)
11:05	Arrive Brighton. Taxi to Avon Hotel (the Grand Hotel was fully booked)
12:00	Taxi to PRJ Offices on Hove Street
12:30	Welcome party in the executive lounge
1:00	Lunch*
2:00	Tour of PRJ Design studios – Jim Paton
3:30	Overview of the new advertising campaign – Mark Cohen
5:30	Delegates taken back to their hotel
7:30	Reservations for dinner at the King's Restaurant

*A special lunch menu has been arranged as requested

---

1. A schedule for some visitors
2. Details of a tour of Brighton
3. Plans for a visit to Malaysia
4. An outline of a food tour

Test tip

Use the preparation time to pick out key information

You have 30 seconds to study the schedule before the first question. Use this time to pick out key information, e.g. the topic (what is it?), what is happening at specific times of the day (morning, afternoon, evening). Also if there are any notes, read them carefully as they are sometimes relevant.

unit
4

Try to remember where key information is

Note where key information is in the schedule. It may help to split the day's events into natural sections, e.g. morning, afternoon, and evening, and summarize what is happening in each section.

B Look at the agenda in A and put events a–c in order of when they will happen 1–3.

   a. tour and overview   b. hotel and dinner   c. travel and welcome party

1. morning   _____

2. afternoon   _____

3. evening   _____

C Find the note in the agenda in A. Which of these questions relate to the information in the note?

1. I just wanted to confirm that food for the Welcome party should be delivered to the cafeteria. That's where it will be held, right?

2. I just want to remind you that we got a request for special meals for our guests. Alex hasn't forgotten to take care of lunch, has she?

3. Hi, I'm afraid that I have misplaced my agenda. Just to confirm, I am meeting you tonight for dinner at 5:30 at English's Restaurant, yes?

Test tip

Question 7 asks for details

Question 7 requires you to answer a question on specific information (*Who, What, When, Where, How*) found in the agenda or schedule.

unit

4

D Read questions 1–4. They are all Question 7-type questions. For each one, complete steps a–c below. The first one has been done for you.

a. Underline the key words in the question.

b. Quickly skim the agenda in A and find the answer.

c. Rephrase the language used in the question to make your answer.

1. Could you tell me <u>which terminal</u> I <u>should</u> be <u>meeting</u> them at?

   <u>(Terminal 3)</u>   *You should meet them at Terminal 3.*

2. What time are they thinking of having lunch?

   _____

3. Do you have any idea who is going to give the overview of the ad campaign?

   _____

4. What time have they scheduled dinner for and where are we going?

   _____

Test tip

Answer with full sentences

Do not give one- or two-word answers. Use full sentences for each question. Pick out words from the question that you can use in your answer.

E 🎧 Listen to questions 1–6. Pick out the key words. Find the answers in the agenda in A. Write your answers rephrasing words used in the question.

1. _____

2. _____

3. _____

4. _____

5. _____

6. _____

Test tip

Question 8 asks for confirmation

This question asks you to correct misinformation or make an inference e.g. asks whether it will be possible to get a special kind of meal. You must check the information, give the answer, and, if necessary, explain why the thing is not possible.

F Read questions 1–4. They are all Question 8-type questions. For each one, complete steps a–c below. The first one has been done for you.

a. Underline the key words in the question.

b. Skim the agenda in A and find the answer.

c. Rephrase the language used in the question to make your answer. For "no" answers, use appropriate introductory phrases.

1. We've got to meet them at Terminal 1, right?
   Yes /(No)
   No, actually you are supposed to meet them at Terminal 3.

2. Mark told me that the Malaysian visitors are coming in on a flight from Bangkok.
   Is that correct?
   Yes / No

   _____

Test tip

Give reasons for *no* answers

If the answer to the question is *no*, then you must politely say so and give a reason. Remember to use full sentences.

3. I understand that we are going to catch the shuttle bus down to Brighton. Can you confirm this?
   Yes / No

   _____

4. Did you manage to get reservations for them at the Grand Hotel? It has always been popular with our visitors.
   Yes / No

   _____

G 🎧 Listen to questions 1–6. Pick out the key words. Find the answers in the agenda in A. Write your answers rephrasing words used in the question.

1. _____

2. _____

3. _____

4. _____

5. _____

6. _____

unit
4

☑ Read the heading to find out what the topic is.

☑ Describe what is happening at different times of the day.

☑ Look for any notes giving extra information about the agenda.

☑ Listen for key words in the questions.

☑ Scan the agenda to find the information you need quickly.

☑ Answer in full sentences, using phrases to refer back to the agenda or to introduce bad news.

☑ Include explanations when answering.

unit

4

B Tactic practice

🎧 Take 30 seconds to read the agenda in Task A. Then, in pairs, take turns to listen and answer questions 1–2 following the steps in the Test technique. Repeat the steps for Tasks B and C.

Task A

Green Valley Tours

6-hour Green Valley Tour, available for small or large groups.
Tour-bus ($95 per person) or Mini-bus ($125 per person).

9:30	Pick up (available from any Green Valley hotel location)
10:30	Arrive Green Valley Inn
10:30–12:30	Tour of Green Valley (including the Fine Arts Museum)
12:30	Picnic lunch at scenic Harwood Estate*
1:30	Depart for historic Freemark Abbey
2:00–3:30	Tour of Freemark Abbey
3:30	Return

* $25 extra for picnic lunch

Task B

World Movie Premiere of *Crystal Dreams*   March 6
Starring Owen Hillsborough

Itinerary for Mr. Hillsborough:

2:00 PM	*Drive from hotel to LAX*
3:00 PM	*Arrive at Sanchez Restaurant for pre-screening party*
5:30 PM	*Media session in front of Sanchez Restaurant (Question and Answer, photo shoot)*
6:00 PM	*Leave Sanchez to drive to Pyramid Theatre, central LA*
6:45 PM	*Red Carpet arrival, meet the fans and autograph-signing session*
7:30 PM	*Movie starts (note change of start time)*
9:30 PM	*Cast party*
12:00 AM	*Limousine to Hotel (Charlotte Hills)*

Task C

Allwright Orientation Seminar

Venue: Allwright Co., Central Office, Lakeview Rd. **Time:** 10:00

10:00–10:30	Welcome to the team – Max Miller, Company President
10:30–11:30	Company overview – Ted Williams, Vice President
11:30–12:30	Paperwork, contract details – Myriam Marshall, Personnel Director
12:30–1:30	Lunch*
1:30–2:30	Tour of Head Office – groups of 5, various supervisors
2:30–3:30	Introduction to On-the-Job Training – Stephen Waits, Personnel
3:30–4:00	Review of schedules for Day Two – Myriam Marshall, Personnel Director

* Trainees are free to use this time as they like. Cafeteria services will not be available due to renovations.

In natural spoken English, sounds are sometimes changed, combined, or dropped. Listen to a native speaker saying the following sentences and write in the words they say.

_____ be able to tell me when the meeting is likely to end?

_____ happen to know the flight number?

_____ tell me which terminal?

Check your answers in the Key on page 12.

Listen again and practice these sentences with the correct sound and rhythm.

C Mini-test

Now apply the Test tactics to answer the following questions. Use the recommended test time for Questions 7–9.

Important

In the test, Questions 7–9 appear together as you will find here in the Mini-test. In this book, Questions 7–8 and Question 9 are covered in separate units. For information and practice on Question 9, see Unit 10.

**Questions 7–9:
Respond to questions
using information
provided**

unit
4

TOEIC Speaking

Questions 7–9: Respond to questions using information provided

Directions: In this part of the test, you will answer three questions based on the information provided. You will have 30 seconds to read the information before the questions begin. For each question, begin responding immediately after you hear a beep. No additional preparation time is provided. You will have 15 seconds to respond to Questions 7 and 8 and 30 seconds to respond to Question 9.

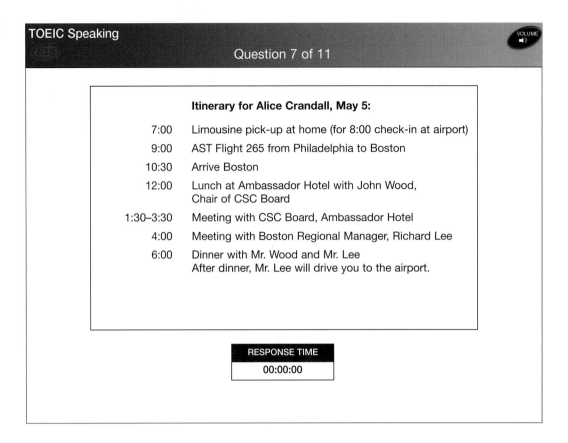

TOEIC Speaking

Question 7 of 11

VOLUME

Itinerary for Alice Crandall, May 5:

7:00	Limousine pick-up at home (for 8:00 check-in at airport)
9:00	AST Flight 265 from Philadelphia to Boston
10:30	Arrive Boston
12:00	Lunch at Ambassador Hotel with John Wood, Chair of CSC Board
1:30–3:30	Meeting with CSC Board, Ambassador Hotel
4:00	Meeting with Boston Regional Manager, Richard Lee
6:00	Dinner with Mr. Wood and Mr. Lee After dinner, Mr. Lee will drive you to the airport.

RESPONSE TIME
00:00:00

Question 7
🎧 Listen to the question. You have 15 seconds to respond.

Question 8
🎧 Listen to the question. You have 15 seconds to respond.

Question 9
🎧 Listen to the question. You have 30 seconds to respond.

If you want to do the follow-up unit to this test item now, please go to Unit 10, page 106.

A Focus: Responding to complaints

In the test

← **Sample test pp28–31**
Speaking Test Question 10

- In Question 10, you will hear a telephone voice message. The caller will make either a request or a complaint.
- You will then be given 30 seconds to prepare a response to the message.
- You will only hear the message once, and it does not appear as text on the screen.
- You have 60 seconds to give your spoken response. In your response, you must show you recognize the problem and propose a way of dealing with it.
- You will be scored on dealing with the task in a suitable way, using the correct level of formality, and providing an answer that is clear and well-organized.
- In Unit 11, we will focus on responding to requests.
- In this unit, we will focus on responding to complaints.

1 Language building: Introducing messages, apologizing, explaining the cause of problems, and suggesting solutions

Test tip

Practice leaving messages

The language you use in messages will differ from the language you use in a conversation. The language we practice in Units 5 and 11 will give examples of the sort of language to use. It is important to practice leaving messages to get used to this.

A Sentences 1–3 would come at the start of a telephone reply call. Match them to their uses shown in a–c.

1. Hello! This is a message for [Heather Gill]. _____

2. This is [Andrew McKelvey] from [Ace Trucking] returning your call. _____

3. I got your message regarding [the problem with the delivery]. _____

a. acknowledge the message you received
b. say who you are, where you are from (if relevant), and why you are calling
c. say who the message is for

unit
5

Test tip

Remember the caller's name

You will hear the caller's name at the beginning and the end of the message you listen to. Remember it, and use it in your opening sentence.

B With a partner, practice introducing your message to the people in scenarios 1–5. The first one is done for you.

1. Person who called: Jenny Pollard
   Person returning call: Alex Thomas (Central Heating)
   Message: new heating system broken again

   Hi. This is a message for Jenny Pollard. This is Alex Thomas from the Central Heating Company returning your call. I got your message regarding the fact that your new heating system is broken again ...

2. Person who called: Tara Smith
   Person returning call: Fran Turner (Davenport Language School)
   Message: has not received information requested

3. Person who called: Will Burns
   Person returning call: Jan Mothersole (Trust Bank)
   Message: lost bank card

4. Person who called: Peter McFarland
   Person returning call: Andy Wilson (Natural Flooring)
   Message: color of floor doesn't match the sample floor tile

5. Person who called: Melody Thompson
   Person returning call: Charlie Green (A to Z Travel)
   Message: wants deposit refunded

Test tip

Recognize the caller's problem

Make an apology and summarize the caller's problem to help them feel like their situation is being addressed appropriately.

C After the introduction, you should apologize to the caller and acknowledge the complaint. Read examples 1 and 2. <u>Underline</u> the phrases that are used to apologize.

1. You made a mistake on a bill to a customer:
   I am very sorry about the mistake on your bill.

2. A customer bought a defective product in one of your company's stores:
   We'd like to apologize for the defective product you bought in our store.

D Make similar apologies about problems 1–5. Use the phrases given.

I'm / We're sorry about …
I'm / We're very sorry for …
I'm / We're sorry that …
I / We'd like to apologize for (the mistake with …)
Please accept my / our apologies for this …
We sincerely hope you will accept our apologies for this situation.

1. You misspelled a customer's name on a bill.

   _____

2. Your company delivered an order one week late.

   _____

3. The customer claims that a salesperson in your company was very rude.

   _____

4. Something sold in your store was missing some important parts.

   _____

5. A truck driver with your company damaged a customer's car.

   _____

unit
5

Test tip

Give background reasons for the problem

The person making the complaint may expect you to tell them what went wrong and why. Generally, it's a good idea to include an explanation of the problem and its cause.

E After apologizing, it is a good idea to explain what went wrong.
Read sentence beginnings 1–4 and match them to endings a–d.
The phrases in **bold** introduce reasons for the problem and are useful to learn.

1. **It seems there was some kind of problem with** our computer records, so … _____

2. **I believe there was some confusion over** the tools your team ordered … _____

3. **I'm afraid that** the wrong delivery date was put on your order, which … _____

4. **There appears to have been a problem at** the factory … _____

a. meant that the warehouse sent it out one week later than you expected.
b. and you were sent the wrong equipment.
c. and these defective items were mistakenly sent out to our stores.
d. your order was sent to the wrong address.

F Make similar explanations about the problems in 1–5. Use some of the phrases in **bold** from E. The first one is done for you.

1. Cold weather – pipes froze and broke
   It seems that because of the cold weather last night your water pipes froze and broke.

2. New delivery driver got lost – deliveries were late
   _____

3. Mistake in warehouse – wrong color chair was shipped
   _____

4. Airline strike in Europe – delay in parts being sent
   _____

5. You made a mistake – CDs weren't delivered to salesperson
   _____

Test tip

Explain your solution

Tell the caller what you would like to do to solve the problem. If the problem can't be fixed, explain how you will avoid similar problems in future, and perhaps offer some financial benefit as compensation.

G Read the phrases in **bold** in 1–5, which introduce solutions. <u>Underline</u> any time phrases that state when the problem will be fixed. Which sentence is offering a financial benefit as they cannot correct the problem?

1. **We're going to arrange for someone** to fix the problem this afternoon.
2. **We'd like to send** the missing parts **by courier to** your office this evening.
3. **I'd like to offer you** a new one / a replacement this week.
4. **We will fix the problem** in the system **immediately,** so that this problem will never happen again.
5. **Because this is our mistake, we would like to** offer you a 20% discount on your next purcase.

H Make similar sentences stating when the problem will be fixed for problems 1–5 in B. Use some of the phrases in **bold** from G.

1. _____

2. _____

3. _____

4. _____

5. _____

Follow up: Compare answers with your partner.

2 Test tactic: Listening for key information, using your imagination, and organizing your response

A 🎧 When you hear the telephone message, it is important that you listen for and remember key information. Listen and read the transcript of a complaint and complete the missing information a–d.

Transcript of the complaint (this will not be shown on the actual test)

Hi, this is John Lord in apartment 16. Listen, I've just noticed that the water in my apartment doesn't seem to be working. I just turned on the tap, and a little bit came out, but now it's stopped. Now I need to take a shower, and I've got to wash my clothes and things, and I need water to cook. And I will definitely need it tomorrow before I go to work. This is really a problem, and I'd appreciate it if you could call me back and let me know what you are going to do about this. I really need this to be taken care of today. Thanks a lot. This is John Lord in apartment 16.

a. Name of the complainant

   _____

b. Complaint

   _____

c. Special conditions (e.g. time, deadlines, or other issues)

   _____

d. Your role

   _____

Use your imagination in the preparation time

Use your imagination to think of an explanation about why the problem happened. Then think of a solution to the problem.

B Listen to three more complaints and note the same information.

1.

a. Name of the complainant

_____

b. Complaint

_____

c. Special conditions (e.g. time, deadlines, or other issues)

_____

d. Your role

_____

2.

a. Name of the complainant

_____

b. Complaint

_____

c. Special conditions (e.g. time, deadlines, or other issues)

_____

d. Your role

_____

3.

a. Name of the complainant

_____

b. Complaint

_____

c. Special conditions (e.g. time, deadlines, or other issues)

_____

d. Your role

_____

unit
5

Always give a solution

Question 10 is called *Propose a solution*, so it is very important to include a solution in your answer. Even if you don't understand the whole message, listen for the complaint and think of a solution. It will help if you practice thinking of solutions.

C Match complaints 1–5 with an explanation a–e and a solution f–j.

Complaints

1. The train was very late and I arrived one hour after my interview was due to begin. ____ ____
2. The store was closed before the time advertised, so we couldn't buy what we needed. ____ ____
3. The computer we bought was missing a cable, so we haven't been able to use it. ____ ____
4. The waiter wouldn't allow us in the restaurant with our children, so we had to go home. ____ ____
5. The new DVD we bought didn't work when we tried it. My children were very disappointed. ____ ____

Explanations

a. I'm afraid it could have been damaged during delivery.
b. I believe there have been a few problems with the packing department recently.
c. It seems that there was a problem with the engine, causing the train to be delayed.
d. I'm afraid the power went out, so we were forced to close early.
e. The waiter appears to have misunderstood our policy.

Solutions

f. We'd like to send you the missing cable by courier today.
g. I'd like to offer you a replacement DVD. We will courier it to your home immediately.
h. Because this is our mistake, we would like to offer you and your family a free meal this weekend.
i. We have fixed the problem and bought a new generator, so this problem should never force us to close early again.
j. We're going to change the system to make sure each train has at least two drivers who are trained mechanics, so this problem shouldn't happen again. To compensate you for your inconvenience, we would like to offer you a free monthly pass.

D With a partner, think of explanations and solutions for complaints 1–3 in B.

1. _____

   _____

2. _____

   _____

3. _____

   _____

unit
5

Understand the organization of typical complaint responses

Polite complaint responses usually follow a set pattern. If you know this pattern, you can build a complete and appropriate response out of short, and reasonably simple, parts.

You can use a fake name and company

If you don't want to use your own name, you can memorize a fake one like *John/ Mary Smith*. Also to save time thinking of a company name, you can always use something like *ABC*.

Use your imagination

You must use your imagination to think of possible causes and solutions to the problem. Try to remember similar situations that you, your friends or family may have experienced or something similar you may have seen on TV.

E Read steps 1–6 explaining how to organize a typical response. Match example sentences a–f below to the appropriate step.

1. **Polite greeting confirming names**
   Greet the person using their name and introduce yourself and your position (if appropriate).

   e.g. ＿＿＿

2. **Reason why you are calling**
   Say that you got their message and give a short summary of the problem.

   e.g. ＿＿＿

3. **Apology / Sympathetic response**
   Say you are sorry to hear about the problem.

   e.g. ＿＿＿

4. **Explanation of problem and its cause**
   Use your imagination to think of a possible explanation of what happened, and why.

   e.g. ＿＿＿

5. **Your solution (and financial benefit if appropriate)**
   Use your imagination to think of a way to fix the problem and say when it will be fixed. Or offer financial benefit as compensation (e.g. one month free; a discount).

   e.g. ＿＿＿

6. **Sincerest apologies**
   Finish the conversation with an apology phrase.

   e.g. ＿＿＿

unit
5

a. We're sending someone out this afternoon to repair the pipes.
b. I'm really sorry to hear that your water has stopped.
c. I received your message about the water problem in your apartment.
d. Hello. This is a message for Mr. Lord. This is John Smith from ABC Building Management returning your call.
e. Once again, I am very sorry for any inconvenience this has caused.
f. It seems that the cold weather last night caused your water pipes to freeze.

F 🎧 Listen to the three complaints in B again. Choose one of the complaints and make responses to those problems. Use the notes you made in B and D. Use the headings 1–6 in E as a checklist.

_____

_____

_____

_____

_____

_____

Follow up: Read your response to your partner. In pairs, make similar responses for the other problems.

Test technique

☑ Listen carefully for key information (name, problem, special conditions).

☑ Determine what your role is.

☑ Use the preparation time to brainstorm possible causes of the problem, and your solution.

☑ Follow a model:
 • greeting
 • reason for call
 • initial apology
 • explanation
 • solution
 • final apology

B Tactic practice

A 🎧 Listen to complaints 1–4.

Use the Test tactics you have practiced to complete the following information. Follow the steps in the Test technique. After each step, compare answers with your partner.

1.
a. Name of the complainant

_____

b. Complaint

_____

c. Special conditions (e.g. time, deadlines, or other issues)

_____

d. Your role

_____

2.
a. Name of the complainant

_____

b. Complaint

_____

c. Special conditions (e.g. time, deadlines, or other issues)

_____

d. Your role

_____

3.

a. Name of the complainant

_____

b. Complaint

_____

c. Special conditions (e.g. time, deadlines, or other issues)

_____

d. Your role

_____

4.

a. Name of the complainant

_____

b. Complaint

_____

c. Special conditions (e.g. time, deadlines, or other issues)

_____

d. Your role

_____

B Take turns making your responses. In each response, be sure to recognize the caller's problem, and propose a way of dealing with it.

🎧 Using natural English

In natural spoken English, sounds are sometimes changed, combined, or dropped. Listen to a native speaker saying the following sentences and write in the words they say.

I'm very sorry about the mistake in _____ bill.
This is Alex Thomas, returning _____ call.
I got _____ message regarding the problem.

Check your answers in the Key on page 15.

Listen again and practice these sentences with the correct sound and rhythm.

C Mini-test

Now apply the Test tactics to draft an outline for the following question. Use the recommended test time for Question 10.

Question 10:
Propose a solution

Question 10: Propose a solution

Directions: In this part of the test, you will be presented with a problem and asked to propose a solution.

You will have 30 seconds to prepare. Then you will have 60 seconds to speak.

In your response, be sure to
- show that you recognize the problem, and
- propose a way of dealing with the problem.

🎧 Listen to the message.

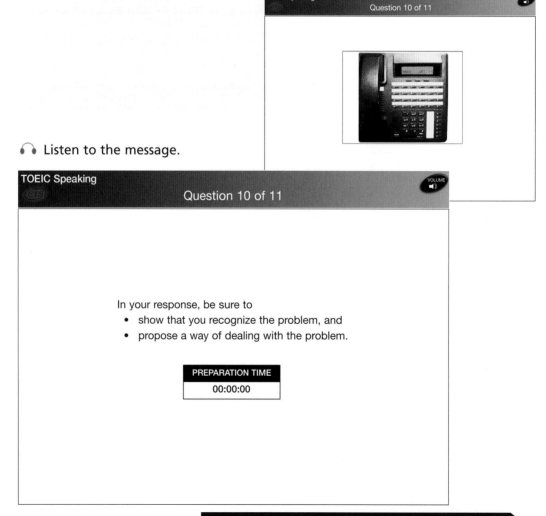

If you want to do the follow-up unit to this test item now, please go to Unit 11, page 116.

A Focus: Planning and delivering an opinion

In the test

← **Sample test pp32–34**
Speaking Test Question 11

- In this question, you will be asked to give your opinion on a topic.
- The directions and the task will appear written on the screen, and will also be spoken.
- The focus of the question will vary, but it will always be an informal and familiar context.
- You will have 15 seconds to prepare your response.
- You will have 60 seconds to give your opinion and support it with reasons and examples.
- Speak slowly and clearly, but say as much as you can in the time allowed.
- In this unit, we will practice how to express and develop an opinion and how to link your ideas.
- In Unit 12, we will focus on personalizing opinions, opposing arguments, and hesitation devices.

1 Language building: Language for stating and linking your ideas

Test tip

Become familiar with common ways of stating your opinion

The wording of the question gives clues as to the appropriate way to state your opinion. Listen carefully and choose an appropriate form.

Test tip

Give a clear opinion

You may be asked to give your opinion based on two choices. Make sure you choose one and give reasons for your choice.

A Match the common question types 1–8 to the opinion phrases a–h. The first one is done for you.

1. Many people think (X) is better than (Y). Which do you think is better? _a_

2. Would you rather (X) or (Y)? _____

3. Would you prefer (X) or (Y)? _____

4. "People should (X)." Do you agree or disagree? _____

5. "It has recently been announced that (X) may change." Would you support or oppose this plan? _____

6. If you could change one important thing about (X), would you change (Y) or (Z)? _____

7. What is your opinion on this issue? _____

8. Are you in favor of companies/governments doing (X)? _____

a. I think/believe …
b. If I could (change) one thing, I would …
c. I agree/disagree that …
d. I would prefer …
e. I would support/oppose …
f. I am in favor of/I am against …
g. My opinion (on X) is …
h. I would rather …

unit
6

Show what it is you are agreeing with, preferring, or supporting.

One way to do this is by restating the relevant part of the question in your first sentence.

B Read the questions and opinion statements. The <u>underlined</u> words in 1 show the part of the question that is being restated. <u>Underline</u> the restated words in the sentences in *italics* in 2 and 3.

1. Would you prefer to work at home or in an office?

    I think I would prefer to <u>work at home</u>.

2. Do you agree or disagree that dogs make better pets than cats?

    I disagree that dogs make better pets than cats.

    Or

    I disagree with this statement. I think cats make better pets than dogs.

3. Your town is planning to build a new shopping mall close to where you live. Do you support or oppose this plan?

    I would oppose the plan for building a new shopping mall close to where I live.

C Complete sentences 1–5 to make opinion statements which restate the question. Use the examples in B to help you.

1. Would you prefer to find a job in your hometown or in a different city?

    I would prefer to _____

2. There is a plan to hold the Olympics near your town. Are you in favor of this idea?

    I am in favor of _____

3. Some people believe private cars should be banned from city centers. What do you think?

    I think _____

4. Would you rather play an individual sport or a team sport?

    I would rather _____

5. "People should stop working at the age of 60." Do you agree or disagree with this statement?

    I disagree that _____

unit
6

D Practice making similar opinion statements with your partner by doing the task below.

Student A: Read the task below.

Student B: Look at Activity File Unit 6 on page 225.

Student A

Take turns asking each other questions 1–3. When it is your turn to answer, give an opinion statement only. Ask Student B these questions.

1. Some people like to buy goods or services in person. Other people prefer to shop using the Internet, catalogs, or TV. Which way of shopping do you prefer, and why?
2. Some people like to travel with a group. Others would rather travel by themselves. Which do you prefer, and why?
3. Would you prefer to work in a large group, or with just a few people? Explain why.

Test tip

Use sequence words to introduce and order your supporting reasons

This will help keep your answer well organized.

E Read the sequence words and put them in the appropriate part of the table.

First   Finally   I also think that   First of all   The final reason is
Another reason why is   The second reason is   The first reason is   Also

Use	Sequence words
To introduce your first supporting point	
To add your second / other supporting points	
To add your last supporting point	

F 🎧 Read example question 1 and the notes on the left. Then listen and read the example answer. <u>Underline</u> the sequence words.

Example:

1. Would you prefer to find a job in your home country or a different country?

   I would rather find a job in my home country.

   The first reason is I wouldn't have any trouble with the language.

   Also, I like the local food very much.

   Finally, I would miss my family very much if I went overseas.

Prefer home country
– no language trouble
– I like local food very much
– miss my family

G For questions 2 and 3, join the ideas given in the boxes. Use the sequence words in E.

2. There is a plan to hold the Olympics near your town / city. Are you in favor of this idea?

   _____

   _____

   _____

   _____

In favor
– I am a sports fan
– good for local business
– make my town / city famous

3. Some people believe private cars should be banned from downtown areas. What do you think?

Agree
– fewer cars mean less pollution
– no more traffic jams downtown
– city less noisy

_____

_____

_____

H Give your own opinion for questions 4 and 5. Prepare notes in the boxes on the left, then write a paragraph to practice organizing your ideas. (In the test, you will have 15 seconds to plan your ideas in your head.)

4. Would you rather play an individual sport or a team sport?

_____

_____

_____

_____

5. "People should stop working at age 60." Do you agree or disagree with this statement?

_____

_____

_____

_____

Follow up: With a partner, cover your notes and practice answering questions 4 and 5.

Note: The paragraphs above are the outline of your answer. In the next section and in Unit 12, you will practice expanding each reason you give.

2 Test tactic: Preparation and delivery

Test tip

Focus clearly on the task

To answer the question correctly you must first understand the task. Quickly read the question and summarize it into one single question.

A Read the question and choose the sentence a–c that summarizes it best.

Some people prefer to fix or build things by themselves. Others prefer to pay other people to do these types of things. Which way do you prefer, and why? Use specific reasons and details to support your answer.

Summary:

a. What do you do when things break?

b. Do you prefer to fix and build things by yourself or pay someone to do it?

c. Why don't you usually pay others to repair things for you?

B Write a short summary sentence for questions 1–3.

1. You have just won a contest, and for your prize you can choose either a small car or an airline ticket. Which would you choose? Use specific reasons and details to support your answer.

   Summary:

   _____

2. Do you agree or disagree with the following statement? "Competition is a fact of life, and children should learn to be competitive when they are young." Use specific reasons to support your answer.

   Summary:

   _____

3. If you were hiring a new employee, would you prefer to choose someone who is very intelligent or someone who is very reliable? Use reasons and examples to explain your choice.

   Summary:

   _____

Test tip

Decide on your answer and plan your supporting points

You only have 15 seconds to do this, so you must think quickly. The supporting points will form the body of your talk, but you must add reasons and/or examples for each.

C Decide your opinion on the questions in B.
Then take turns making opinion statements. Look at Language building C on page 80 to help you.

D Take turns preparing reasons for your opinion on one of the questions in B. You will have 10 seconds to brainstorm three supporting points for your opinion. Very short sentences or a couple of words are OK. Your partner will time you.

Test tip

Choose an opinion and stay with it

If you don't have a very strong opinion on the topic, it is best to choose one opinion and stick to it. Otherwise your answer will be unclear.

unit
6

E 🎧 Read the supporting points for the example question *Do you prefer to fix and build things by yourself or pay someone to do it?* Then listen to and read the example paragraph for point 1. Do you agree with the points the speaker makes?

Some people prefer to fix or build things by themselves. Other people prefer to pay others to do these types of things. Which way do you prefer, and why? Use specific reasons and details to support your answer.

Test tip

Think of reasons / examples for each supporting point

You should include these after introducing each of the points.

Prefer to do it myself	**Prefer to pay someone**
Point 1 – It can save money	Point 1 – Professionals do a better job
Point 2 – You can learn new skills	Point 2 – You don't waste your time
Point 3 – It gives you a good feeling	Point 3 – It can be dirty and tiring

Example:

When things break, I usually prefer to fix things myself if I can. The first reason for this is that it saves money. Many things can be repaired easily once you have a little bit of experience. Once you have bought a set of tools, which could last forever, the actual cost for a repair is usually only in time and effort and not really any financial cost to you.

Test tip

Keep a steady pace and watch your timing

Speak at a careful, steady pace to allow yourself time to think.

F With your partner, take turns introducing a statement (from the six points above or your own ideas), then talk about it for about 15 seconds, giving examples and reasons. Your partner will time you.

B Tactic practice

Use the Test tactics you have practiced to give your opinions on questions 1–4. Follow the four steps summarized in the Test technique. After each step, pause to see if your partner has understood and if they have any suggestions. Your partner will also time you during your supporting points.

1. There is a plan to hold the Olympics near your town. Do you support or oppose this idea? Use reasons and examples to explain your choice.
2. Some people believe private cars should be banned from downtown areas. Do you agree or disagree? Use reasons and examples to explain your choice.
3. Would you rather play an individual sport or a team sport? Use specific reasons to support your answer.
4. "People should stop work at age the age of 60." Do you agree or disagree with this statement? Use reasons and examples to explain your choice.

unit
6

Test technique

☑ Quickly summarize the task and decide your opinion.

☑ Brainstorm several supporting points.

☑ Make your opinion statement.

☑ Introduce each supporting point and add reasons and examples.

🎧 **Using natural English**

In natural spoken English, sounds are sometimes changed, combined, or dropped. Listen to a native speaker saying the following sentences and write in the words they say.

If I _____ change one thing about my life, I think _____ go to graduate school.

If I _____ live in any other city, _____ prefer to live in Paris.

Check your answers in the Key on page 18.

Listen again and practice these sentences with the correct sound and rhythm.

C Mini-test

Now apply the Test tactics to answer the following question. Use the recommended test time for Question 11.

Question 11:
Express an opinion

Question 11: Express an opinion

Directions: In this part of the test, you will give your opinion about a specific topic. Be sure to say as much as you can in the time allowed. You will have 15 seconds to prepare. Then you will have 60 seconds to speak.

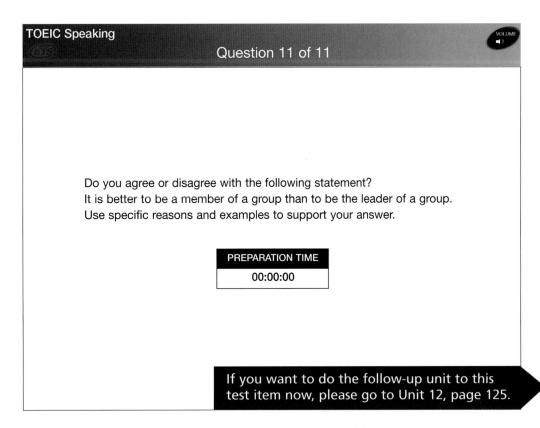

TOEIC Speaking

Question 11 of 11

Do you agree or disagree with the following statement?
It is better to be a member of a group than to be the leader of a group.
Use specific reasons and examples to support your answer.

PREPARATION TIME
00:00:00

If you want to do the follow-up unit to this test item now, please go to Unit 12, page 125.

A Focus: Stress and intonation

In the test

← **Sample test pp15–17**
← **Unit 1 p39**
Speaking Test Questions 1–2

- In each of these questions, you will be given a paragraph of 40–60 words to read aloud.
- You will be given 45 seconds to prepare and 45 seconds to read the text aloud.
- You will be scored on your pronunciation, and the intonation and stress of your sentences.
- In Unit 1, we focused on the pronunciation and stress of individual words and intonation in lists and questions.
- In this unit, we will focus on stress and intonation with transition words.

1 Language building: Stress and pausing

Test tip

Use the punctuation marks to help

Periods and commas signal the places to pause to give your listener time to understand what you have said. After periods and commas, pause briefly.

Test tip

Don't pause in the middle of a *thought group*

Try to avoid pausing in the middle of a thought group. This will make your message easier to follow. Look for groups of words that have a single idea and make sure that you read these as a group.

A 🎧 Listen to a native speaker reading the paragraph. The marks (✓) indicate when the reader pauses. What effect does punctuation have on pauses? Where else does the speaker pause?

The Thornburg Summer festival got off to a terrific start today. (✓) As usual, (✓) large crowds were in attendance for the strong man, (✓) wood-chopping, (✓) and pie-baking contests this afternoon, (✓) and we expect the fun to continue (✓) until the closing fireworks on Sunday evening. (✓)

Pronunciation note

Thought groups

Complex sentences in spoken English are divided up into shorter chunks, each with a separate idea. These are called "thought groups". The last content word (noun, verb, adjective, or adverb) may be followed by a slight pause.

B 🎧 Listen again to the paragraph in A being read. Listen and repeat each phrase.

1. The Thornburg Summer festival got off to a terrific start today.
2. As usual,
3. large crowds were in attendance for the strong man,
4. wood chopping,
5. and pie-baking contests this afternoon,
6. and we expect the fun to continue
7. until the closing fireworks on Sunday evening.

C 🎧 In each read-aloud task, there will be a complex sentence. Read sentences 1 and 2 and divide them into thought groups. Then listen and repeat each sentence.

1. We would like to thank Paul for all his hard work over the years, and wish him the very best for his retirement.
2. While you are waiting, you may wish to enjoy the comfort of our visitors' lounge, or alternatively, take in the view from our roof-top terrace.

unit
7

D 🎧 Listen again to the first sentence of the text in A. Repeat the sentence putting a stress on the marked sounds.

●   ●   ●   ●   ●   ●   ●
The Thornburg Summer festival got off to a terrific start today.

Test tip

Auxiliary verbs aren't usually stressed

Statements using auxiliary verbs (e.g. *is, are, can, have, will*) are usually unstressed. This means that the vowel sound becomes shorter and consonants may change or be dropped, e.g. "He can…" may sound more like /hɪːkʌn/.

E Look back at the sentence in D and answer questions 1–3.

1. What parts of speech are stressed?
2. What parts of speech are not stressed?
3. What happens to the pronunciation in unstressed words?

F 🎧 <u>Underline</u> the words in the first sentence that you think will be stressed. Then listen to the recording and check your answers. Now do the same with the remaining sentences. Check your answers in the Key on page 19.

1. Thank you for calling the Central Library.
2. May I have the attention of passengers traveling to Rome?
3. On Sunday, June 6, we will be doing essential work on the server.
4. Welcome, and thank you for joining us today.
5. Attention all shoppers in the home and garden department.

G 🎧 Listen to the words and sentences in 1–5. Repeat them aloud. Do the auxiliary words sound the same on their own as they do in a sentence?

1. could   I could finish the document this evening.
2. have   Where have they left the files?
3. can   They can play tennis.
4. did   Where did you put the key?
5. are   All of our parts are made in this city.

🎧 *Follow up*: Listen again to the sentences in G. Repeat what you hear. <u>Underline</u> the words in the sentences that are unstressed.

H 🎧 Listen to the words and sentences in 1–3 being read aloud. Repeat them aloud. Do the sounds of the negative auxiliaries change in the same way as in G?

1. can't   She can't speak Spanish.
2. didn't   He didn't say goodbye.
3. couldn't   He couldn't finish the project.

I 🎧 Read sentences 1–6 and <u>underline</u> any auxiliary verbs and the other words that are normally weak. Listen to the sentences and repeat what you hear. Check your answers in the Key on page 19.

1. The builder couldn't fix the leak in the roof.
2. He thinks the project will be canceled.
3. What did his boss say?
4. Sorry, you can't get a discount on this stereo.
5. The Grand is the most expensive hotel.
6. Ms. Smith didn't leave a forwarding address.

2 Test tactic: Intonation with transition words

Test tip

Each paragraph will contain at least one transition word, e.g. *because, although, also, until, however.* These show how the clauses in a sentence relate to each other. Transition words that appear at the beginning of a sentence, or following a comma, are often marked by a rise in intonation.

A 🎧 In this part of the test, the text you read aloud will include a transition word. Make sure you are familiar with the common intonation pattern for transition words. Listen to the sentence and repeat. Try to imitate the intonation used by the speaker.

↗

Although this beautiful house was damaged by fire in 1962, Lyle had it completely rebuilt.

B 🎧 In pairs, read sentences 1–4 aloud and mark the intonation of the words in **bold**. Then listen, repeat, and check your answers.

1. **Until** further notice, the slow train to Maine will be canceled.
2. The main entrance will be closed over the weekend. **However,** staff will be able to gain access through the side gates.
3. You shouldn't call the technician **unless** there is a problem with the system.
4. **Because** the museum is closed for refurbishment at the moment, we won't be able to visit it during our stay.

C Read the paragraph and <u>underline</u> the transition word. Then divide the paragraph into thought groups and mark the pauses.

To the left of the bus, we can see the home of the famous movie star, Lyle Randleman. Although this beautiful house was damaged by fire in 1962, Lyle had it completely rebuilt. A new wing decorated in Italian marble, teak from Indonesia, and Canadian redwood was also added at this time.

🎧 *Follow up*: Listen to a native speaker reading the text in C and check your answers.

D Read paragraphs 1 and 2, and mark the pauses and stressed words.

1. Hi. This is Bill Thomson from apartment nineteen. Unfortunately, I am still waiting for someone to come up and take care of my garbage disposal. It is making a loud noise, liquid is leaking from the bottom, and there is definitely something seriously wrong with it. When is something going to be done about this?

2. For almost fifteen years now, Charlie Simpson has been one of our top sales people, trained our new sales staff, and coached our winning softball team. So, on behalf of all the employees of Jenkins Interiors, I would like to wish him the very best for the future.

E Look again at the paragraphs in D. Find the transition word, the list, and the question (if there is one). How should you pronounce these? Look back at Unit 1, pages 42–43 for help if necessary.

Follow up: With your partner, choose one paragraph each from D to read aloud. Be careful to use appropriate pauses, stress, and intonation.

B Tactic practice

Prepare paragraphs 1–4 following the steps in the Test technique and the Remember notes on the next page. After each step, compare answers with your partner. Then choose one text each and read it aloud.

1.

Still searching for a health club that's right for you? Well, look no further than Buster's Health Club and Spa. Buster's has modern equipment, experienced trainers, and spa facilities, that other clubs can't match at double the price. Come on down and see for yourself, and we guarantee we'll make you a happy customer.

Test technique

☑ Do not rush. Keep a steady pace, and pause at commas and periods.

☑ Do not pause in the middle of thought groups.

☑ Think about which words to stress and how to say the unstressed words.

☑ Watch for transition words and use an appropriate intonation.

Remember

☑ Watch for any unknown words or words that are difficult to pronounce.

☑ Think about where the stress goes on individual words.

☑ Look for the list and remember the up, up, down pattern.

☑ Are there any questions? Remember the common intonation patterns in questions.

Test tip

Numbers will be written out in full

In this part of the test, any numbers will usually be written out in full to help you. These questions do not test your ability with numbers in English, but how to pronounce English when speaking aloud.

2.

Attention passengers with tickets on the four-thirty express train bound for Bloomington, Forest Hill, and Rosedale. Unfortunately, this train has been delayed for thirty minutes. It will now be leaving at five o'clock on track thirteen. We apologize for any inconvenience.

3.

Welcome to the Midville City museum. This month we have a special display of colonial era items. Please visit our special gallery to see the collections of seventeenth-century clothing, furniture, and weapons. Be sure to come early, however, as this is a very popular exhibit.

4.

May I have your attention? All participants who have signed up for courses in Spanish, Latin, or Italian will be attending an orientation session in the Fraser Building, directly in front of the main offices. Please go immediately to the lobby, where you will be able to find class lists for these courses.

🎧 Using natural English

In natural spoken English, sounds are sometimes changed, combined, or dropped. Listen to a native speaker saying the following sentences and write in the words they say.

Large crowds were in attendance _____ the contests.

We would like to thank Paul _____ all his hard work.

Thank you _____ calling the Central Library.

Check your answers in the Key on page 20.

Listen again and practice these sentences with the correct sound and rhythm.

C Mini-test

Now apply the Test tactics to prepare for and read aloud the following text. Use the recommended test times for Questions 1–2.

Questions 1–2: Read a text aloud

Directions: In this part of the test, you will read aloud the text on the screen. You will have 45 seconds to prepare. Then you will have 45 seconds to read the text aloud.

Question 1

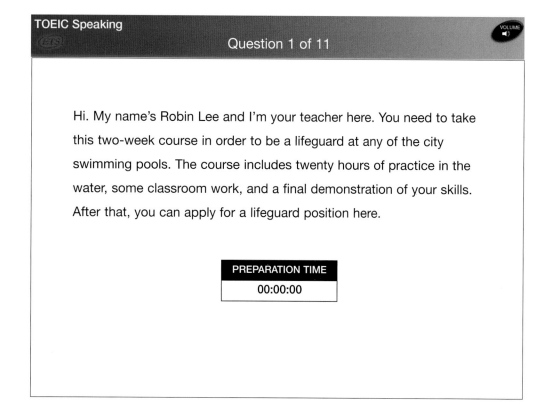

TOEIC Speaking

Question 1 of 11

Hi. My name's Robin Lee and I'm your teacher here. You need to take this two-week course in order to be a lifeguard at any of the city swimming pools. The course includes twenty hours of practice in the water, some classroom work, and a final demonstration of your skills. After that, you can apply for a lifeguard position here.

PREPARATION TIME
00:00:00

Question 2

Ladies and gentlemen, welcome. There'll be a short break after the first half of the show tonight, and you'll have about twenty minutes to buy coffee, soft drinks, and other refreshments in the lobby. However, we do want to resume the performance promptly after the break, so please return to your seats when you hear the bell ring.

RESPONSE TIME
00:00:00

Speaking Test
Question 3 — Describe a picture

A Focus: Speculating on a picture

In the test

← **Sample test pp18–19**
← **Unit 2 p47**
Speaking Test Question 3

- In this part of the test, you will be given a picture to describe in as much detail as you can.
- In Unit 2, you practiced how to describe the scene and the people, and how to plan and organize your response.
- This unit will focus on how to speculate and talk about details in the picture that you are unsure about and how to organize your reply.

unit
8

1 Language building: Language for speculation and uncertainty

1.

2.

3.

4.

Test tip

Learn useful phrases to indicate that you are speculating

If you aren't 100% sure of *who, what or where,* then use the phrases in **bold** to describe what you think is shown in the picture. This will give you more to say and will make your description more interesting.

A Match sentences 1–6 to the pictures 1–4 they are describing.

1. He **appears to be** writing a report. _____
2. They **look like** they are leaning against a car. _____
3. **I think** the woman is the girl's mother. _____
4. He **looks like** a dentist or a doctor maybe. _____
5. It **seems like** they are having a good time. _____
6. She **seems to be** pointing at something. _____

Test tip

Talk about things that are possible (in the present / past / future)

Expand your description to talk about things that may be about to happen or have already happened, or things that are probably true, but aren't visible in the picture.

B Take turns making two more sentences for each picture 1–4. Ask your partner to guess which picture you are describing. Use the phrases and the words in the box to help you.

He / This looks like / as if …
I think this is …
It / They seem(s) to be …
He / She appears to be …

doctor's office	game	soup	map	family
friends	lost	cook	medical information	

C Match sentences 1–5 to the pictures 1–4 on page 93 they speculate about. <u>Underline</u> the probability words.

1. He could be a scientist.
2. It's probably a birthday party – they look like they're playing a game.
3. They may be lost, so they're looking at a map.
4. Perhaps they've made some homemade soup.
5. They might be playing a children's game.

Note: The adverbs *probably, perhaps,* and *maybe* often come at the beginning of the sentence.

D Match the sentence beginnings 1–6 to the correct ending a–f to describe picture 1 on page 93.

1. This man is …	_____	a. be lost.
2. They **may** have been …	_____	b. stopped for a break.
3. **Perhaps** they are driving …	_____	c. across the U.S.A. for a vacation.
4. They **might** be trying …	_____	d. **probably** the father.
5. **Maybe** they have …	_____	e. driving a long way.
6. They **could** …	_____	f. to find a motel.

E Take turns making more sentences about pictures 2–4.

Test tip

Use language that is more general when you aren't exactly sure

If you aren't sure of things like numbers, ages or other exact details use words and phrases to show this.

Test tip

Try to say as much as you can about the picture

In order to score well, you must demonstrate as fully as possible what you can say. Try to give as complete an answer as possible and speak for the full 45 seconds.

F Complete sentences 1–5 using the words a–e to indicate that the information is an estimation or guess. More than one answer may be possible.

1. The man looks _____ 40 years old.

2. There are _____ eight to ten kids in the picture.

3. Maybe it is _____ stew.

4. I think they are playing a game, _____ .

5. He looks _____ confused.

a. around
b. about
c. a little
d. some kind of
e. or something

G Take turns making two more sentences about each picture 1–4 on page 93 using the phrases in F.

H Take turns speculating as much as possible about picture 5.

5.

🎧 *Follow up*: Listen to the sample answer.

2 Test tactic: Providing a complete answer including visible features and speculation

1.

2.

3.

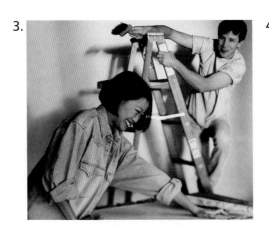

4.

Test tip

Speculate about the scene

Give extra information about the scene and what is happening, has happened, or will possibly happen in the picture to add further detail to your description.

Test tip

Speculate about the characters

When you have described what you can see in as much detail as possible, begin to speculate about the characters. If there is not a main character, focus on the group.

A For pictures 1–4, begin by making two sentences for each picture about what you can see. (See Unit 2, p50 for help.)

B Look at the main characters in pictures 1–4. Choose one person and think of possible answers to these questions.

- How old is he/she? (e.g. *in her thirties, around fifty.*)
- What is his/her job? (e.g. *He looks like a banker.*)
- What does he/she do in his/her free time? (e.g. *She probably does a lot of sport.*)
- What is his/her emotional state? (e.g. *They look happy.*)
- What is his/her relationship to the other people? (e.g. *mother, boss, coworker.*)

C Take turns making sentences to speculate about the character you chose. Give reasons for your ideas. For example, *She's probably an athlete because she looks fit. / I think he's just seen a friend because it looks like he's smiling at someone.*

D Look at the background and scene in pictures 1–4. Choose one picture and think of possible answers to these questions.

- Where are they? (e.g. *It looks like they're in a conference room.*)
- What season/time of year/day is it? (e.g. *It could be summer.*)
- Has something just happened or is something going to happen?

- What adjective would describe this place? (e.g. *fancy, dirty, fashionable*)
- If the picture shows an outdoor scene, what is the weather like? Has it changed/will it change? (e.g. *It's rather cloudy, so it may rain later.*)

E Take turns making sentences to speculate about the background. Give reasons for your ideas. For example, *It's probably winter because the people are wearing heavy coats. I think it has been raining, because the road is wet.*

🎧 *Follow up*: Listen to the sample answer. Which picture is being described?

unit
8

B Tactic practice

☑ Brainstorm vocabulary and plan introductory sentences (30 seconds).

☑ After your introduction, describe what you can see using adjectives, adverbs, and prepositions.

☑ Expand your answers with speculation on the character and scene.

☑ Use uncertain and speculative language when you aren't 100% sure.

☑ Say as much as you can in the time allowed.

Describe each of the pictures 1–4 following the steps in the Test technique. After each step compare your answers with your partner.

1.
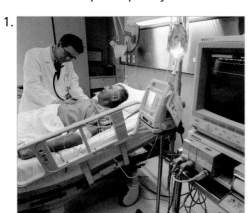

2.

3.

4.

🎧 **Using natural English**

In natural spoken English, sounds are sometimes changed, combined, or dropped. Listen to a native speaker saying the following sentences and write in the words they say.

She _____ pointing at something.

He _____ writing a report.

She _____ giving a presentation.

Check your answers in the Key on page 23.

Listen again and practice these sentences with the correct sound and rhythm.

C Mini-test

Now apply the Test tactics to draft an outline for the following question. Use the recommended test time for Question 3.

**Question 3:
Describe a picture**

Question 3: Describe a picture

Directions: In this part of the test, you will describe the picture on your screen in as much detail as you can. You will have 30 seconds to prepare your response. Then you will have 45 seconds to speak about the picture.

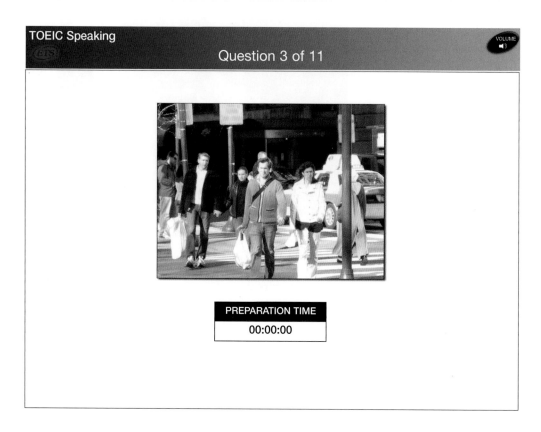

9 Speaking Test
Question 6 — Respond to questions

A Focus: Answering extended description and opinion questions

> **In the test**
>
> ← **Sample test pp20–23**
> ← **Unit 3 p54**
> **Speaking Test Questions 4–6**
>
> - In Questions 4–6, you will be asked to imagine that you are taking part in a market research telephone interview.
> - You will be asked to respond to three related questions without preparation.
> - The questions will be about familiar topics that relate to your personal experience: entertainment, purchases, dining out, family and friends, health, housing, news, shopping, or travel.
> - You will be scored on using relevant vocabulary and structures and answering the question appropriately.
> - In Unit 3, we focused on Questions 4–5.
> - In this unit, we will look at how to answer Question 6, which asks you to give a longer response of 30 seconds.
> - In this unit, we will learn some phrases for describing objects, people, and experiences, and for giving explanations and opinions. We will also look at how to introduce opposing arguments, and how to make your answer cohesive using linking devices.

unit
9

1 Language building: Phrases for describing and giving opinions

A 🎧 Read and listen to the model phrases a–c used to introduce *Describe your favorite X* questions.

> **Describe your favorite (sport)**
>
> a. *Well, there are a lot of (sports) I like, but if I had to choose one, it would have to be (football).*
> b. *I would have to say that my favorite (sport) is (ice hockey).*
> c. *I like a lot of (sports), but I think my favorite is (tennis).*

B Use the model phrases in A to answer questions 1–3. Write your answers in 1. Take turns answering questions 2 and 3.

1. Describe your favorite restaurant.

   a. *Well, there are a lot of (restaurants) I like, but if I ...*

   b. _____

   c. _____

2. Describe your favorite movie actor.
3. Describe your favorite way to travel.

Test tip

Become familiar with phrases to introduce your opinions

For questions that ask you to give your opinion on an issue or ask you to suggest ideas, you should quickly decide on an opinion or idea you can easily speak about, and then use an appropriate phrase to make your introductory statement.

C 🎧 Read and listen to the model phrases a and b used to introduce *Describe a(n) X* questions.

> **Describe (a popular place for shopping) in your community.**
> a. Well, there are quite a few (places to shop), but one very popular one is (Sheridan Mall).
> b. OK, one (popular place for shopping) that I can think of is (Kensington market).

D Use the models in C to answer questions 1–3. Write your answer in 1. For questions 2 and 3, make your answers in pairs.

1. Describe a place that people in your community like to visit on weekends.

   a. *Well, there are quite a few places that people like to visit, but ...*
   _____

   b. _____
   _____

2. Describe a special gift you have received.
3. Describe a summer activity that is popular in your community.

E 🎧 Use the opinion phrases in the table to answer questions 1–6. Begin your sentence with *In my opinion ... , I think ... , I believe ... .* First listen to an example. Which question does it answer?

Strong positive opinion	Positive opinion	Negative opinion	Strong negative opinion
I really believe that the best way to ... is to ...	... is quite important ...	I believe that it is not very important to ...	I really don't believe ... that ... is important at all.
		I don't think it's very important to ...	

1. What type of entertainment facility would you like to see opened in your community? Why?
2. How important is it to buy brand-name goods? Why?
3. Do you think it is a good idea for families to have pets? Why?/Why not?
4. How important is it for children to take part in sports or regular physical education in school? Why?
5. How do you think English education could be improved in your community?
6. Where in your community would you take a visitor from another country? Why?

Test tip

Link your opinions and supporting points clearly

In Question 6, you are expected to talk for 30 seconds. It is important to add supporting sentences to your opinions and use appropriate words to link them together. This will make your answer more structured and easier to follow.

Test tip

You may wish to include some opposing ideas

Adding some points that oppose your opinion can show that you have carefully thought about the opinion. If you include opposing points, you should finish with a sentence that restates your opinion.

F Use the linking words and phrases in the table to complete the example answer below.

Linking word / phrase	Use
the reason I say this is that … one reason for this is …	To give supporting reasons for an opinion
another thing … also …	To add additional supporting sentences
on the other hand, … however, …	To introduce an opposing point
overall, … in spite of that, … … though …	To signal your conclusion after you have mentioned an opposing point

Q: How important is it for people to have a watch? Why?

I think it is very important to have a watch. (1) _____ if you don't know the time you might often be late for things. (2) _____ I think watches look very stylish and professional. (3) _____ is that most watches also tell you the date. (4) _____ , some people use cell phones as an alternative way to tell the time and date, but (5) _____ I think having a watch is very important for me.

G Extend the opinion statements you made in E by following steps 1–4. First listen to an example. Which question does it answer?

1. Choose one of the opinion statements 1–6 you made in E.
2. Think of some supporting reasons (and opposing points if appropriate).
3. Make a new answer by joining your opinion with the supporting (and opposing) points, using the linking words and phrases.
4. End with a short conclusion, restating your opinion.

2 Test tactic: Organizing different question types

Become familiar with how to organize different question types

Responses for different questions require a different organization. Learn different types then choose the appropriate type to answer the question.

unit
9

A 🎧 Listen and read the example for organizing *Describe ...* questions.

Answer model	Example: *Describe your favorite sport.*
1. Begin with an introduction sentence that says what you are describing and includes words from the question.	*I would have to say that my favorite sport is ice hockey.*
2. Give a reason why you chose this thing/place/person.	*The reason I say this is because I think it is a really exciting sport. It is also good exercise, and is a lot of fun to play.*
3. Describe the thing/place/person. Use adjectives (e.g. *helpful, relaxing, expensive, beautiful, delicious*) and words to talk about appearance, character, use, etc. to give as much information as you can.	*It is a team sport played on ice.* *It is very fast.* *You use a stick to shoot.*

B With a partner, answer questions 1–3 following the three steps in the answer model in A. Look back at the language introduced in the Language building section to help you make statements and link your sentences.

1. Describe a family member you have learned a lot from.
2. Describe your favorite way to spend a weekend.
3. Describe a food that is well known in your country.

C 🎧 Listen and read the example for organizing *Opinion* questions.

Answer model	Example: *What animal do you think makes a good family pet?*
1. Begin with an introduction sentence that gives your opinion and includes words from the question.	*In my opinion, a turtle would make a good family pet.*
2. Think of two or three reasons to support your opinion.	*Some of the reasons are because turtles are cheap and they are quiet. Also they are very interesting.*
3. If you can think of any opposing points you may add them.	*However, they aren't very loving.*
4. If you added an opposing point, add a final conclusion sentence.	*In spite of this though, I think they make a very good family pet.*

D With a partner, answer questions 1–3 following the four steps in the answer model in C. Look back at the language introduced in the Language building section to help you.

1. What do you think is a good way to keep fit? Why?
2. If you could change one thing about your home, what would it be? Why?
3. How important is it for children to enjoy reading? Why?

If you aren't sure what to say next, do not leave very long pauses or use words or sounds from your own language. Learn the words, phrases and sounds used in English to help you sound fluent and natural.

E 🎧 Look at the list of common English hesitation devices below, then listen to the recording and repeat them until they are familiar to you.

> Umm …
> Hmmm … that's a good question … uh
> Well, uh … let me think … errr …
> Oh, yes well, basically uh … basically I think … umm …

F Practice using similar hesitation devices with your partner by doing the task below.

Student A: Read the task below.
Student B: Look at Activity File Unit 9 on page 225.

Student A
Take turns asking each other questions 1–3. The person answering the question must talk for as long as possible (maximum 30 seconds) without a silent pause of more than two seconds. If you need time to think, use hesitation devices. Ask Student B these questions.

1. What is the most expensive thing you have ever bought? Describe it.
2. What was the first book you ever read? Describe it.
3. What would you buy if you had a thousand dollars? Explain why.

unit
9

Test technique

☑ Ask yourself what kind of question it is (description or opinion) and decide on your focus.

☑ Follow an appropriate organization model for the question.

☑ Link your ideas together, and if you need time to think, use English hesitation devices.

B Tactic practice

Use the Test tactics you have practiced to answer the following questions. Follow the steps summarized in the Test technique. After each of the three points in the checklist, discuss your ideas with your partner.

1. Describe a piece of furniture in your home that is important to you.
2. How do you think sports facilities could be improved in your community?
3. How important is it for people to have computer skills, and why?
4. Describe your favorite place to go in the evening, and why you like it.

🎧 **Using natural English**
In natural spoken English, sounds are sometimes changed, combined, or dropped. Listen to a native speaker saying the following sentences and write in the words they say.

Ten people _____ around the table easily.
All aspects of life _____ made easier.
Some clubs are expensive and only adults _____ there.

Check your answers in the Key on page 25.

Listen again and practice these sentences with the correct sound and rhythm.

C Mini-test

Now apply the Test tactics to answer the following questions. Use the recommended test time for Questions 4–6.

Important

In this part of the test, you will have to answer three questions (4–6).
In this unit, we have practiced question-type 6.
See Sample test, pages 20–23 or Unit 3 page 54 for practice on Questions 4–5.

Questions 4–6: Respond to questions

unit
9

Questions 4–6: Respond to questions

Directions: In this part of the test, you will answer three questions.

For each question, begin responding immediately after you hear a beep.

No preparation time is provided. You will have 15 seconds to respond to Questions 4 and 5 and 30 seconds to respond to Question 6.

Question 4

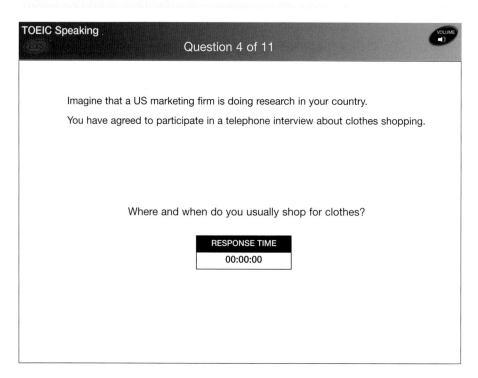

TOEIC Speaking
Question 4 of 11

Imagine that a US marketing firm is doing research in your country.
You have agreed to participate in a telephone interview about clothes shopping.

Where and when do you usually shop for clothes?

RESPONSE TIME
00:00:00

Question 5

Imagine that a US marketing firm is doing research in your country.

You have agreed to participate in a telephone interview about clothes shopping.

How do you decide where you will shop for clothes?

RESPONSE TIME
00:00:00

unit
9

Question 6

Imagine that a US marketing firm is doing research in your country.

You have agreed to participate in a telephone interview about clothes shopping.

How important is the way you dress at work and why?

RESPONSE TIME
00:00:00

A Focus: Summarizing multiple pieces of information

Important

In the test, Questions 7–9 appear together. In this book, Questions 7–8 are covered in Unit 4. Question 9 is covered here in Unit 10.

In the test

← **Sample test pp24–27**
← **Unit 4 p60**
Speaking Test Questions 7–9

- In Questions 7–9, you will be given 30 seconds to read a written agenda or schedule.
- You will then be asked three questions by a "caller" who needs information from your written schedule.
- You will only hear the questions once, and they do not appear as text on the screen.
- You will be scored on using relevant vocabulary and structures and for giving accurate information. You will need to speak clearly.
- In Unit 4, we focused on how to answer Questions 7–8, which allow you 15 seconds to make your response for each question.
- In this unit, we will focus on how to answer Question 9, which allows you 30 seconds to make your response.
- In this unit, we will also focus on summarizing multiple pieces of information, building notes into full paragraphs, and selecting relevant information from an agenda.

unit
10

Test tip

Practice building notes into full sentences

The information found on agendas is usually in note form. You must use the information on the agenda to make clear, well-formed sentences.

1 Language building: Building notes into full sentences

A Read examples 1–3 showing how notes can be made into full sentences. <u>Underline</u> the words that have been added to the notes to make the sentences. What tense is used? Why?

1. 7:45   Arrive flight NA39 from Toronto

   At 7:45, you will arrive on flight NA39 from Toronto.

2. 8:15   Meet Walter Gallant at arrival gate

   At 8:15, you will meet Walter Gallant at the arrival gate.

3. 9:15   Shuttle bus to Royal Hotel

   At 9:15, you will take a shuttle bus to the Royal Hotel.

Test tip

Be careful of verb tenses and particles

In most cases you will be talking about the future, so you will usually use either *will* or *going to*. Look for places where you will need to add prepositions, e.g. *at* before times, and remember that you will often need to add articles.

B Read the notes in 1–5 and make them into full sentences. Use the future *will* and add verbs, articles, and prepositions as required.

1. 12:00   Arrive head office

2. 12:30   Meet members of sales team

3. 1:00   Lunch – El Greco restaurant

4. 3:00   Tour of work areas

5. 5:30   Return to hotel

C Read the Grammar note. Then read the notes in 1–5 and complete the sentences using the correct structure.

> ### Grammar note
>
> You can describe the items on an agenda using a future form to say what is planned in different ways:
>
> *You / We / They will (go) …* To describe a scheduled action that the subject will do, use *will* future.
>
> *You / We / They will be (picked up) by …* To describe a scheduled action that someone else will perform, use the passive. The verb is often followed with the preposition *by*.
>
> *There will be …* To describe a scheduled event, use *there will be* for both singular and plural events.

1. 9:00   Taxi to printing factory

   At 9:00, _____ by taxi to the printing factory.

2. 9:30   Meet members of management team

   At 9:30, _____ members of the management team.

3. 10:30   Break for coffee

   At 10:30, _____ a break for coffee.

4. 11:00   Tour of printing plant

   At 11:00, _____ a tour of the printing plant.

5. 12:30   Limousine to head office

   At 12:30, _____ to the head office.

D Write your own sentences based on the information given in 1–5 below. The first one is done for you.

1. 11:30 a.m.   Arrive flight Terminal 2, Newark Airport

   At 11:30, you will arrive at Terminal 2 at Newark Airport.

2. 12:00 p.m.   Taxi to hotel

   _____

3. 1:00 p.m.   Reception lunch in Green Suite

   _____

4. 2:30 p.m.   Conference registration

   _____

5. 3:00 p.m.   Opening session

   _____

Follow up: Take turns reading the sentences aloud. Compare your sentences with your partner's.

Include related information

Often agendas will include extra details, e.g. where something will happen or who will be running an event, or similar extra details. You may wish to include this information in the same sentence or put it in an extra sentence.

E Read example sentences 1 and 2 showing how additional information may be added. <u>Underline</u> the words that have been added to the notes or any other changes that have been made to form the sentences.

1. 9:30   Overview of the new franchise project
             – Geoff France (Asia Development head)

At 9:30, we will be given an overview of the new franchise project by Geoff France, who is the head of Asia Development.

2. 10:45   Seminar "New production techniques"
             – Bill Grieve (Production Manager, Chase Metals)

At 10:45, we will attend a seminar on new production techniques. This will be given by Bill Grieve, who is the Production Manager for Chase Metals.

F Write your own sentences based on the information given in 1–5.

1. 12:00 p.m.   Demonstration of new hardware
                     – Dr. DeZote (Research and Development)

2. 1:30 p.m.   Presentation "Communication and Management"
                     – Stephen Burns (Human Resources)

Use common words and phrases to organize your answer

When you are answering Question 9, you should use linkers, time markers, and phrases to introduce choices to make your answer easier to follow.

3. 2:00 p.m.   Tour of offices/introduce development staff
                     – Thomas Smith (Office Manager)

4. 3:45 p.m.   Tour admin building (including new high-security wing)

5. 7:30 p.m.   Dinner reservation, Oliphant Restaurant
                     – Mary Grant (Accounting) will join us

Follow up: Take turns reading the sentences aloud. Compare your sentences with your partner's.

G Look at the chart showing common words and phrases. Match headings a–c to the appropriate column.

a. Extra information markers   b. Choice markers   c. Time markers

1. _____	2. _____	3. _____
after (dinner, arriving …), and then … then, after that … at 7:30 … finally, …	… and … (there is) also … … and also … in addition, …	You have two choices/ options … You can choose (either X or Y) Also, at the same time, there is … You have to choose one of these …

H Read the paragraph based on the agenda below. Complete gaps 1–6 using the words given.

1:00	Lunch
2:00	Meet John Sewell – discuss recent sales trends and plan next month's conference
3:30	Meet Rob Bechard (PDH President) – advertising campaign
6:30	Limousine to airport for flight to London (stay at Grand Hotel or Old Lodge?)

finally   then, after that   and also
you can choose   after   you have two options

(1) _____ lunch, you will be meeting John Sewell to discuss recent sales trends, (2) _____ to plan next month's conference. (3) _____ you will be meeting with Rob Bechard, who is the PDH President, to discuss the advertising campaign. (4) _____ , at 6:30, you will be taken by limousine to the airport to catch your flight to London. (5) _____ for hotels in London. (6) _____ either the Grand Hotel or the Old Lodge.

I 🎧 Listen to the question and then respond with a short paragraph using extra information markers, time markers, and choice markers from G.

Meeting Agenda for April 1st

Presenters: Josh Andrews, Ryan Martin, Phil Greenaway
Chair: Scott Humphreys

11:30	Review of minutes from last month's meeting
12:00	Presentation: "Maximizing sales performance" – Josh Andrews
1:00	Presentation: "Overseas markets" – Phil Greenaway (buffet lunch will be served)
2:00	Presentation: "Cost management" – Ryan Martin
3:00	Group discussion on issues raised in Day Three's presentations
4:00	Meeting adjourned

Please confirm attendance by phone or e-mail, at least one week prior to the meeting.

🎧 ***Follow up***: With a partner, cover your response and practice answering the question in I. Then listen to a sample answer.

2 Test tactic: Picking out key words and locating your answer

Test tip

Listen for key words to identify which section you will be discussing

You will be asked to summarize only some of the events. Listen for key words, such as prepositions and times that will tell you which information you must include, e.g. *in the morning, after lunch, before 2:00.*

A Look at the agenda. Think about how the day is broken up, e.g. with breaks or by activity type. Then divide it into three sections. Any of the three sections could be the focus of Question 9.

Graphic Design **Conference**

Date: May 23rd   Cost: $50   Venue: Harpur, Beamville

8:30–9:00	Introduction, Aims of the conference
9:00–10:00	"Use of image in the 21st Century" – Simon Yeats, Graphica (conference organizer)
10:00–10:15	1st break
10:15–11:15	"3-D design techniques" – Oliver Biggs, Myth Design
11:15–12:00	"Maintaining consistent colors" – Tomas Nole, Maya Design
12:00–1:00	Lunch in the cafeteria
1:00–2:00	Keynote address: "Developing and sharing design ideas" – Duncan Simms, Think Design
2:00–2:45	Plenary discussion and Closing statements

B Read questions 1–5 and <u>underline</u> the key words that refer to which element of an agenda you should focus on. The first one is done for you.

Test tip

Give the correct factual information

When answering questions, be careful not to change the information you give from the agenda. The response you give should reflect accurate information.

1. Do you know what Mr. Sutton is planning to do <u>following the training session</u>?
2. Could you give me information about the activities in the morning?
3. What do we have on the schedule after the managers' meeting finishes?
4. Could you tell me what other products are going to be on display?
5. Can you remind me which companies the speakers come from?

C 🎧 Look at the agenda in A and listen to questions 1–4. Write down the questions and then <u>underline</u> the key words. If you don't understand the whole question, just write down the key words you hear.

1. _____

2. _____

3. _____

4. _____

Follow up: Compare your questions in C with a partner. Then take turns answering the questions by locating the relevant information in the agenda in A. Make paragraphs similar to the one in Language building I.

D 🎧 Look at the agenda in A. Then listen to the question, taking note of the key words. Answer the question.

_____

_____

_____

_____

Test tip

Include part of the question in your opening sentence

You should respond as though you are actually talking to the person. It is appropriate to start by acknowledging their request, e.g. *Certainly … , Yes, of course*, and include an introduction that contains part of the question. By adding a phrase like *just a moment* or *just let me have a look*, you also gain some time to read the agenda without creating an awkward silence.

E In this part of the test, it is a good idea to begin your answer with the words/phrases below. This will make your answer more natural and give you time to think. Write the beginnings of answers to questions 1–5 in B, beginning with an introductory sentence. The first one is done for you.

> Certainly …
> Sure, …
> OK, just let me have a look. Yes …
> Yes, of course, just a second …

1. *Certainly, just let me have a look. Yes, after the training Mr. Sutton is planning to …*

2. _____

3. _____

4. _____

5. _____

☑ Read the heading and events.

☑ Be aware of extra information.

☑ Listen for key words.

☑ Answer in full sentences and include explanations.

☑ Use phrases from Unit 4 to refer back to the agenda or to introduce bad news.

B Tactic practice

🎧 Listen to three questions for each Task A–C. Follow the steps summarized in the Remember box and Test technique. After each of the points in the checklists, discuss your ideas with your partner.

Task A

National Dental Association Annual Dinner

Hillsdale Golf Club 7:00~11:00 p.m. Invitation only*

7:00	Guests arrive at the Hillsdale Golf Club
7:30	Drinks and snacks served in the Main Reception Area
8:00	Dinner served in the Dining Room
9:00	Musical entertainment – *Shalimar*
	(note: Cheryl Rhodes, scheduled to sing, had to cancel due to illness)
10:00	Prize raffle
10:30	Awards presentation
11:00	Closing speech – NDA Chairman, Dominic Simons

*Members may bring one guest with them.

☑ Listen carefully for the key words that indicate the things you will summarize.

☑ Start with an appropriate introductory statement.

☑ Use accurate information to make well-formed and well-linked sentences.

Task B

November 12th, Business Schedule for Jane Goldwin

07:00 a.m. Taxi to Newark	**2:30 p.m.** Meeting with PSG Board at Main Street offices to discuss recent sales trends
09:00 a.m. Northern Air Flight 132 from Newark to Chicago	**4:00 p.m.** Meeting with Orlando Hart, PSG President, to discuss merger plans
12:30 p.m. Arrive Chicago. PSG Sales Manager, Brian Rice, will meet you at the airport	**6:30 p.m.** Limousine back to the airport
1:00 p.m. Lunch with Mr. Rice at Oakview restaurant *(note: originally planned to use Bluebird restaurant, but fully booked)*	**7:30 p.m.** Northern Air Flight 139 from Chicago to Newark

---

Task C

Swinsdale Jazz Festival

Date: Saturday 3rd–Sunday 4th August, 12:00–Late
Venue: Central Park

Price: One-day pass – $75
Two-day pass – $125

Saturday		*Sunday*	
12:00	The Alan Carter Four	12:00	Phil Hart's Big Band
1:30	Panama	1:30	The Crush
3:00	Mary Albarn	3:00	The Soft Tones
5:00	Dangerfield	5:00	Abel Wizzard
7:00	Lazarus	7:00	Ian Walker Five
9:00	The Turtles	9:00	Penelope Gray

Refreshments available on-site (not included in cost)

---

unit **10**

🎧 Using natural English

In natural spoken English, sounds are sometimes changed, combined, or dropped. Listen to a native speaker saying the following sentences and write in the words they say.

Can you _____ know what time?

Just _____ look at the agenda.

_____ look at your schedule.

Check your answers in the Key on page 28.

Listen again and practice these sentences with the correct sound and rhythm.

C Mini-test

Now apply the Test tactics to answer Questions 7–9. Use the recommended test time for Questions 7–9.

Important

In the test, Questions 7–9 appear together as you will find here in the Mini-test. In this book, Questions 7–8 and Question 9 are covered in separate units. For information and practice on Questions 7–8, see Unit 4.

Questions 7–9: Respond to questions using information provided

| TOEIC Speaking | |

Questions 7–9: Respond to questions using information provided

Directions: In this part of the test, you will answer three questions based on the information provided. You will have 30 seconds to read the information before the questions begin. For each question, begin responding immediately after you hear a beep. No additional preparation time is provided. You will have 15 seconds to respond to Questions 7 and 8 and 30 seconds to respond to Question 9.

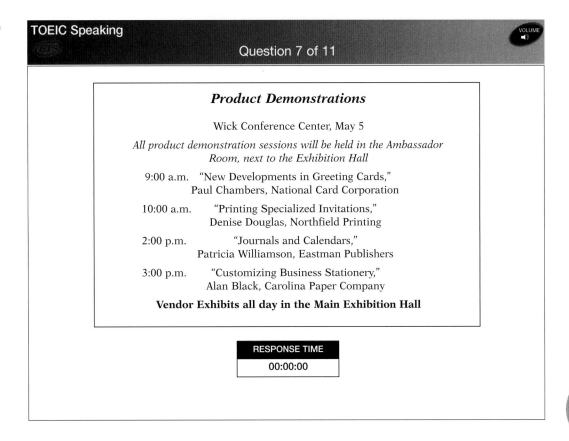

TOEIC Speaking

Question 7 of 11

Product Demonstrations

Wick Conference Center, May 5

All product demonstration sessions will be held in the Ambassador Room, next to the Exhibition Hall

9:00 a.m. "New Developments in Greeting Cards,"
Paul Chambers, National Card Corporation

10:00 a.m. "Printing Specialized Invitations,"
Denise Douglas, Northfield Printing

2:00 p.m. "Journals and Calendars,"
Patricia Williamson, Eastman Publishers

3:00 p.m. "Customizing Business Stationery,"
Alan Black, Carolina Paper Company

Vendor Exhibits all day in the Main Exhibition Hall

RESPONSE TIME
00:00:00

Question 7

🎧 Listen to the question. You have 15 seconds to respond.

Question 8

🎧 Listen to the question. You have 15 seconds to respond.

Question 9

🎧 Listen to the question. You have 30 seconds to respond.

11 Speaking Test
Question 10 — Propose a solution

A Focus: Responding to requests

> **In the test**
>
> ← **Sample test pp28–31**
> ← **Unit 5 p69**
> **Speaking Test Question 10**
>
> - In Question 10, you will hear a telephone voice message. The caller will make either a request or a complaint.
> - You will then be given 30 seconds to prepare a response to the message.
> - You will only hear the message once, and it does not appear as text on the screen.
> - You have 60 seconds to give your spoken response. In your response, you must show you recognize the problem and propose a way of dealing with it.
> - You will be scored on dealing with the task in a suitable way, using the correct level of formality, and providing an answer that is clear and well-organized.
> - In Unit 5, we focused on responding to complaints.
> - In this unit, we will focus on responding to requests.

1 Language building: Giving reasons why the request may be difficult, giving possible solutions, and ending your message

Test tip

Acknowledge the problems with granting the request

Request tasks in Question 10 will always include an urgent or immediate problem for you to fix. In such situations it is common to give an explanation of why the request is difficult to grant.

A Read sentences 1 and 2 explaining why it may be difficult to grant a request. <u>Underline</u> the phrases that are used to introduce the explanation. Which one begins with an apology, and which refers to some evidence?

1. Wants car fixed – very short time (by tomorrow)

   I'm afraid that fixing your car by tomorrow would be very difficult.

2. Wants meeting Wednesday – schedule says closed on Wednesday

   As you can see from the schedule, we are closed on Wednesday.

B Read the situations 1–4. Complete the explanations using the phrases given.

> I'm afraid that … is out of the question.
> As it says in the ad,
> Unfortunately, it won't be possible
> As you can see from the notice,

1. This person wants individual Spanish lessons – ad says you only give group lessons.

   _____ I only give group lessons.

2. This person wants their car repaired quickly – one week is not enough time.

   _____ to repair this car in just one week.

Test tip

Present a possible solution

You must show you have understood the request and provide a reasonable solution.

3. This person wants to stay in the hostel – the notice says it is full.

_____ the hostel is full.

4. This person wants to do a tour of your factory on Friday – you're in a meeting on Friday.

_____ doing the tour on Friday

_____

Test tip

Tell the person that is the best you can do

Sometimes the thing the caller requests may be very difficult to grant. In that case offer to do what you can, then finish by saying, *I'm sorry, but that is the best we / I can (do).*

C Write sentences about situations 1–3 using the phrases in B. Read them aloud to your partner.

1. This person wants a sudden appointment at the dentist, but can only come in the evening – dentist has another engagement this evening.

_____

2. This person would like a travel brochure on Australia – travel agent has none left.

_____

3. This person would like some information about the exhibition sent by mail – company doesn't have enough staff to send out leaflets and prefers to send electronic information.

_____

D Match solutions a–d to the situations 1–4 in B. If you introduce a reason why the request is difficult to grant, the words in **bold** are ways to help introduce a solution.

a. ***On the other hand,*** *we do also offer* camping facilities.

b. ***The only thing I can suggest is*** that I could spare you about half an hour at lunch time.

c. ***However, as this is an emergency, if you can*** bring your car in now, I can have a look at it.

d. ***... but I'll tell you what, if you*** come in, we may be able to arrange some individual lessons for you.

E Solutions c and d in D use conditionals. Read the information in the grammar note. Complete sentences 1 and 2 on the next page by putting the verbs in the correct form.

unit
11

Grammar note		
Talking about possibilities	If + can + infinitive, can + infinitive OR	If you **can wait** till Monday, I **can see** you then.
	If + present tense, can + infinitive	If you **don't mind** paying extra, we **can ship** it express.
Talking about less likely possibilities	If + could + infinitive, could + infinitive	If you **could send** me the plans, I **could give** you an estimate.

Talking about possibilities

1. I'm afraid that fixing your car by tomorrow would be very difficult. However, if you _____ (bring) your car in, we _____ (try) to fix it as soon as possible. I'm sorry, but that is the best we can promise.

Talking about less likely possibilities

2. As you said, we are closed on Wednesdays. The only thing I can suggest is that, if you _____ (come) by at 9:00 on Thursday morning, I _____ (meet) with you early in the morning.

F Match solutions a–c to the situations in C.

a. Contact the tour operators and ask them to send a brochure directly to the person if he or she can give us an address. _____

b. On this occasion make an exception and send the details by mail. _____

c. Give them the details of another emergency dentist who works evenings. _____

G With your partner, make solution sentences based on the notes in F. Use the phrases in D and E to help you. Practice reading them out aloud.

1. _____

2. _____

3. _____

H Match phrases 1–6 for future contact situations to meanings a–c.

1. I will call you (tomorrow) to confirm this. _____

2. If this sounds OK, please stop by or give us a call. _____

3. So please expect a call later on tomorrow. _____

4. If this is good for you, please call me immediately and we can get started. _____

5. Please call me and let me know if this is OK for you. _____

6. So as soon as you get this message, please call me right away. _____

a. Time is very important, so call soon.

b. Call whenever you have free time, if you are interested.

c. I will check something and call you back.

Follow up: Choose the most appropriate sentence in H for each of the situations in C.

2 Test tactic: Listening for key information and organizing your response

Test tip

Listen for the key information

You will only hear the message once, so you must pick out the key information you need to make a complete response, including the person's name and what they are requesting.

A 🎧 Read and listen to the transcript of a request. Then complete the missing information a and b, and work out the answers for c and d.

a. Name of the requestor

_____

b. Request

_____

c. What you propose to do

_____

d. Your role

_____

Transcript of the request (this will not be shown on the actual test)

Hello, is this Kramer Furniture Design? My name is Tom Jenkins, and I'm a contractor and I need a custom-made table for a special customer I have, and, unfortunately, the table he wants to put in is quite an unusual shape and size. So what I would like you to do, is to make this table for me. Unfortunately, this needs to be done by next week. I realize that this is very short notice, but this is a very important job for me. I'd appreciate it if you could call me back and let me know what exactly you can do for me on this job. Thanks very much. This is Tom Jenkins, and my number is 555-3368.

B 🎧 Listen to three more requests and note the same information.

1.

a. Name of the requestor

_____

b. Request

_____

c. What you propose to do

_____

d. Your role

_____

unit
11

2.

a. Name of the requestor

_____

b. Request

_____

c. What you propose to do

_____

d. Your role

_____

3.

a. Name of the requestor

_____

b. Request

_____

c. What you propose to do

_____

d. Your role

_____

C Match requests 1–3 with solutions a–c.

Requests
1. Want to book a table in a restaurant tonight – restaurant is full
2. Need to have a TV repaired before weekend – technician too busy
3. Want to learn how to ski next week – group lessons fully booked

Solutions
a. They could offer them private lessons.
b. They could pick the TV up and lend them a TV while it is repaired.
c. They could fit them in before 8 p.m.

D With a partner, think of suitable explanations and solutions for requests 1–3 in B.

1. _____

_____

2. _____

_____

3. _____

_____

Test tip

Understand the organization of typical responses to requests

Responses to requests usually follow a fairly set pattern. If you know this pattern you can build a complete and appropriate response out of small, reasonably simple parts.

Remember

☑ Use your imagination

☑ You can respond as yourself or use a fake name and company

E Read steps 1–5 explaining how to organize a typical response. Match the example sentences a–e to the appropriate step.

1. **Polite greeting confirming names**
   Greet the person by name and introduce yourself and your position (if appropriate).
   e.g. _____

2. **Reason why you are calling**
   Say that you got their message and give a short summary of the request.
   e.g. _____

3. **Difficulties or conditions**
   Use your imagination to think of possible reasons why it is difficult, or give extra conditions.
   e.g. _____

4. **Your solution**
   Give a response that you think fits what the person wants and the problem you noted.
   e.g. _____

5. **Close**
   Finish the response with a thank you. If appropriate you may wish to add a request for further contact to confirm they accept your solution.
   e.g. _____

   a. If you don't mind paying the extra charge, we can put extra workers on the project.
   b. Usually it takes at least three weeks to make custom furniture. To do it so quickly will be much more expensive. We will have to add an extra charge.
   c. Hello, Mr. Jenkins? This is John Smith from Kramer Furniture Design.
   d. I received your message about the special table you need made.
   e. If this is OK with you, please call me immediately and we can get started. Thanks a lot.

F 🎧 Listen to the three requests in B again. Choose one of the requests and respond to the problems. Use the notes you made in B and D. Use the headings 1–5 in E as a checklist.

_____

_____

_____

_____

_____

_____

_____

Follow up: Read your response to your partner. In pairs, make similar responses for the other requests.

Test technique

B Tactic practice

☑ Listen carefully for key information (name, request, problem).

☑ Use the preparation time to brainstorm possible reasons for the problem, and your solution.

☑ Follow the model:
  • Greeting
  • Reason for call
  • Difficulties or conditions
  • Solution
  • Close

A 🎧 Listen to requests 1–4. Use the Test tactics you have practiced to complete the following information. After each step in the Test technique discuss your ideas with your partner.

1.

a. Name of the requestor

_____

b. Request

_____

c. What you propose to do

_____

d. Your role

_____

2.

a. Name of the requestor

_____

b. Request

_____

c. What you propose to do

_____

d. Your role

_____

3.

a. Name of the requestor

_____

b. Request

_____

c. What you propose to do

_____

d. Your role

_____

4.

a. Name of the requestor

_____

b. Request

_____

c. What you propose to do

_____

d. Your role

_____

B Take turns making your responses. In each response, be sure to summarize the caller's request, mention the problems with granting the request, and propose a way of dealing with it.

unit
11

🎧 **Using natural English**

In natural spoken English, sounds are sometimes changed, combined, or dropped. Listen to a native speaker saying the following sentences and write in the words they say.

If _____ bring your car in, we'll fix it.
As _____ can see from the schedule … .
I can give _____ their details.

Check your answers in the Key on page 32.

Listen again and practice these sentences with the correct sound and rhythm.

C Mini-test

Now apply the Test tactics to draft an outline for the following question. Use the recommended test time for Question 10.

Question 10:
Propose a solution

Question 10: Propose a solution

Directions: In this part of the test, you will be presented with a problem and asked to propose a solution.

You will have 30 seconds to prepare. Then you will have 60 seconds to speak.

In your response, be sure to
- show that you recognize the problem, and
- propose a way of dealing with the problem.

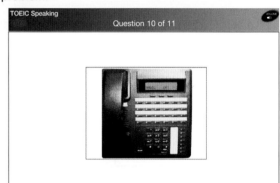

🎧 Listen to the message.

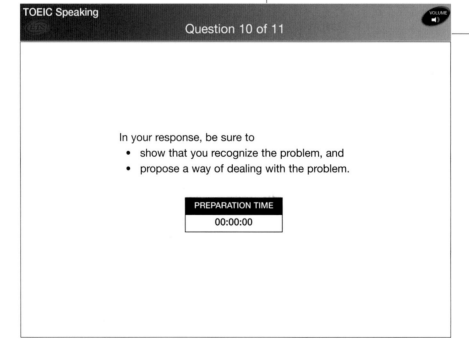

In your response, be sure to
- show that you recognize the problem, and
- propose a way of dealing with the problem.

PREPARATION TIME
00:00:00

A Focus: Personalizing opinions, mentioning opposing arguments and useful expressions for giving opinions

In the test

← Sample test pp32–34
← Unit 6 p79
Speaking Test Question 11

- In this question, you will be asked to state an opinion and give reasons for that opinion.
- You will have 15 seconds to prepare and 60 seconds to give your opinion and support it with reasons and examples.
- In Unit 6, we practiced how to express and develop an opinion and how to link your ideas.
- In this unit, we will focus on useful expressions, opposing arguments and restating your opinion.

Test tip

Learn words and phrases to state and support an opinion

Question 11 will ask you to state a position or a stance on a particular topic. Learn words and phrases that clearly state an opinion and introduce supporting details like examples, reasons, etc. that you can use throughout your answer.

Test tip

Personalize your response

You may want to give examples or reasons that are based on your own experience or that are relevant to life in your country. Learn phrases to introduce these examples.

1 Language building: Personalizing opinions, opening phrases and hesitation devices

A Match the sentence beginnings 1–5 to the endings a–e. Take note of the useful personalization phrases in **bold**.

1. **For me**, eating healthily is really important because … ____
2. **The main reason I think** huge shopping malls shouldn't be built … ____
3. **In my country**, this is a much talked about issue, … ____
4. **In my experience**, it is always better to do a job you enjoy, … ____
5. **This actually happened to me once, and on that occasion** I … ____

a. so I have thought about it a lot.
b. because it is more important to feel happy than to have lots of money.
c. it affects your body and your mind.
d. decided it was better to go to the police than to deal with it myself.
e. is the effect they have on smaller stores.

B Read the question below. Write three sentences giving your opinion. Use the personalization phrases in **bold** in A.

Some people think it is important to dress in expensive and fashionable clothes for work, while others prefer to feel comfortable and dress in their own individual style. What is your opinion on dress code for work?

1. _____

2. _____

3. _____

unit
12

Test tip

Use phrases to give you time to think

Sometimes you may need a bit more time to organize your thoughts before you start your answer. Give yourself more time by using a phrase to introduce what you are going to say.

C Read the phrases below. Then with a partner, answer Questions 1–3, by opening with one of the phrases and then using words from the question to start your answer (as practiced in Unit 6, page 80).

> Well, that's a hard question, but … (I guess the most important thing is X).
>
> There are many things that I (would change), but if I had to (choose one, I guess I would say …)
>
> I think there are pros and cons for (this issue), but if I had to choose, I would say …

Question 1

Some people think children should be taught how to cook at school, others think that it is their parents' responsibility to teach them. What is your opinion and why?

Question 2

Do you agree or disagree with this statement?

If you choose to go and live in another country, you should be willing to learn the language and to adapt your ways to fit into the new society. Give reasons and examples to support your opinion.

Question 3

Some people prefer to live downtown, close to shops, restaurants and sports facilities. Others choose to live in the countryside where it is peaceful and relaxing. Which do you prefer and why?

D 🎧 Look at the common English hesitation devices below. Then listen to six examples of native speakers giving their opinions and write the number of the speaker next to the devices you hear them use.

er …	_____	I mean …	_____	let me see …	_____
uhh …	_____	sort of/kind of …	_____		
mmm …	_____	you know …	_____		

Test tip

Use hesitation devices to give you time to think

You should try to avoid long pauses during your speech. All languages have some words or sounds (called hesitation devices) that people use when they need time to think of what to say. Try to avoid using the ones in your own language because they can sometimes make it difficult for a listener to understand you or follow your message.

E 🎧 Now listen to extracts from D and repeat the phrases you hear.

F Practice using similar hesitation devices with your partner by doing the task below.

Student A: Read the task below.
Student B: Look at Activity File Unit 12 on page 225.

Student A

Take turns asking each other Questions 1–3. The person answering the question must talk for 20 seconds without a silent pause of more than two seconds. If you need time to think, use hesitation devices. Ask Student A these questions.

1. If you could live anywhere in the world now, would you live somewhere hot or cold? Explain why.
2. What skill would you most like to develop your ability to do art or math? Why?
3. What is the most important thing you look for in a friend – loyalty or being fun to be with? Give reasons for your choice.

2 Test tactic: Mentioning an opposing argument and restating your opinion

Test tip

Use language to show you have considered the other side of the argument

Although you are only expected to give your own opinion and reasons, in some questions you may wish to include some opposing points, before giving your final conclusion. This can help show that you have carefully considered the question. It is important to make it clear what your overall opinion is.

A Study the outline for planning below. Then read Question 1 and the example notes.

Outline for planning your opinion

1. Decide your opinion on the issue (e.g. agree or disagree? / support or oppose?).
2a. Brainstorm two or three supporting reasons for your opinion.
2b. (Optional) If appropriate, mention a reason that supports the other opinion, but be sure to make clear that your main supporting reasons are more important.
3. Restate your opinion.

Example

Question 1

If the government announced that it was planning to build a new superhighway near where you live, would you support or oppose the plan? Explain your position.

1. My opinion – *oppose*
2a. Support my opinion – *noisy, pollution, more traffic*
2b. Possibly include support for other opinion and reason why your opinion not changed – *good for local business, but this is not enough to outweigh the negative effects*
3. Restate my opinion – *oppose.*

B Write planning notes for Questions 2 and 3.

Question 2

Some people prefer to travel by public transport. Other people prefer driving their own cars. Which do you prefer? Use specific examples to support your preference.

1. My opinion – _____

2a. Support my opinion – _____

2b. Possibly include support for other opinion and reason why your opinion not changed _____

3. Restate my opinion – _____

Question 3

In order to become more profitable your company has decided to invest more money in either increased advertising or research and development of new products. Which plan would you support? Give specific reasons to support your answer.

1. My opinion –

   _____

2a. Support my opinion –

   _____

2b. Possibly include support for other opinion and reason why your opinion not changed.

   _____

3. Restate my opinion –

   _____

C Read the example sentences with the common words/phrases to introduce opposing arguments in **bold**. Then make similar sentences to compare the opposing arguments of the things listed in 1–4. Use the words in the box to help you.

Comparing two things:

dogs / cats

*I prefer dogs because they make excellent pets. They are friendly, loyal and good company. **However,** I know cats can be good company too. **But, to me,** it's not quite the same – there's nothing like a dog.*

cars / bicycles

*I like cars the best as they are more convenient. You can travel further distances and use them in all weather. I know, sometimes cars can be slow in heavy traffic, **whereas** bicycles may move more freely, **but** I **still** think cars are more convenient.*

---

quiet	more space	expensive	exciting
useful	efficient	interesting	fast

1. travel by boat / travel by plane

   _____

   _____

2. football / chess

   _____

   _____

3. houses / apartment

_____

_____

4. study alone / study with others

_____

_____

D Read the example sentences for comparing/contrasting the pros and cons of one thing. Then make similar sentences using the words/phrases in **bold** for sentences 1–4.

The pros and cons of one thing:

cars

I love cars as they are so convenient. You can travel from A to B very easily and quickly. **On the other hand,** _cars are very expensive to run._ **However,** _this doesn't change what I think about them, cars are by far the most flexible and comfortable form of transport._

dogs

Dogs are very friendly, loyal and good company, **although** _they can sometimes be noisy._ **Then again,** _their noise could also act as a deterrent to burglars._

1. living in the city – convenient / expensive

_____

_____

2. motorcycles – fast / dangerous

_____

_____

3. build a new factory – more jobs / more pollution

_____

_____

4. the Internet – a lot of information / wastes time

_____

_____

If you have stated some possible arguments against your opinion, restate your opinion using phrases like: *That being said, I still believe that ... , Overall I would say ... .*

Test tip

Choose an answer you can say a lot about

Don't worry about giving an answer you strongly believe. Choose the one you think you can talk about most easily.

E Complete sentences 1–3 with the phrases below.

All things considered I would …
That being said, I still believe that …
Overall I would say …

1. _____ that I still prefer the idea of living in the countryside.
2. _____ have to agree that people should dress smartly for work.
3. _____ it is the responsibility of parents to teach children to cook.

F Read the outline for presenting your opinion.
1. Begin with your opening opinion statement by restating part of the question and using one of the phrases from Language building C. (This will both clarify what you are talking about and give you time to think of what you will say next.)
2a. Say each of your supporting points (adding reasons and examples).
2b. If appropriate, include an example of the other opinion, introducing it with a conjunction (however, on the other hand, etc.) but also clearly state that this is not as important as your main points.
3. Restate your opinion.
   (Don't forget to use the language for hesitating, introducing, personalizing, presenting and sequencing your ideas covered in Unit 6 and Unit 12.)

G 🎧 Listen to and read the developed plan for Question 1 in A. Then with your partner underline the following:

• Introduction and personalization phrases
• Words for presenting and sequencing ideas
• Comparing and contrasting words
• Phrases indicating a transition back to your own opinion

Question 1

Mmm … There are many pros and cons for this issue, but I think I would oppose this kind of building plan for several reasons.

First of all, the main reason I would be against it is that a superhighway would create a lot of noise. One of the reasons I chose to live where I do is because it's so quiet. But I don't think even people who are used to a bit of noise would really like the constant noise a superhighway would cause.

Also, a very important factor is that it would increase pollution. This isn't healthy for anyone, but is especially dangerous for children and elderly people. Really superhighways shouldn't be built near any type of housing at all.

In my country, whenever new superhighways have been built, they've always brought more traffic problems with them. I wouldn't want this for the area that I live in, so I would definitely be against such a plan.

On the other hand, I can imagine that a new superhighway might bring more business for local companies. However, this is only a minor benefit. Overall, the negative affects from noise, extra traffic, and pollution far outweigh this.

All things considered, I would definitely vote strongly against this plan.

Pace your talk carefully

Use the following rough guide to time your essay.

Opinion Statement: 5–10 seconds

Support (with reasons and examples): 40–50 seconds

Conclusion: 5–10 seconds statement

H Prepare your answers for Questions 2 and 3 based on the notes you made in B.

Question 2

_____

_____

_____

_____

_____

_____

_____

_____

_____

Question 3

_____

_____

_____

_____

_____

_____

_____

_____

_____

_____

_____

Follow up: With a partner, practice reading aloud your answers to Questions 2 and 3.

unit
12

☑ Choose the side you will defend.

☑ Present your opinion (with a restatement of the question).

☑ Introduce each supporting point and talk for around 15 seconds (adding reasons and examples) and remember to use hesitation devices to avoid long pauses.

☑ If appropriate, add an opposing point before concluding with your opinion.

☑ Be sure to include your reason why this does not convince you to change your mind.

B Tactic practice

Use the Test tactics you have practiced to give your opinions on Questions 1 and 2. Follow the steps summarized in the Test techniques. After each step, pause to see if your partner has understood and if they have any suggestions. Your partner will also time you during your supporting points.

1. Recently plans were announced to build a new airport near your community. Do you support or oppose this plan? Explain your position.

2. Some people like to go to the gym to do exercise. Others prefer to cycle to work and take the stairs instead of the elevator. Which way do you prefer to keep healthy? Give reasons for your opinion.

∩∩ Using natural English

In natural spoken English, sounds are sometimes changed, combined, or dropped. Listen to a native speaker saying the following sentences and write in the words they say.

_____ convenient.

_____ good pets.

_____ fast.

Check your answers in the Key on page 35.

Listen again and practice these sentences with the correct sound and rhythm.

C Mini-test

Now apply the Test tactics to answer the following question. Use the recommended test time for Question 11.

Question 11:
Express an opinion

Question 11: Express an opinion

Directions: In this part of the test, you will give your opinion about a specific topic. Be sure to say as much as you can in the time allowed. You will have 15 seconds to prepare. Then you will have 60 seconds to speak.

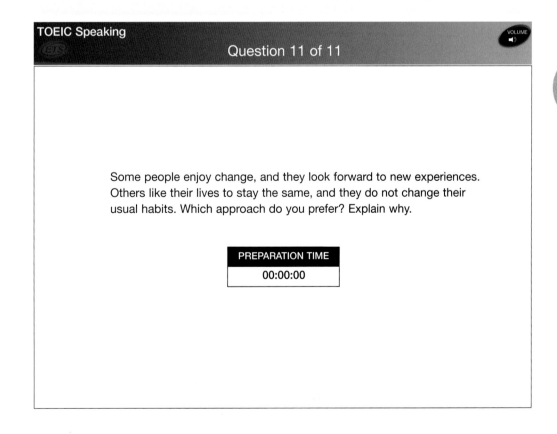

Some people enjoy change, and they look forward to new experiences. Others like their lives to stay the same, and they do not change their usual habits. Which approach do you prefer? Explain why.

PREPARATION TIME
00:00:00

Phonetic Alphabet

Vowels

iː	see	/siː/
ɪ	sit	/sɪt/
e	ten	/ten/
æ	hat	/hæt/
ɑː	arm	/ɑːm/
ɒ	got	/ɡɒt/
ɔː	saw	/sɔː/
ʊ	put	/pʊt/
uː	too	/tuː/
ʌ	cup	/kʌp/
ɜː	fur	/fɜː/
ə	ago	/əˈɡəʊ/
eɪ	page	/peɪdʒ/
əʊ	home	/həʊm/
aɪ	five	/faɪv/
aʊ	now	/naʊ/
ɔɪ	join	/dʒɔɪn/
ɪə	near	/nɪə(r)/
eə	hair	/heə(r)/
ʊə	pure	/pjʊə(r)/

Consonants

p	pen	/pen/
b	bad	/bæd/
t	tea	/tiː/
d	did	/dɪd/
k	cat	/kæt/
ɡ	got	/ɡɒt/
tʃ	chin	/tʃɪn/
dʒ	June	/dʒuːn/
f	fall	/fɔːl/
v	voice	/vɔɪs/
θ	thin	/θɪn/
ð	then	/ðen/
s	so	/səʊ/
z	zoo	/zuː/
ʃ	she	/ʃiː/
ʒ	vision	/vɪʒn/
h	how	/haʊ/
m	man	/mæn/
n	no	/nəʊ/
ŋ	sing	/sɪŋ/
l	leg	/leg/
r	red	/red/
j	yes	/jes/
w	wet	/wet/

TOEIC®
Writing Test

The TOEIC Writing Test: An Overview

The TOEIC Writing Test is designed to measure the ability to use written English to perform communication tasks that are typical to the international workplace. The test is composed of eight tasks and takes approximately one hour to complete. As with the TOEIC Speaking Test, the range of ability among English learners who will take the TOEIC Writing Test is expected to be broad. The test is designed to provide information about the writing ability of test takers across a range of language proficiency levels.

To this end, the tasks are organized to support the following three claims about test-taker performance:

1. *The test taker can produce well-formed sentences (including subordination).*
2. *The test taker can produce multi-sentence-length text to convey straightforward information, questions, instructions, narratives, etc.*
3. *The test taker can produce multi-paragraph-length text to express complex ideas, using, as appropriate, reasons, evidence, and extended explanations.*

Because these claims are hierarchical, task difficulty increases as the test taker progresses through the test. The first claim describes test takers at lower levels of English language proficiency. Test takers who can successfully complete the tasks that support the second and third claims will probably be very successful at carrying out the tasks that support the first claim. At the same time, the tasks that support the third claim will distinguish between moderately high-level and very high-level writers of English as it is used in workplace settings.

The following chart shows how the tasks in the TOEIC Writing Test are organized:

Question	Task	Evaluation Criteria
1–5	Write a sentence based on a picture	• grammar • relevance of the sentences to the pictures
6–7	Respond to a written request	• quality and variety of your sentences • vocabulary • organization
8	Write an opinion essay	• whether your opinion is supported with reasons and/or examples • grammar • vocabulary • organization

How to Improve Your Score on the TOEIC Writing Test

Like the TOEIC Speaking Test, the TOEIC Writing Test features a variety of timed tasks appropriate for test takers across a broad range of proficiency. There are several areas on which you can focus in order to improve your performance on this test.

Key test-taking strategies

- Familiarity with the test format, instructions, and question types – Although all the instructions are printed at the start of each test part, knowing these beforehand will save you time and energy on the day of the test.
- Time management – The tasks in the Writing Test are timed. Understanding how much time you have to complete each of the various tasks and maintaining an appropriate pace as you prepare and produce your responses will help you to improve your overall performance.

Linguistic skills

- Grammar knowledge – The Writing Test will require you to write sentences, paragraphs, and longer texts. An understanding of grammatical form, meaning, and use will help you to construct clearly written sentences. Maintaining a consistent level of accuracy will improve your overall performance on the Writing Test and will also help you in your writing in everyday situations.
- Knowledge of key vocabulary and useful phrases – Vocabulary, both in single words and in phrases, is a key area contributing to scores in each part of the test. This course provides a selection of high-frequency vocabulary and phrases that are appropriate to the tasks in the test.
- Reading comprehension skills – Tasks in the Writing Test will require you to read some information and respond appropriately. Good reading comprehension skills are important in completing these tasks successfully.
- Understanding of organizational conventions – Some of the language tasks in the Writing Test, such as responding to an e-mail or giving an opinion, are easier to complete if you can follow standardized organizational patterns in English. An understanding of the ways ideas are organized, and of the words and phrases that are often used to join ideas together, will also help you to be understood in English in the real world.

TOEIC Writing Claims

The tasks in the Writing Test are designed to capture evidence about a test taker's writing abilities as defined in the TOEIC Writing Claims.

General Claim: The test taker can use written English to perform typical international workplace communication tasks.

Claims for specific tasks

Claim 1: The test taker can produce well-formed sentences (including subordination).

This claim is supported by the following task:

Questions 1–5: Write a sentence based on a picture

The test taker writes a sentence about each of five photographs using the key words provided beneath each photograph. In two of the sentences, a complex sentence with a subordinate clause is required.

> **For this task, the test taker will be measured on the following criteria:**
> *Grammar*
> *Relevance of the sentence to the photograph*

Claim 2: The test taker can produce multi-sentence-length text to convey straightforward information, questions, instructions, narratives, etc.

This claim is supported by the following task:

Questions 6–7 Respond to a written request

The test taker responds to each of two e-mail messages; for example, by giving information, explaining a problem, making a suggestion, and/or asking questions. The response should be written in language that is appropriate to the audience (the person who will read the response).

> **For this task, the test taker will be measured on the following criteria:**
> *Quality and variety of sentences*
> *Vocabulary*
> *Organization*

Claim 3: The test taker can produce multi-paragraph-length text to express complex ideas, using, as appropriate, reasons, evidence, and extended explanations.

This claim is supported by the following task:

Question 8: Write an opinion essay

The test taker develops an essay on a topic of general interest, appropriate to the TOEIC test-taking population.

> **For this task, the test taker will be measured on the following criteria:**
> *Support for the opinion with reasons and/or examples*
> *Grammar*
> *Vocabulary*
> *Organization*

Sample TOEIC® Writing Test

TOEIC Writing Test Directions

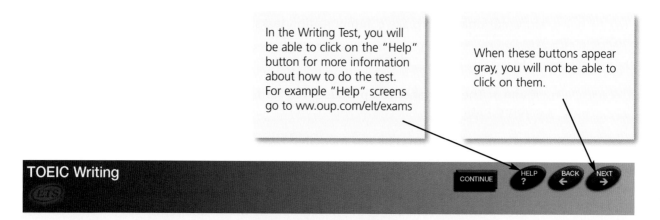

In the Writing Test, you will be able to click on the "Help" button for more information about how to do the test. For example "Help" screens go to ww.oup.com/elt/exams

When these buttons appear gray, you will not be able to click on them.

Writing Test Directions

This is the TOEIC Writing Test. This test includes eight questions that measure different aspects of your writing ability. The test lasts approximately one hour.

Question	Task	Evaluation Criteria
1–5	Write a sentence based on a picture	• grammar • relevance of the sentences to the pictures
6–7	Respond to a written request	• quality and variety of your sentences • vocabulary • organization
8	Write an opinion essay	• whether your opinion is supported with reasons and/or examples • grammar • vocabulary • organization

For each type of question, you will be given specific directions, including the time allowed for writing.

Click on **Continue** to go on.

Questions 1–5: Write a sentence based on a picture

Questions 1–5: Write a sentence based on a picture

Directions: In this part of the test, you will write ONE sentence that is based on a picture. With each picture, you will be given TWO words or phrases that you must use in your sentence. You can change the forms of the words and you can use the words in any order. Your sentences will be scored on

- the appropriate use of grammar and
- the relevance of the sentence to the picture.

In this part, you can move to the next question by clicking on **Next**. If you want to return to a previous question, click on **Back**. You will have 8 minutes to complete this part of the test.

Example

write / notebook

Sample response

The man is writing in a notebook.

Click on **Continue** to go on.

Question 1: Write a sentence based on a picture

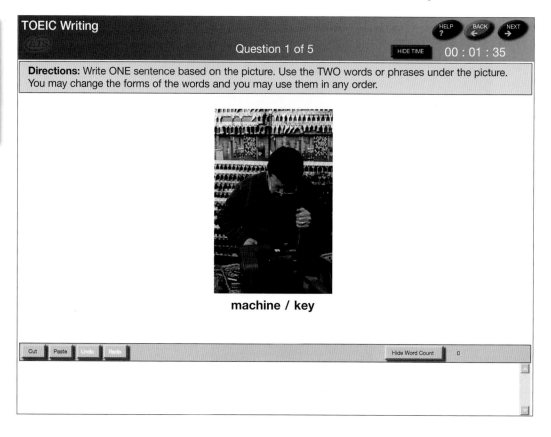

In this part of the test, you can click on "next" to go to the next question, whenever you are ready.

Directions: Write ONE sentence based on the picture. Use the TWO words or phrases under the picture. You may change the forms of the words and you may use them in any order.

machine / key

Cut   Paste   Undo   Redo   Hide Word Count   0

Question 1 Score, response, and examiner's comments

Score Point 3

> **He is using a machine to make keys.**

This response is a 3 because it consists of one sentence that uses both key words appropriately, has no grammatical errors, and is consistent with the picture.

Score Point 2

> **A man is looking into with his machine to find his keys.**

This response is a 2 because it consists of one sentence that uses both words correctly and that is consistent with the picture. However, it cannot receive a higher score because there is a grammatical error: "looking into with his".

Score Point 1

> **There is a man reparimg**

This response is a 1 because it omits both key words. In addition, it does not complete the task of writing a grammatically correct sentence that is consistent with the picture.

Question 2: Write a sentence based on a picture

From Question 2 onwards, you can also click on the "back" button to review the previous questions.

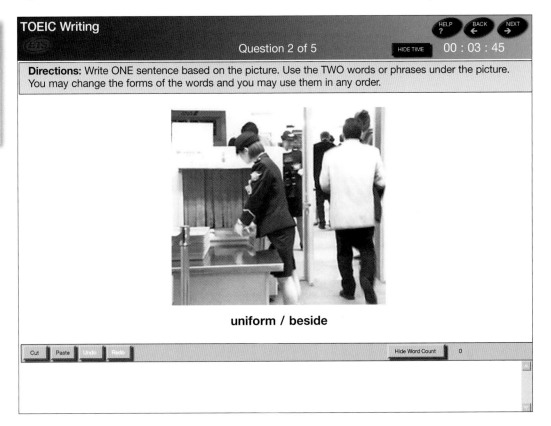

Question 2 Score, response, and examiner's comments

Score Point 3

> **A man is walking beside a lady wearing a uniform.**

This response is a 3 because it has no grammatical errors, it contains both key words used appropriately, and it is consistent with the picture.

Score Point 2

> **The man is walking beside a woman wear uniform .**

This response is a 2 because it consists of one sentence that uses both words correctly and is consistent with the picture. However, it cannot receive a higher score because there is a grammatical error: "…a woman wear…".

Score Point 1

> **Woman who work fligt center check garbages.**

This response is a 1 because it omits both of the key words. In addition, it contains several errors that interfere with meaning.

Question 3: Write a sentence based on a picture

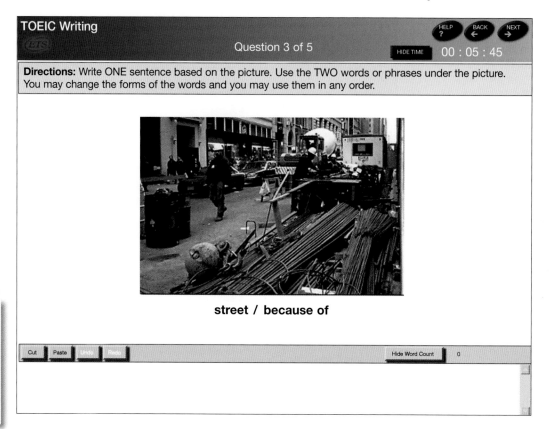

Remember that responses will be marked down if errors interfere with meaning. At times, punctuation errors can interfere with meaning. Therefore, it is a good strategy to use accurate punctuation in your responses.

Question 3 Score, response, and examiner's comments

Score Point 3

> the street is blocked because of the construction.

This response is a 3 because it has no grammatical errors, it contains both key words used appropriately, and it is consistent with the picture.

Score Point 2

> **The street seem crowded because of many pipes.**

This response is a 2 because it consists of one sentence that uses both words correctly and is consistent with the picture. However, it cannot receive a higher score because there is a grammatical error: "The street seem …".

Score Point 1

> **IN NEWYORK,THE STREETS ARE MATERIAL**

This response is a 1 because it omits one of the key words and contains errors that interfere with meaning.

Question 4: Write a sentence based on a picture

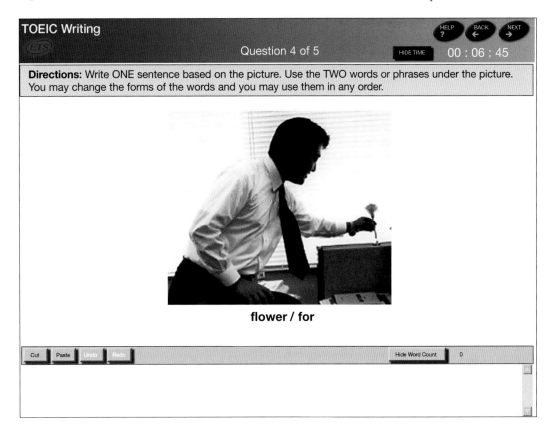

Directions: Write ONE sentence based on the picture. Use the TWO words or phrases under the picture. You may change the forms of the words and you may use them in any order.

flower / for

Cut   Paste   Undo   Redo   Hide Word Count   0

Question 4 Score, response, and examiner's comments

Score Point 3

> **he is putting a flower on his desk for himself.**

This response is a 3 because it has no grammatical errors, it contains both key words used appropriately, and it is consistent with the picture.

Score Point 2

> **The man in the office is looking a small flower. He uses this for arrangement of his office.**

This response is a 2 because, although it contains both key words, they are not used in the same sentence. In addition, the word "for" is not used properly. Both sentences contain grammatical errors: "… is looking a small …" and "… for arrangement of his office".

Score Point 1

> **She like flower.**

This response is a 1 because it omits one of the key words.

Question 5: Write a sentence based on a picture

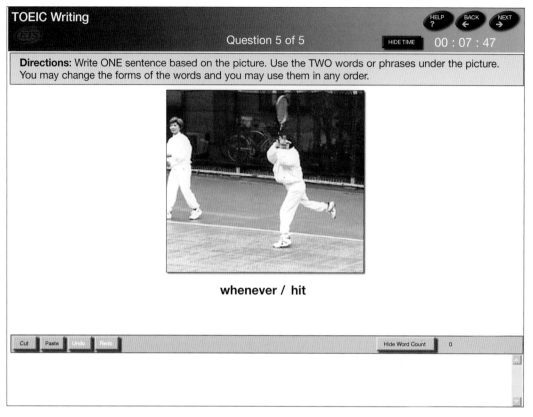

Question 5 Score, response, and examiner's comments

Score Point 3

> **whenever she plays tennis, she hits many balls.**

This response is a 3 because it has no grammatical errors, it contains both key words used appropriately, and it is consistent with the picture.

Score Point 2

> **Whenever the person try to hit the ball, his racket wouldn't hit the ball.**

This response is a 2 because it consists of one sentence that uses both words correctly and is consistent with the picture. However, it cannot receive a higher score because there is a grammatical error: "… the person try …".

Score Point 1

> **whenever hit the ball, he lacket**

This response is a 1 because it contains errors that interfere with meaning.

In the test, you will see this screen after 8 minutes, when the time given for answering Questions 1–5 is complete.

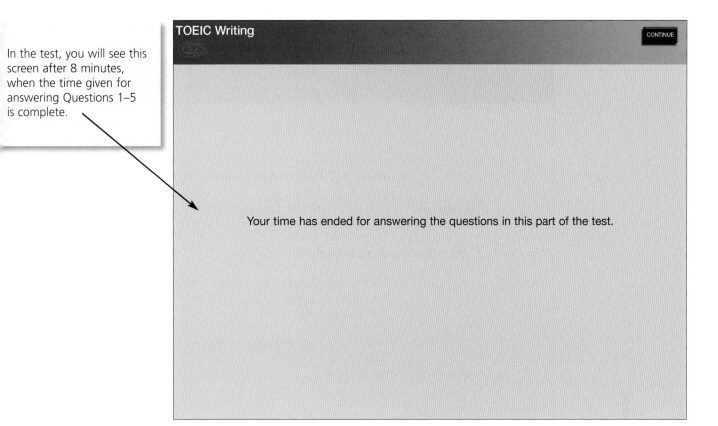

Questions 1–5: Write a sentence based on a picture
Scoring Guidelines

3   The response consists of ONE sentence that:
- has no grammatical errors; AND
- contains forms of both key words used appropriately; AND
- is consistent with the picture.

2   The response may consist of one or more sentences that:
- have one or more grammatical errors that do not obscure the meaning; AND
- contain BOTH key words, but they may not be in the same sentence and the form of the word(s) may not be accurate; AND
- are consistent with the picture.

1   The response:
- has errors that interfere with meaning; OR
- omits one or both key words; OR
- is not consistent with the picture.

0   The response is blank, written in a foreign language, or consists of keystroke characters.

Question 6: Respond to a written request

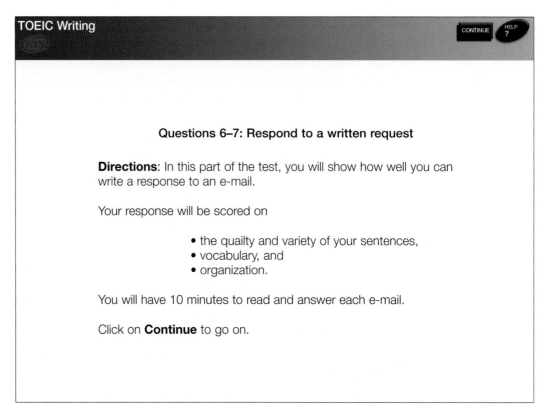

TOEIC Writing

CONTINUE   HELP ?

Questions 6–7: Respond to a written request

Directions: In this part of the test, you will show how well you can write a response to an e-mail.

Your response will be scored on

- the quailty and variety of your sentences,
- vocabulary, and
- organization.

You will have 10 minutes to read and answer each e-mail.

Click on **Continue** to go on.

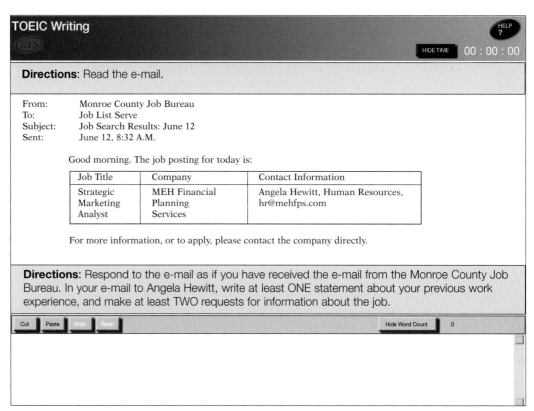

TOEIC Writing

HELP ?

HIDE TIME   00 : 00 : 00

Directions: Read the e-mail.

From: Monroe County Job Bureau
To: Job List Serve
Subject: Job Search Results: June 12
Sent: June 12, 8:32 A.M.

Good morning. The job posting for today is:

Job Title	Company	Contact Information
Strategic Marketing Analyst	MEH Financial Planning Services	Angela Hewitt, Human Resources, hr@mehfps.com

For more information, or to apply, please contact the company directly.

Directions: Respond to the e-mail as if you have received the e-mail from the Monroe County Job Bureau. In your e-mail to Angela Hewitt, write at least ONE statement about your previous work experience, and make at least TWO requests for information about the job.

Cut   Paste   Undo   Redo   Hide Word Count   0

Question 6 Score, response, and examiner's comments

Score Point 4

> **Dear Ms. Angela Hewitt,**
> **I am interested in your company. I used to work in MNO Financial Group**
> **as a strategic marketing analyst for 5 years.**
> **Please send me your company's profile in details. And please tell me the**
> **due date of the application.**
> **I'm looking forward to your quick reply.**
> **Thank you and best regards,**

This response is a 4. It effectively addresses all the tasks in the prompt using multiple sentences that clearly convey the information required by the prompt. The response uses organizational logic, and the tone and register of the response are appropriate.

In the test, you will see this screen after 10 minutes, when the time given for answering each e-mail question is complete.

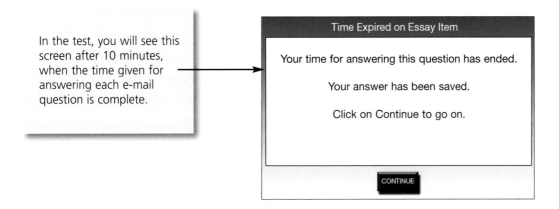

Time Expired on Essay Item

Your time for answering this question has ended.

Your answer has been saved.

Click on Continue to go on.

CONTINUE

Score Point 3

> **Hello Ms.Angela Hewitt,**
>
> **Thank you for your information about a job. It seems suitable for me. Because I had been working as a manager of marketing section for 5years. Then I'd like to receive this job. I have 2 more questions about the job. When the job as the post start if I have been employed? And, how much the salary for it? I will be glad if I can have your answer by tomorrow. Thank you, and best regards,**

This response is a 3. It is mostly successful but falls short in addressing one of the tasks required by the prompt. The response gives at least one statement about the writer's previous working experience and makes one successful request for information about the job. However, the other request for information about the job is unsuccessful due to errors in grammar and usage: "When the job as the post start if I have been employed?" The errors in this sentence obscure the writer's meaning and therefore, the task is unsuccessful.

Score Point 2

> **Thanks you to make me a chance to request for a new job. I want to make a request to a strategic Marketing Analyst for MEH Financial Planning Services. I have expereinced the same job for ABC Financial company in Tokyo. I want to have an appointment to Angela, Human Resources whenever she want.**

This response is a 2. It successfully addresses only one of the tasks required by the prompt in that it makes a statement about previous work experience. It does not, however, make two requests for information about the new job. The meaning of the first stated request is unclear; it uses the language of requesting and then merely inserts the title of the job from the stimulus e-mail. The second attempt at making a request concerns making an appointment; no request for information about the job is made. In addition, the response shows a limited awareness of audience, and errors in grammar and usage obscure meaning in the first two sentences.

Score Point 1

> **Good morning.My job is Strategic Marketing Analyst,isn't it? I'm to go the MEH Financial Planning Services by 10:00 P.M. Is this time OK?If I have something not to kown,I send a e-mail to that company.**

This response is a 1. It addresses none of the required tasks, the connections between ideas are missing, and the errors in grammar and usage obscure the writer's meaning.

Question 7: Respond to a written request

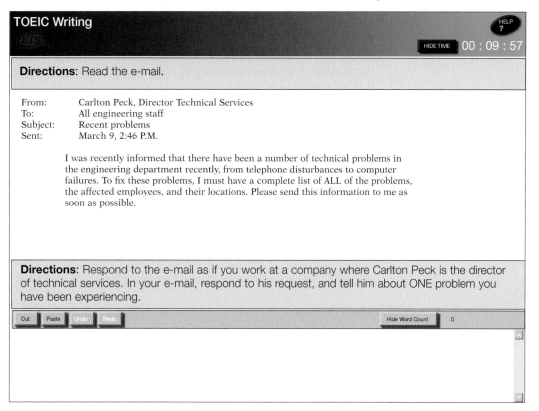

Directions: Read the e-mail.

From: Carlton Peck, Director Technical Services
To: All engineering staff
Subject: Recent problems
Sent: March 9, 2:46 P.M.

I was recently informed that there have been a number of technical problems in the engineering department recently, from telephone disturbances to computer failures. To fix these problems, I must have a complete list of ALL of the problems, the affected employees, and their locations. Please send this information to me as soon as possible.

Directions: Respond to the e-mail as if you work at a company where Carlton Peck is the director of technical services. In your e-mail, respond to his request, and tell him about ONE problem you have been experiencing.

Question 7 Score, response, and examiner's comments

Score Point 4

> I have found some technical problems in the engineering department since I worked the site.
> There are total 4 problems to fix, and here is the list of them.
>
> 1. Telephone disturbances.
> 2. Computer Failures.
> 3. Network Connecting Failures.
> 4. Interphone Disturbances.
>
> I have been often experiencing Network Connecting Failures since I work at Information Center at 7th floor.
> Whenever I need to connect lines between 7th floor and 4th floor, it didn't work.
> Please fix it right away.
>
> Information Center at 7th floor is the most affected by these technical problems, but all of offices at the 7th floor are known t

This response is a 4. It effectively addresses all the tasks required by the prompt. It uses organizational logic to create coherence among sentences. Although the writer does not address Mr. Peck in the e-mail, the tone and register are appropriate to the intended audience. Isolated errors in usage do not interfere with meaning.

Score Point 3

> **Dear Mr. Carlton Peck.**
>
> **Regarding your e-mail about the problems, I have several things to tell you. There have been frequent black-out in my office – Human Resources Department. I remember it's three times only in this month, so we had lost lots of important data.**
> **You should have informed the black-out in advance.**
> **There many be some miscommunication.**
> **Please, let this happen again.**

This response is a 3. It is mostly successful, but falls short in addressing one of the tasks required by the prompt. Two of the required tasks are successfully completed: telling Mr. Peck about one problem the writer is experiencing and the location ("my office – Human Resources Department"). However, one of the required tasks, indicating which employees are affected, is not completed. The writer notes that "we had lost . . . data" but does not elaborate on who "we" are. In addition, noticeable errors in grammar and usage are present. The response shows some awareness of the audience and uses organizational logic.

Score Point 2

> **dear Carlton Peck**
> **I have a troble on my personal computer distributed from my company to apply the work. My pc does not reach a condition to use it. In some case afer swithing on It can not start windows OSrestart by himself,again and again**

This response is a 2. It addresses only one of the tasks required by the prompt: telling Mr. Peck about one problem the writer is experiencing. The response does not include information about other employees affected or their locations. In addition, errors in grammar and usage obscure meaning in the first two sentences and then again at the very end.

Score Point 1

> **In my department, A number of technical problems have occur recently. The problem's cause is very complex. But**

This response is a 1. It addresses none of the required tasks, although it includes some content relevant to the stimulus.

Questions 6–7: Respond to a written request
Scoring Guidelines

4   The response e-mail effectively addresses all the tasks in the prompt using multiple sentences that clearly convey the information, instructions, questions, etc., required by the prompt.

 • the response uses organizational logic or appropriate connecting words or both to create coherence among sentences
 • the tone and register of the response is appropriate for the intended audience
 • a few isolated errors in grammar or usage may be present but do not obscure the writer's meaning

3   The response e-mail is mostly successful but falls short in addressing one of the tasks required by the prompt.

 • the response may omit, respond unsuccessfully, or respond incompletely to ONE of the required tasks
 • the response uses organizational logic or appropriate connecting words in at least part of the response
 • the response shows some awareness of audience
 • noticeable errors in grammar and usage may be present; ONE sentence may contain errors that obscure meaning

2   The response e-mail is marked by several weaknesses:

 • the response may address only ONE of the required tasks or may unsuccessfully or incompletely address TWO OR THREE of the required tasks
 • connections between ideas may be missing or obscure
 • the response may show little awareness of audience
 • errors in grammar and usage may obscure meaning in MORE THAN ONE sentence

1   The response e-mail is seriously flawed and conveys little or no information, instructions, questions, etc., required by the prompt.

 • the response addresses NONE of the required tasks, although it may include some content relevant to stimulus
 • connections between ideas are missing or obscure
 • the tone or register may be inappropriate for the audience
 • frequent errors in grammar and usage obscure the writer's meaning most of the time

0   A response at this level merely copies words from the prompt or stimulus, rejects the topic or is otherwise not connected to the topic, is written in a language other than English, consists of keystroke characters that convey no meaning, or is blank.

Question 8: Write an opinion essay

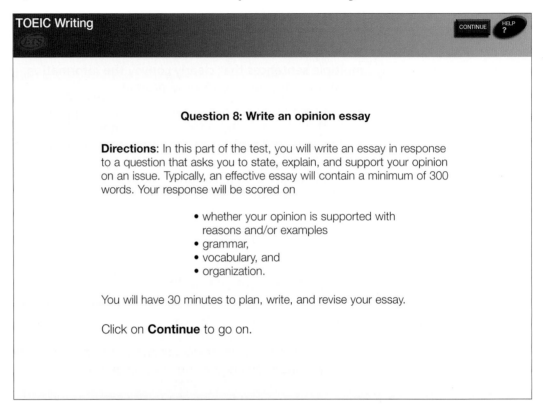

Question 8: Write an opinion essay

Directions: In this part of the test, you will write an essay in response to a question that asks you to state, explain, and support your opinion on an issue. Typically, an effective essay will contain a minimum of 300 words. Your response will be scored on

- whether your opinion is supported with reasons and/or examples
- grammar,
- vocabulary, and
- organization.

You will have 30 minutes to plan, write, and revise your essay.

Click on **Continue** to go on.

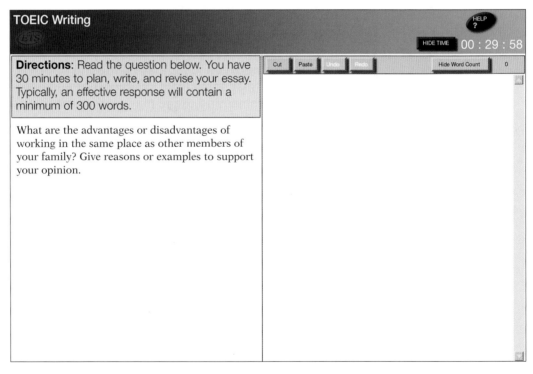

TOEIC Writing

HIDE TIME 00 : 29 : 58

Directions: Read the question below. You have 30 minutes to plan, write, and revise your essay. Typically, an effective response will contain a minimum of 300 words.

What are the advantages or disadvantages of working in the same place as other members of your family? Give reasons or examples to support your opinion.

Cut | Paste | Undo | Redo | Hide Word Count | 0

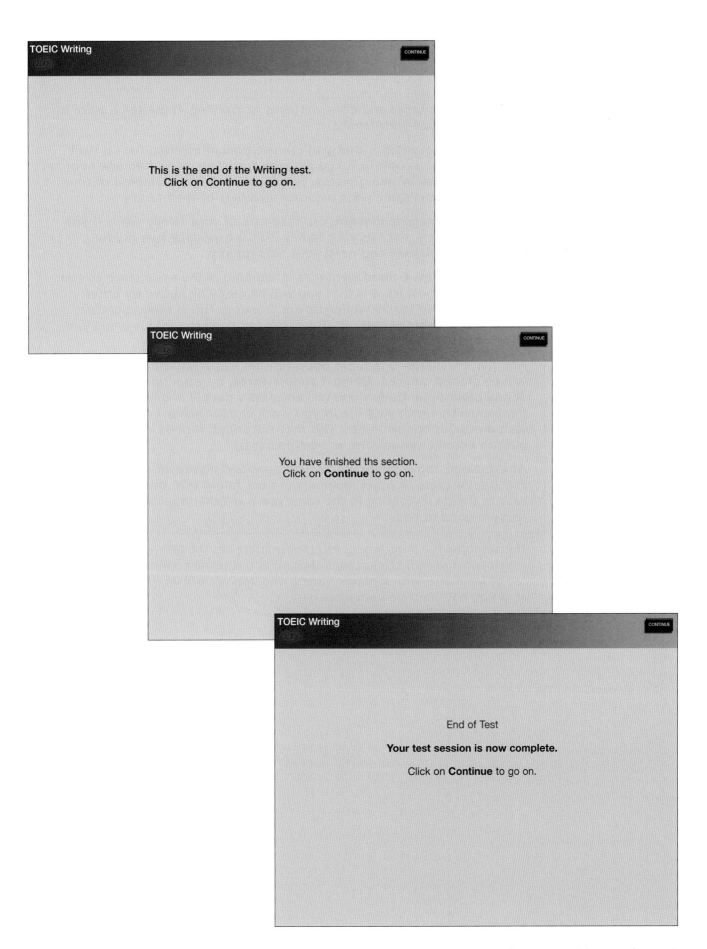

TOEIC Writing

This is the end of the Writing test.
Click on Continue to go on.

CONTINUE

TOEIC Writing

You have finished ths section.
Click on **Continue** to go on.

CONTINUE

TOEIC Writing

End of Test

Your test session is now complete.

Click on **Continue** to go on.

CONTINUE

Score Point 5

> There are advantages and disadvantages of working in the same place as other members of your family.
>
> The biggest adavanteg is that you can use time effectively. As it is well known, average people in Tokyo area are spending more than one hour to commute to their working places. People can save great amount of time by working in the same place as other members of their family.
>
> Another advantage is that you can take care of your family easily if you work in the same place as your family. This is especially true if your children are still small and need your help greatly.
>
> There are, however, disadavantages in working in the same place as your family. The biggest issue is that you will be easily disturbed by other members of your family while you are working. This is especially true when you have small children. This issue can be very seruous when you have an important and urgent work to be done.
>
> Another advantage is that the opportunities to participate in outer society will be greatly reduced. As most people agree, by working in a company or any other organization you will encounter people and learn many things, which enrich your life. If you work in your home, you will lose such precipous opportunities. This may not sound serious in the first place but can become serious one as time passes by.
>
> As explained above, there are adavantages and disadvanteges in working in the same place as other members of your famiy. It is, therefore, not easy to decide if working in the same place as other members of your famiy is good or bad.

This response is a 5 because it effectively addresses the task with well-developed and well-organized writing. It also displays consistent facility in the use of language, with syntactic variety and appropriate word choice. Minor errors do not interfere with meaning.

The advantage of working in the same place as oher members of family is that the knowledge can be shared easily.

For example, In case of the family members who are staying together, Even if the company is very big and is making some difficulties in communincating each other, The more easily they communicate, the better the information can be shared. Since they are always together, the information can be shared easily unless they are hating each other, at least they are trying to communicate in terms of the bussines. So it defenately can be said as one of the advantages.

On the other hand, The one of the disadvantages is the position each family member has.

Though It has the difficulty talking about the each case, It could be said that some of people are judging the person with the position they have.This means that depending on the position they have, some criterias are also different, like the job they are given, salary they get monthly and so on, Those differences are thought to produce kind of the feeling like jerousy and other nagaive passion against the person.So that makes me say it as one of the disadvantages in working in the same place with family members.

So in one sence,It depends on what type of company they work in and how they think the job and the position they own.

In conclusion, no matter how they feel against the position they have and what type of job they are doing, The family has respect each other, cause everything has advantage and disadvantage.

This response is a 4 because it addresses the topic and task well, though some points could be better elaborated. It is generally well organized and displays progression and coherence, but displays occasional redundancy. In addition, noticeable errors in structure, word choice, and word form are present. These do not interfere with meaning, but they are frequent enough that they prevent the higher score.

Score Point 3

> When we work with other menber,there are mainly two advantages, I think.
>
> First,if coworkers are family,they can keep the good communication.Because they deeply understand thier charactors each other.So even if there is no time to dscuss the issue,they know how partnaers think and what to do.
>
> Second,they will same distiny.they are not the relationship with enployee and enployment.So they have same problem and feel same stress.They wil do their best for the issue without unsatisfaciton.
>
> In other hand,they also have some disadvantage then.
> They know private and working life each other.
> So it is easy to lose their temper.
> There are much more mouth fihgt than normal working place.
>
> However,if the company is too small less than about 30 emplyee,it is a big advantage to work with other family menbers.But if the company are big,there are not good for them.Becuse menbers aroud them will have to pay attention to their relationships.That will make thier working some problem.

This response is a 3 because it addresses the topic with somewhat developed explanations and a steady progression of ideas. However, it also shows inconsistent facility in sentence formation and word choice, resulting in a lack of clarity and occasionally obscured meaning.

Score Point 2

> In my opinion, the advantage of working in the same
> place is to easy to work together regulary.
> That is to say, Working in the same place gives
> us friendly team mind and working order sysytematically.
> Especially It suits for routin work.
> Contraly, the disadevantage of that is to hard to dealing with something different and new challenges.
> Because they have same knowlege and skill.
> And their information is limited.
> If we want to expand our business widely.
> We should work with many kinds of people.

This response is a 2 because it shows limited development in response to the task. Explanations and details are sometimes insufficient to support generalizations, and connections between ideas are not always clear. The response also displays an accumulation of errors in usage and word form.

Score Point 1

> I think it is good for my family to be working the same place.Because my family fits on this place.There are a lot of friends and good parks and good shops.If we move the place never have been,we are nervece.
> But, if I am alone,I would like to work a lot of place because of my skil's up.
> I tink it is important to communicate a lot of people.If I have been working in the same place,I think I prefer safety to inovetion.It is denger because I don' notice the wrong or if it is wrong,I think it is no plomblem because of usual.

This response is a 1 because it is underdeveloped in relationship to the task and is full of irrelevant information. Serious and frequent usage errors tend to obscure meaning.

Question 8: Write an opinion essay
Scoring Guidelines

5   An essay at this level largely accomplishes all of the following:
- effectively addresses the topic and task
- is well organized and well developed, using clearly appropriate explanations, exemplifications, and/or details
- displays unity, progression, and coherence
- displays consistent facility in the use of language, demonstrating syntactic variety, appropriate word choice, and idiomaticity, though it may have minor lexical or grammatical errors

4   An essay at this level largely accomplishes all of the following:
- addresses the topic and task well, though some points may not be fully elaborated
- is generally well organized and well developed, using appropriate and sufficient explanations, exemplifications, and/or details
- displays unity, progression, and coherence, though it may contain occasional redundancy, digression, or unclear connections
- displays facility in the use of language, demonstrating syntactic variety and range of vocabulary, though it will probably have occasional noticeable minor errors in structure, word form, or use of idiomatic language that do not interfere with meaning

3   An essay at this level is marked by one or more of the following:
- addresses the topic and task using somewhat developed explanations, exemplifications, and/or details
- displays unity, progression, and coherence, though connection of ideas may be occasionally obscured
- may demonstrate inconsistent facility in sentence formation and word choice that may result in lack of clarity and occasionally obscure meaning
- may display accurate but limited range of syntactic structures and vocabulary

2   An essay at this level may reveal one or more of the following weaknesses:
- limited development in response to the topic and task
- inadequate organization or connection of ideas
- inappropriate or insufficient exemplifications, explanations, or details to support or illustrate generalizations in response to the task
- a noticeably inappropriate choice of words or word forms
- an accumulation of errors in sentence structure and/or usage

1   An essay at this level is seriously flawed by one or more of the following weaknesses:
- serious disorganization or underdevelopment
- little or no detail, or irrelevant specifics, or questionable responsiveness to the task
- serious and frequent errors in sentence structure or usage

0   An essay at this level merely copies words from the topic, rejects the topic, or is otherwise not connected to the topic, is written in a foreign language, consists of keystroke characters, or is blank.

Writing Scores

How your responses are rated

Responses to all TOEIC Writing tasks are sent to ETS's Online Scoring Network. Overall, the responses from each test taker are scored by at least three different human raters. In addition, some of the individual tasks are each scored by two raters to ensure the reliability of the scores.

Interpreting your scores

Scaled scores
After you have taken the TOEIC Writing Test, you will receive a scaled score indicating your overall performance on the test. The scaled scores range from 0 to 200 in increments of 10. Your scores indicate the general proficiency in writing that you have demonstrated by your performance on the test.

Raw scores
Before your scaled score can be calculated, your performance on each task must be considered. The Writing Test is made up of tasks of different levels of difficulty that are rated on individual scales. The *Write a sentence based on a picture* tasks are rated on a scale of 0–3 according to the Scoring guidelines on page 145. The *Respond to a written request* tasks receive an overall rating on a scale of 0–4 in accordance with the Scoring guidelines on page 151. The *Write an opinion essay* task is rated on a scale of 0–5, according to the Scoring guidelines on page 157.

Converting raw scores to scaled scores
The test is designed so that the earlier tasks require less proficiency in written English than the later tasks do; in fact, the test progresses in a series of steps. Your performance on the higher-level tasks contributes more to your overall score than does your performance on the lower-level tasks.

Although the formulas that ETS uses to calculate your scaled score are complicated, the basics of how your performance is converted into the score are quite simple. If you have someone who can give you accurate ratings of your responses, look at the table below to get an approximate estimate of your score and level. Begin by looking at your performance on the last task on the TOEIC Writing Test, the Opinion Essay task.

In this table you can see some frequently observed patterns of scores. Not all possible patterns are represented here. Note that, across different forms of the TOEIC Writing test, the same raw scores will not always translate exactly to the same scaled scores.

WRITING LEVEL	WRITING SCALED SCORE	Opinion Essay Task	Respond to a Written Request Task	Picture-Sentence Task
1	0–30	no response or off topic	no response or off topic	no response or off topic
2	40	1	2, 1 or 1, 1	nearly all 1
3	50–60	1	2, 1 or 1, 1	mostly 1
4	70–80	2	2, 1 or 1, 1	some 1, some 2
5	90–100	2	3, 2 or 2, 2	mostly 2
6	110–130	3	3, 2 or 2, 2	mostly 2
7	140–160	3	4, 4 or 4, 3 or 3, 3	mostly 2
7	140–160	4	3, 2 or 2, 2	mostly 2
8	170–190	4	4, 4 or 4, 3	all or nearly all 3
9	200	5	4, 4 or 4, 3	all or nearly all 3

Official scores on the test are given by trained ETS raters. These raters complete a rigorous training program and are required to pass a certification test before they can score the test. Keep in mind that people who are not authorized/certified by ETS to assign scores may not be able to give you a completely accurate rating of your response.

Proficiency Levels

Depending on where your total score falls on the scaled score range of 0 to 200, you will be provided with a description of your level of writing proficiency. There are 9 proficiency levels covering the 0–200 total score range for the Writing Test. The proficiency level descriptors outline the types of general skills and abilities in written English that are common for most people who have achieved a score similar to yours. The descriptor associated with the level that you have achieved will help you understand the strengths and weaknesses of your written English.

WRITING Scaled Score	WRITING Proficiency Level
0–30	1
40	2
50–60	3
70–80	4
90–100	5
110–130	6
140–160	7
170–190	8
200	9

These descriptors will appear on individual score reports. For further information go to www.ets.org/toeic

Writing Proficiency Level Descriptors

Level 9   Scale score   200
Typically, test takers at level 9 can communicate straightforward information effectively and use reasons, examples, or explanations to support an opinion.

When using reasons, examples, or explanations to support an opinion, their writing is well-organized and well-developed. The use of English is natural, with a variety of sentence structures and appropriate word choice, and is grammatically accurate.

When giving straightforward information, asking questions, giving instructions, or making requests, their writing is clear, coherent, and effective.

Level 8   Scale score   170–190
Typically, test takers at level 8 can communicate straightforward information effectively and use reasons, examples, or explanations to support an opinion.

When giving straightforward information, asking questions, giving instructions, or making requests, their writing is clear, coherent, and effective.
When using reasons, examples, or explanations to support an opinion, their writing is generally good. It is generally well-organized and uses a variety of sentence structures and appropriate vocabulary. It may also include one of the following weaknesses:

- occasional unnecessary repetition of ideas or unclear connections between ideas
- noticeable minor grammatical errors or incorrect word choices.

Level 7 Scale score 140–160

Typically, test takers at level 7 can effectively give straightforward information, ask questions, give instructions, or make requests but are only partially successful when using reasons, examples, or explanations to support an opinion.

When attempting to explain an opinion, their writing presents relevant ideas and some support. Typical weaknesses at this level include:

- not enough specific support and development for the main points
- unclear connections between the points that are made
- grammatical errors or incorrect word choices

When giving straightforward information, asking questions, giving instructions, or making requests, their writing is clear, coherent, and effective.

Level 6 Scale score 110–130

Typically, test takers at level 6 are partially successful when giving straightforward information or supporting an opinion with reasons, examples, or explanations.

When giving straightforward information, asking questions, giving instructions, or making requests, the message omits important information or is partly unintelligible.

When attempting to explain an opinion, their writing presents relevant ideas and some support.

Typical weaknesses at this level include:

- not enough specific support and development for the main points
- unclear connections between the points that are made
- grammatical errors or incorrect word choices

Level 5 Scale score 90–100

Typically, test takers at level 5 are at least partially successful when giving straightforward information. However, when supporting an opinion with reasons, examples, or explanations, they are mostly unsuccessful.

When giving straightforward information, asking questions, giving instructions, or making requests, the message omits important information or is partly unintelligible.

When attempting to explain an opinion, significant weaknesses that interfere with communication occur, such as:

- not enough examples, explanations, or details to support the opinion or they are inappropriate
- inadequate organization or connection of ideas
- limited development of ideas
- serious grammatical errors or incorrect word choices

Level 4 Scale score 70–80

Typically, test takers at level 4 have some developing ability to express an opinion and to give straightforward information. However, communication is limited.

When attempting to explain an opinion, significant weaknesses that interfere with communication occur, such as:

- not enough examples, explanations, or details to support the opinion or they are inappropriate

- inadequate organization or connection of ideas
- limited development of ideas
- serious grammatical errors or incorrect word choices

When giving straightforward information, asking questions, giving instructions, or making requests, the responses do not successfully complete the task because of:
- missing information
- missing or obscure connections between sentences and / or
- many grammatical mistakes or incorrect word choices

At level 4, test takers have some ability to produce grammatically correct sentences, but they are inconsistent.

Level 3   Scale score   50–60
Typically, test takers at level 3 have limited ability to express an opinion and to give straightforward information.

When attempting to explain an opinion, the responses show one of the following serious flaws:

- serious disorganization or underdevelopment of ideas
- little or no detail or irrelevant specifics
- serious and frequent grammatical errors or incorrect word choices

When giving straightforward information, asking questions, giving instructions, or making requests, the responses do not successfully complete the task because of:
- missing information
- missing or obscure connections between sentences and/or
- many grammatical errors or incorrect word choices

At level 3, test takers have some ability to produce grammatically correct sentences, but they are inconsistent.

Level 2   Scale Score   40
Typically, test takers at level 2 have only very limited ability to express an opinion and give straightforward information.

When attempting to explain an opinion, the responses show one of the following serious flaws:

- serious disorganization or underdevelopment of ideas
- little or no detail or irrelevant specifics
- serious and frequent grammatical errors or incorrect word choices

At level 2, test takers cannot give straightforward information. Typical weaknesses at this level include:

- not including any of the important information
- missing or obscure connections between ideas
- frequent grammatical errors or incorrect word choices

At level 2, test takers are unable to produce grammatically correct sentences.

Level 1   Scale score   0–30
Test takers at level 1 left part or parts of the TOEIC Writing Test unanswered. Test takers at level 1 may need to improve their reading ability in order to understand the test directions and the content of test questions.

13

Writing Test Questions 1–3 | Write a sentence based on the picture

A Focus: Subjects/objects, verbs, modifiers, and prepositions

Important

In the test, Questions 1–5 appear together. In this book, Questions 1–3 and 4 & 5 are covered in separate units.

In the test

← Sample test pp139–145
Writing Test Questions 1–3

- In this part of the test, you will see a picture with two words or phrases under it.
- You must write one sentence using both words.
- You may change the form and order of the words if necessary.
- The sentence must relate to the picture and must be grammatically accurate.
- The types of words given in Writing Questions 1–3 may be a combination of a noun, verb, adjective, adverb, coordinating conjunction, or preposition.
- This unit will focus on making simple Subject-Verb-Object sentences.
- In Unit 17, we will focus on function words.

1 Language building: Identify the type of word and where to place it in a sentence

Test tip

Become familiar with basic SVO constructions

One of the most useful sentence patterns for the easy Questions 1–3 is Subject-Verb-Object. Practice making sentences with this pattern to help you write simple but correct sentences in this part of the test.

A Match the nouns to the items labeled in pictures 1 and 2.

dessert	desk	chef	telephone	man	hat	pen

Test tip

Think about the subject

The subject of the sentence may be people or things. Given nouns will always be singular, so you may have to change them to the plural form. Your sentence could also be about the location of certain objects in the picture, e.g. *There are two pens on the desk.*

B Match each verb with two nouns (using one as a subject and one as an object) from A. You may make the nouns plural, use them more than once, or use other nouns as necessary. The first one is done for you.

talk	sit	prepare	wear	hold

1. *man – talk – telephone* _____
2. _____
3. _____
4. _____
5. _____

Choose the verb tense carefully

Verbs will always appear in the base form. You must change them to fit the sentence. The present continuous tense can be the most appropriate tense if you are describing an action, e.g. … *is talking* … . The present simple tense is useful for talking about a state, something permanent, or something generally true.

Use modifiers appropriately

One of the words may be a modifier. These are adjectives and adverbs which give more information about the subject/object or verb. Understanding how to identify them, and their position in a sentence, will help you make well-formed sentences.

C Underline the correct tense in sentences 1–6.

1. The woman **wears** / **is wearing** a red shirt and blue jeans today.
2. He **has** / **is having** a bag in his hand.
3. The person on the left **watches** / **is watching** a TV program at the moment.
4. She **likes** / **is liking** meeting a friend.
5. Right now, the man **reads** / **is reading** the newspaper.
6. The plant **is** / **is being** on the table.

Follow up: The nouns and verbs in sentences 1–6 are all in singular form. In the test, the key words will be in singular form, but you may want to make them plural, depending on the details in the picture. Practice making sentences 1–6 plural and make sure you change the articles and verb forms as necessary. Take care with irregular plurals (e.g. "man" becomes "men").

D Write sentences based on the words you matched in B. Think carefully about the tense. You may make the nouns plural. The first one is done for you.

1. *The man is talking on the telephone.* _____
2. _____
3. _____
4. _____
5. _____

> **Grammar note**
>
> **Modifiers**
>
> Adjectives describe nouns. They can come before a noun, e.g. *an* **expensive** *car*, or after the verbs *be*, *look*, *seem*, *feel*, e.g. *I feel* **happy**.
>
> A few adverbs of manner (ones that can be shown clearly in the picture, e.g. *together*, *alone*) also appear in the test. These generally appear after the verb.

E Rewrite each sentence using the adjective / adverb given.

1. The man has a desk.   neat

   _____

2. The chefs are finishing the desserts. together

   _____

3. The man is in the room.   alone

   _____

4. The chefs are wearing uniforms.   white

   _____

Follow up: Write one more sentence about each picture using these words.

kitchen   work   relaxed   busy

F Complete the sentences about pictures 1 and 2 with the correct preposition.

at   in   on   in front of   next to

1. There are two pens _____ the desk.

2. The desserts are _____ the chefs.

3. The man is sitting _____ a desk.

4. He is holding a pen _____ his hand.

5. The chefs are _____ each other.

Follow up: Write two similar sentences about things you can see around you in the room. Take out the prepositions and see if your partner can put in the missing words.

2 Test tactic: Think about what words you need to complete the sentence

Grammar note

Sentences often have more than one object

In "*He is giving money to the man*", *He* is the subject, *giving* is the verb, and *money* is the direct object (person/thing the verb is directly affecting). *The man* is an indirect object.

A Read the words under each picture and identify how each of the words might be used in the sentence. Write each word next to the category you feel it fits best. The first one is done for you.

1.

2.

man / newsstand

subject   *man*

verb   _____

direct/indirect object   *newsstand*

modifier   _____

preposition   _____

wait / line

subject   _____

verb   _____

direct/indirect object   _____

modifier   _____

preposition   _____

Test tip

Work out what's missing

Once you have identified what your words refer to, you must add the parts you need to make a complete sentence (e.g. subject, verb, preposition).

3.

read / beside

subject   _____

verb   _____

direct/indirect object   _____

modifier   _____

preposition   _____

Test tip

Keep it simple, and check your work

Do not try to make very complex sentences unless you are very sure how to make them. Simple is best, e.g. for subjects, use *The man* …, *The people* …, or *The books* … .

B   Each sentence must have a subject and a verb and will often need an object to make sense. For each picture 1–3, think of appropriate words related to the picture to complete the sentence.

Follow up: Check with your partner that you agree on the missing parts, and compare the words you have chosen.

C   Use the words under the pictures and the missing words you added to make sentences. After you have written each one, check carefully that the words are in the correct form and position. Check for any other errors.

1. _____

2. _____

3. _____

Follow up: Exchange sentences with your partner and check each other's work. Can you spot any problems or suggest any changes?

B Tactic practice

For each picture, complete steps 1–4. After each step, compare answers with your partner.

1. Read the two words and decide what types of words you have been given (as in Test tactic A).
2. Decide what is necessary to make a good sentence and choose words to match the picture.
3. Write the two words you were given and your words into a single sentence that relates to the picture.
4. Check your sentence to make sure
   - you have written only one sentence
   - you have used both of the given words in your sentence (remember, you can change the form of the words)
   - you haven't made any obvious grammatical mistakes.

1.

hold / basket _____

2.

man / meet _____

3.

on / table _____

4.

woman / smell _____

5.

walk / in front of _____

C Mini-test

Now apply the Test tactics at the approximate test speed for Questions 1–3.

Questions 1–5: Write a sentence based on a picture

Questions 1–5: Write a sentence based on a picture

Directions: In this part of the test, you will write ONE sentence that is based on a picture. With each picture, you will be given TWO words or phrases that you must use in your sentence. You can change the form of the words and you can use the words in any order. Your sentences will be scored on

- the appropriate use of grammar and
- the relevance of the sentence to the picture.

In this part, you can move to the next question by clicking on **Next**. If you want to return to a previous question, click on **Back**. You will have 8 minutes to complete this part of the test.

Example

write / notebook

Sample response

The man is writing in a notebook.

Click on **Continue** to go on.

Question 1

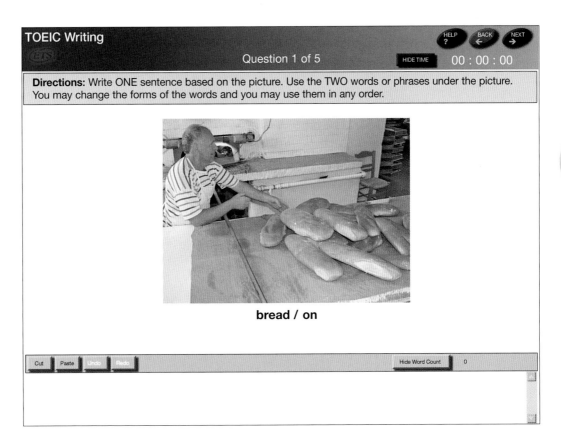

Directions: Write ONE sentence based on the picture. Use the TWO words or phrases under the picture. You may change the forms of the words and you may use them in any order.

bread / on

Cut   Paste   Undo   Redo   Hide Word Count   0

Question 2

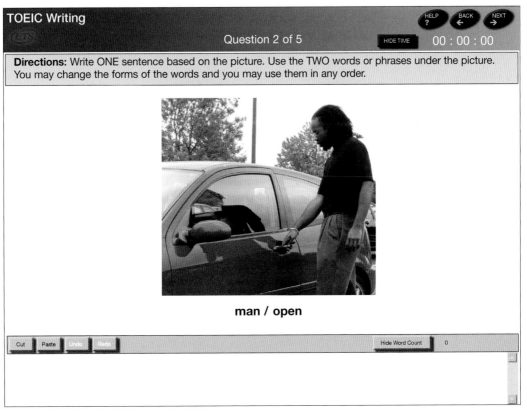

Directions: Write ONE sentence based on the picture. Use the TWO words or phrases under the picture. You may change the forms of the words and you may use them in any order.

man / open

Cut   Paste   Undo   Redo   Hide Word Count   0

unit
13

Question 3

unit
13

Directions: Write ONE sentence based on the picture. Use the TWO words or phrases under the picture. You may change the forms of the words and you may use them in any order.

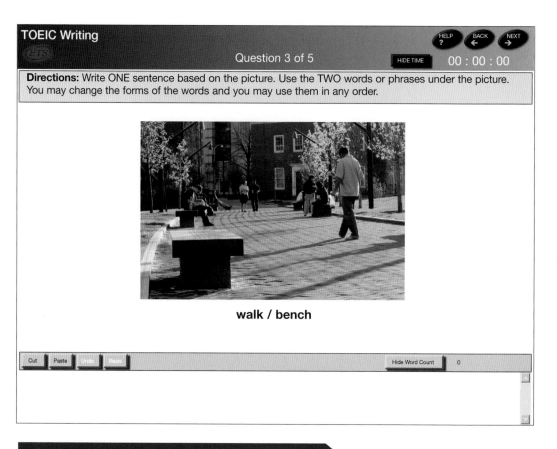

walk / bench

Cut · Paste · Undo · Redo · Hide Word Count · 0

If you want to do the follow-up unit to this test item now, please go to Unit 17, page 194.

A Focus: Writing sentences with subordinate clauses

In the test

← **Sample test pp139–145**
Writing Test Questions 4–5

- In this part of the test, you will see a picture with two words or phrases under it.
- You must write one sentence using both words.
- You may change the form and order of the words if necessary.
- The sentence must relate to the picture and must be grammatically accurate.
- One of the words given in Writing Questions 4–5 will be a noun, verb, adjective, adverb, or spatial preposition directly related to picture. The other word will be a subordinating conjunction (e.g. *because, so, while, before*).
- This unit will focus on subordinating conjunctions of time, location, and cause/effect.
- In Unit 18, we will focus on subordinating conjunctions of contrast and condition.

unit
14

1 Language building: Subordinate clauses of time / location and cause / effect

Time and location

Grammar note

Subordinate clauses and subordinating conjunctions

Some sentences have more than one idea joined together with a subordinating conjunction.

Example:
*We ate in the garden **because** it was a nice day*.

We ate in the garden is an independent clause, which means it could stand alone as a complete sentence. However, *because it was a nice day* cannot stand by itself, so it is what is called a subordinate clause. The subordinating conjunction *because* is used to show the relationship between the two ideas: in this case, to show the reason why *we ate in the garden*.

A Sentences 1–5 include a subordinate clause (underlined). Match the time / location conjunctions (in **bold**) with the description in a–e. The first one is done for you.

1. His cup is in a place **_where_** he can reach it easily.   _b_
2. They are probably going bowling **_after_** they finish work.   ___
3. The man is drinking coffee **_while_** he is driving.   ___
4. The people can't go into the theater **_until_** they open the doors.   ___
5. Paul always takes the train **_whenever_** he has to go into the city.   ___

The conjunction is used to describe

a. two actions happening at the same time.
b. the location.
c. an action that is true up to the noted time only.
d. an action that happens every time the main clause happens.
e. the order of two actions.

B Complete sentences 1–8 with the time conjunctions.

whenever   by the time   while   before

1. The man is having a snack _____ he is watching TV.
2. _____ it rains, people want to buy umbrellas.
3. The players are doing some stretches _____ they play football.
4. The train had already left _____ she got to the station.

when   after   since   until

5. _____ dinner, he usually has a cup of coffee.
6. She is waiting _____ the rain stops.
7. She was very happy _____ she saw her great test score.
8. _____ being promoted, he has had to travel a lot.

Follow up: Practice making similar sentences with your partner using the same conjunctions.

Cause and effect

C Sentences 1–5 combine a main clause and a subordinate clause (underlined). Match the cause/effect conjunctions (in **bold**) with the appropriate functions a–c.

1. ***Now that*** <u>the bus has arrived</u>, he can get aboard. _____
2. She is reading the book ***so that*** <u>she can learn about accounting</u>. _____
3. Please complete this form ***so*** <u>we may process your order</u>. _____
4. ***As*** <u>the library is closed</u>, the children won't be able to get any books. _____
5. He lost his job ***because*** <u>he was often late</u>. _____

The conjunction indicates
a. the purpose/goal of the main clause.
b. the completion of an action in the subordinate clause.
c. the reason why the subordinate clause is true.

D Match the sentence beginnings 1–5 to the endings a–e.

1. He can't reach the books … _____ a. **as** the printer is out of paper.
2. **Now that** spring has arrived, … _____ b. they have reduced prices.
3. He had to buy a car … _____ c. **because** the shelf is too high.
4. **So** they can attract more customers, … _____ d. most of the snow has melted.
5. She can't print her document … _____ e. **so that** he could get to work on time.

Follow up: With your partner, write new endings for the sentence beginnings 1–5 above.

unit
14

Subordinate clause order

Note that the order of the clauses can be switched without affecting the meaning.

Example:

*He took the bus to work **because** it was raining.*

***Because** it was raining, he took the bus to work.*

Both sentences have the same meaning. You will notice that if the subordinate clause (the one with the conjunction) comes first, it is followed by a comma.

E   Read each clause below. Then write another clause to complete the sentence using the words in parentheses.

1. The man is reading the newspaper (while / breakfast)

    _____ .

2. The woman has taken off her shoes (because / tight)

    _____ .

3. (when / eat) _____ , my tooth hurts.

4. (save / so that) _____ they can buy a new house.

5   He must cook the meat (before / eat) _____ .

6. The woman is studying hard (so / exam) _____ .

Test tip

Identify the meaning of the subordinating conjunction

As soon as you have identified the subordinating conjunction, think of how it is used in a sentence.

Test tip

Keep it simple

Even though Questions 4 & 5 require you to write two clauses linked by the conjunction given, keep the clauses simple.

2   Test tactic: Answering questions with a subordinating conjunction

a.   Look at picture 1 on page 174 and the pair of words given. <u>Underline</u> the conjunction, and think about its use.

b.   Look at the other word and the picture. Use the other word to write a short, simple sentence that describes the picture.
The presentation is in the main hall.

c.   Write another clause using the conjunction and join the clauses together to make a <u>single</u> sentence. You may have to change the words to make them fit grammatically in your sentence.
When there is a presentation, they use the main hall.

d.   Repeat stages a–c for pictures 2 and 3.

1.

when / presentation _____

2.

seatbelt / before _____

Test tip

Both words could be used in the same clause

The two words given do not have to be placed in separate clauses; they may both be used in the same clause, if appropriate.

Test tip

Don't forget the instructions!

You must write ONE sentence per picture that includes both key words and describes the picture.
You may change the form of the words or the order in which they appear.

3.

fix / so that _____

B Tactic practice

For each picture on page 175, complete steps 1–4. After each step, compare your answers with your partner.

1. Look at the subordinating conjunction and decide what type it is (e.g. time, location, cause/effect). This will tell you the type of information you will need for each clause.

2. Look at the word that is not a conjunction and think of how it relates to the picture. Then make a short, simple sentence with the word, related to the picture.

3. Now write another clause that matches the type of information suggested by the conjunction. Join the clauses into a SINGLE sentence with the conjunction at the start of the subordinate clause.

4. Check and correct any obvious mistakes and make sure you have used BOTH words.

1.

after / taxi _____

2.

award / because _____

3.

call / before _____

4.

read / while _____

5.

children / because _____

Test technique

☑ Use the conjunction to find the relationship between the two clauses.

☑ Relate the other word to the picture and think of a short sentence.

☑ Write another clause with the proper relationship, and join the two clauses with the conjunction.

☑ Check that you have written only ONE sentence that contains both words.

C Mini-test

Now apply the Test tactics at the approximate test speed for Questions 4–5.

Important
In the test, Questions 1–5 appear together. You have 8 minutes to complete the questions. In this book, Questions 1–3 and 4 & 5 are covered in separate units. You have 3–4 minutes to complete Questions 4–5.
The TOEIC directions are printed in this book as they appear in the actual test.

Questions 1–5: Write a sentence based on a picture

Questions 1–5: Write a sentence based on a picture

Directions: In this part of the test, you will write ONE sentence that is based on a picture. With each picture, you will be given TWO words or phrases that you must use in your sentence. You can change the form of the words and you can use the words in any order. Your sentences will be scored on

- the appropriate use of grammar and
- the relevance of the sentence to the picture.

In this part, you can move to the next question by clicking on **Next**. If you want to return to a previous question, click on **Back**. You will have 8 minutes to complete this part of the test.

Example	Sample response
	The man is writing in a notebook.

write / notebook

Click on **Continue** to go on.

Question 4

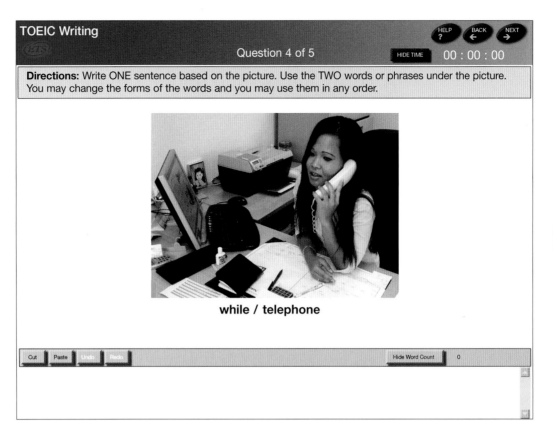

Question 5

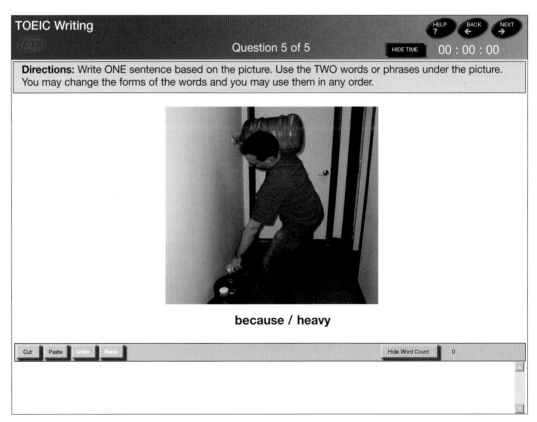

If you want to do the follow-up unit to this
test item now, please go to Unit 18, page 203.

A Focus: Requesting goods, services, and information

Test tip

See Writing Claims page 137

The directions for Questions 6–7 ask you to respond to an e-mail. For example, you may be asked to explain a problem, give information, or make a request on the basis of the information you read in an e-mail.

unit
15

Test tip

Use common request phrases

Making requests is a common task in Questions 6–7. Become familiar with the common words and phrases for making polite requests.

In the test

← Sample test pp146–151
Writing Test Questions 6–7

- In this part of the test, you will be given an e-mail to read and respond to.
- You must make sure that you have completed the THREE tasks specified in the directions at the end of the e-mail.
- You must use suitable language depending on who you are writing to.
- Your reply should be about 4–5 sentences long.
- Sometimes you will be playing the role of a different person.
- This unit will focus on making polite requests.
- In Unit 19, we will focus on giving explanations, descriptions, instructions, and opinions.

1 Language building: Making polite requests

A The sentence beginnings (in **bold**) in 1–6 show common phrases for making polite requests. Match the beginnings to the endings a–f. The first one is done for you.

1. **Please** send us …   _c_
2. **Could you tell me** where …   ____
3. **Would it be possible** to have a …   ____
4. **I was wondering if it would be possible** to … ____
5. **I would appreciate it if you could** have …   ____
6. **Would you mind** …   ____

a. repair person come to fix the air conditioner?
b. get some samples of your product.
c. three boxes of white letterhead paper.
d. your delivery staff use the back entrance.
e. postponing our meeting until the end of May?
f. I could have my car repainted?

B Write the number of each completed sentence (1–6) from A next to the matching description and recipient (a–f) below.

____ a. A request for a recommendation of an automobile service (to the representative of an auto association).

____ b. A request to change a scheduled appointment (to a coworker from another department).

____ c. An order for office supplies (to a stationery store).

____ d. A request for repairs (to the superintendent of your apartment building).

____ e. A request for examples of a company's products (to a manufacturing company).

____ f. A request about how a delivery should be made (to a supplier's shipping department).

Test tip

Identify the tasks

There will always be **three** things you are asked to include in your response. Write these in three separate sentences.

C Use phrases 1–6 in A to complete requests 1–3. Change the period to a question mark if appropriate.

1. Make ONE request for information about a course you are interested in taking (to a community college).

   _____ information on schedules and costs for your certificate course on network management.

2. Order ONE product from a catalog (to a garden supply company).

   _____ one 25 kg bag of garden fertilizer.

3. Make ONE request for details on the advertised job (to a company hiring new employees).

   _____ the training opportunities offered by your company?

2 Test tactic: Identify what you have to write

Test tip

Understand the role you are playing

In the e-mail task, who you are and the person to whom you are writing have an impact on what you write. Before you start writing a response, be sure to understand these roles.

A Read the directions and e-mail. In the test you will have to write a reply. In this task, be sure to follow the directions. Say who you are writing to and reply as you are instructed to do: either as yourself or as another person.

Directions: Read the e-mail.

FROM: H. Thomson, Manager, Teflo Wire Company

TO: All sales reps

SUBJECT: New computers

SENT: March 26, 9:31 A.M.

We will soon be replacing computers for all sales staff. As we would like you to be available when we replace your computer, could you tell us a time convenient for you? Also please let us know if you need any other equipment.

Respond to the e-mail as if you are a sales representative for Teflo Wire Company. In your e-mail, give ONE time you are free and make TWO requests for new equipment.

Test tip

Use salutations

In the test, you may not know if the e-mail was sent by a man or a woman. In this case, you may open your response with either, e.g. *Dear Ms.* or *Dear Mr. Thompson.* Your score will not be affected by your choice.

I am: _____

I am writing to: _____

B In the test, you will always be asked to include three points in your reply. Write the points you have to include in reply to the e-mail on page 179. The first one is done for you.

1. *give convenient time*   _____

2 and 3.   _____

Test tip

Brainstorm ideas, then make sentences

Use your imagination to brainstorm short answers. Then write your ideas into sentences.

C Review the points noted in 2B and brainstorm short answers for each. Add explanations or reasons if possible. The first one is done for you.

1. *Thursday, April 6 (morning) – at a meeting (afternoon)*

2. _____

3. _____

D Write your answers in sentences that clearly respond to the points in the question or e-mail. Remember to use the phrases in 1A on page 178. Use a different phrase for each sentence.

1. *I am available on Thursday, April 6, in the morning only. I will be at a meeting in the afternoon.*

2. _____

3. _____

Test tip

Note the opening and closing sentences

In the test you should write an opening and closing sentence. Look at the Sample test on pages 147–150 for examples of this.

E Complete the e-mail with the two requests you planned in C and D.

Thank you for your e-mail regarding the replacement of my computer. The earliest I will be available in the office is on Thursday, April 6, in the morning only.

_____

_____

_____

_____

_____

_____

Please confirm this equipment will be installed on April 6.

unit
15

B Tactic practice

Test tip

You will not always be writing as yourself

For Questions 6–7, in one question you will respond as yourself, and in the other you will respond as if you are another person.

For each e-mail 1 and 2, read the directions and the e-mail. Then complete steps 1–4. After each step, compare answers with your partner.

1. Identify the three tasks.
2. Note who you are responding to and who you are responding as.
3. Brainstorm brief answers and explanations for each task.
4. Write your answers in sentences that clearly respond to the question or e-mail.

Test technique

- ☑ Read the e-mail and directions and identify the three tasks.
- ☑ Note whom you are writing to and who you are writing as.
- ☑ Brainstorm answers to the three tasks. Then write your ideas as sentences.
- ☑ Add an opening and closing sentence.
- ☑ Check your writing for errors.

1.

> **Directions:** Read the e-mail.
>
> **FROM:**   M. Eaton, Spring Valley Travel
> **TO:**   J. Moore – European Adventure Tours
> **SUBJECT:** Opening for overseas tour guide
> **SENT:**   August 26, 2:54 P.M.
>
> Thank you for your interest in the position of tour guide.
>
> I am attaching an application form for the position. Please let me know if you have any questions about the application or the job itself.
>
> **Directions:** Respond to the e-mail as if you are J. Moore. In your e-mail, ask TWO questions and make ONE request.
>
> Dear M. Eaton,
>
> Thank you for your e-mail and the application form for the position.
>
> _____
> _____
> _____
> _____
> _____
>
> I look forward to hearing from you again.
>
> Sincerely yours,
> J. Moore

Test tip

Use salutations

Use an appropriate opening and closing salutation (*Dear ...*, *Sincerely yours*, etc.) in your response. See page 262 for further information about salutations.

2.

Test tip

Manage your timing carefully

In the test you will have 10 minutes to answer each e-mail. Spend no more than six minutes brainstorming and writing answers for the three tasks.

unit
15

Directions: Read the e-mail.

FROM: memberships@healthsports.com

TO: Dean Towers Tenant

SUBJECT: Special membership deal

SENT: June 11, 12:04 P.M.

Dean Towers Healthsports is pleased to announce special discounts for employees of companies in the Dean Towers complex. Apply within the next month and you can get a full 30% discount off your first year's membership at our fully-equipped and expertly-staffed facility.

Directions: Respond to the e-mail as if you are interested in joining the health club. In your e-mail, ask THREE questions.

Dear Sir or Madam,

I am interested in finding out more about your special offer for employees of companies in the Dean Towers complex.

_____

_____

_____

_____

_____

_____

I look forward to hearing from you soon.

Yours truly.

Test tip

Leave time to finish and check your answer

Allow roughly two minutes for each of the three tasks. You will need the rest of the time to organize and edit your response.

C Mini-test

Now apply the Test tactics at the actual test speed for Questions 6–7.

Important

In the test, it is a good strategy to write an opening and closing sentence in your response. Opening and closing sentences can improve the organizational logic of your answer. Look at the Sample test on pages 147–150 and the e-mails on pages 180–182 for examples of this.

Questions 6–7: Respond to a written request

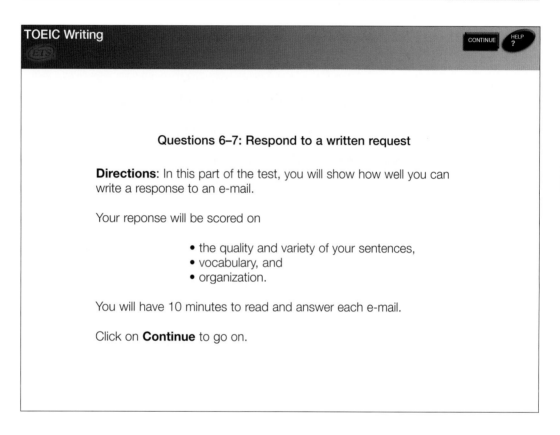

TOEIC Writing   CONTINUE   HELP ?

Questions 6–7: Respond to a written request

Directions: In this part of the test, you will show how well you can write a response to an e-mail.

Your reponse will be scored on

- the quality and variety of your sentences,
- vocabulary, and
- organization.

You will have 10 minutes to read and answer each e-mail.

Click on **Continue** to go on.

Question 6

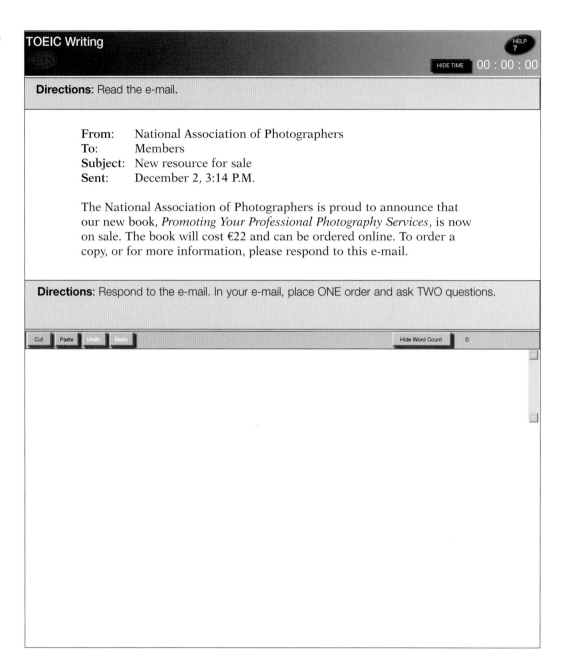

HELP ?

HIDE TIME   00 : 00 : 00

Directions: Read the e-mail.

From: National Association of Photographers
To: Members
Subject: New resource for sale
Sent: December 2, 3:14 P.M.

The National Association of Photographers is proud to announce that
our new book, *Promoting Your Professional Photography Services*, is now
on sale. The book will cost €22 and can be ordered online. To order a
copy, or for more information, please respond to this e-mail.

Directions: Respond to the e-mail. In your e-mail, place ONE order and ask TWO questions.

Cut   Paste   Undo   Redo   Hide Word Count   0

unit
15

Question 7

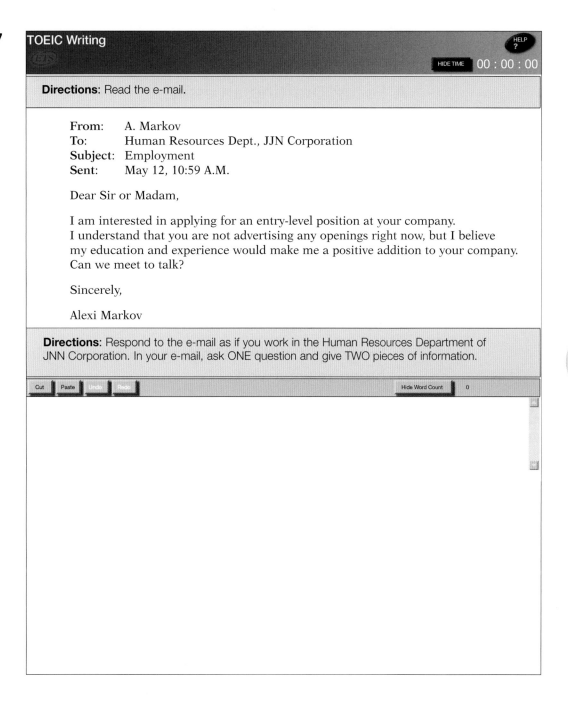

TOEIC Writing

HELP ?

HIDE TIME 00 : 00 : 00

Directions: Read the e-mail.

From: A. Markov
To: Human Resources Dept., JJN Corporation
Subject: Employment
Sent: May 12, 10:59 A.M.

Dear Sir or Madam,

I am interested in applying for an entry-level position at your company.
I understand that you are not advertising any openings right now, but I believe
my education and experience would make me a positive addition to your company.
Can we meet to talk?

Sincerely,

Alexi Markov

Directions: Respond to the e-mail as if you work in the Human Resources Department of JNN Corporation. In your e-mail, ask ONE question and give TWO pieces of information.

Cut   Paste   Undo   Redo   Hide Word Count   0

unit
15

If you want to do the follow-up unit to this test item now, please go to Unit 19, page 209.

A Focus: Drafting an essay

> ### In the test
>
> ← **Sample test pp152–157**
> **Writing Test Question 8**
>
> - In this part of the test, you will be asked to write an essay stating your opinion in response to a given topic.
> - You will have 30 minutes to plan, write, and revise your essay.
> - You will be able to make notes on screen and delete them when you have finished.
> - Your main goal is to answer the question fully, giving reasons for your opinion.
> - Your reply should be 3–5 paragraphs, forming an organized response.
> - This unit will focus on how to express your opinions and organize your essay.
> - In Unit 20, you will learn how to link your ideas and expand on the reasons and examples you have given.

1 Language building: Language to express opinions and organize your work

Test tip

Use language that makes your opinions clear

Using a range of expressions can make it instantly clear whether you have strong opinions about the topic or have mixed feelings. Become familiar with a range of phrases to show your opinions.

unit
16

A   Match opinion expressions 1–8 to descriptions a–c.

Expressing opinions

1. I (strongly / firmly) believe   _____

2. In my opinion   _____

3. I'm totally opposed to   _____

4. It's a difficult choice, but I think I would prefer to   _____

5. I'm completely in favor of   _____

6. If I had to choose, I would pick / say   _____

7. I really don't agree with   _____

8. I would prefer to   _____

a. Positive opinion (strong)
b. Positive position (neutral or weak)
c. Negative opinion (strong)

B   Answer questions 1–3 giving your opinion in ONE sentence. Use the phrases in A to help you. Compare ideas with your partner.

1. Would you rather work in a quiet town or a big city?

   _____

2. Which is the best way to travel to another country, by air or over land?

   _____

3. Do you agree or disagree that health care should be free for the whole population?

   _____

C   Read questions 1–3, then complete the opening sentences using the answers given in parentheses. Use the opinion expressions in A.

1.   Shopping on the Internet is bad for local businesses. People should make more effort to do their shopping locally. **Do you agree or disagree? (disagree – like the Internet for some shopping)**

Many people believe that shopping online is destroying local businesses. However, _____ .

2.   When traveling medium distances, some people prefer to fly. Others prefer to take express trains. **Which do you prefer? (trains)**

Although some people prefer to fly because it is faster,

_____ .

3.   **What do you like most** about your current job? **(long vacations)**

There are several things I like about my current job, but

_____ .

D   Read the question and the essay on page 188. Label paragraphs A–E with the following headings.

Second reason   Conclusion   Introduction   Third reason   First reason

E   Read the essay again and choose the correct phrase from the chart below to complete gaps 1–9. More than one phrase may be suitable.

Phrases for organizing ideas	
First ideas first of all the first (dis)advantage	**Adding to reasons** moreover also what's more
Second ideas another (dis)advantage another point in addition	**To introduce contrasts** on the other hand (at the start of a sentence only) although whereas however
Final ideas a final (dis)advantage a final point	**To conclude** in conclusion

Would you prefer to work longer hours on a daily basis and, as a result, have more vacation time? Give your opinion and explain why.

A
_____

There are a number of advantages and disadvantages to working longer hours and having more days off in compensation. In my opinion, the advantages outweigh the disadvantages.

B
_____

(1) _____, I believe having an extra day of leisure time would make people more relaxed. This would obviously be beneficial to people's general health. (2) _____ being more relaxed would also benefit employers, as their workers would probably concentrate better during their work time and have fewer days off sick.

C
_____

(3) _____ advantage is that if more people had an extra day off during the week, shopping malls and supermarkets would be less crowded on weekends. (4) _____ people would be able to use sports facilities and leisure services at off-peak times.

D
_____

(5) _____ , at least for me, is that two extra hours added on to the day wouldn't seem like a huge addition, (6) _____ a whole day off is an added bonus. (7) _____ , I can understand that the longer day may not be suitable for people with families or for people who have a long commute to work.

E
_____

(8) _____ , (9) _____ working hours may not suit everyone, for me the benefits far outweigh the drawbacks and I would definitely favor this system.

unit
16

F   Add the extra words and phrases 1–6 to the correct place in the chart in E.

1. but	4. all in all
2. finally	5. secondly
3. most importantly	6. too

Follow up: With your partner make more sentences using the contrast words, e.g. *I love living in the city. However, it is rather noisy.*

2 Test tactic: Creating a draft

Test tip

Plan your essay before you start to write

The first and most important stage in writing an essay is to draft a simple outline that clearly answers the question and includes all the main ideas.

A Read Opinion question 1 below and <u>underline</u> the key words. Then summarize the test question. Compare summaries with your partner. See Key page 41 and check your answer.

Opinion question 1

Recently in your town, construction of a new factory that would employ thousands of workers has been halted because it would endanger the wild animals living in the area. Do you agree or disagree with this decision? Give reasons or examples to support your opinion.

B Answer the question you wrote in A with a complete sentence. Use the phrases from Language building A, page 186. This is your thesis statement (statement of your opinion), which you should include in the introduction of your essay.

Test tip

Focus clearly on the task

Begin by picking out the key words. Then summarize the question and make a clear thesis (statement of your opinion).

Example
I strongly agree that they should stop the construction of the new factory.

C Read Opinion question 2 below and complete the same tasks, listed 1–4.

Opinion question 2

Do you agree or disagree with the following statement? *The most important factor you should consider when choosing a job is the salary.* Give reasons or examples to support your opinion.

1. Read the question and <u>underline</u> the key words.

2. Make a sentence that summarizes the question and the task.

3. Write a suitable thesis.

4. Compare answers with a partner.

Test technique

Make a draft outline

☑ Think of three reasons to support your thesis.

☑ If you have time you may want to think of some opposing points, as this will show that you have considered both sides of the question.

☑ Do not worry about grammar or ordering your ideas at this point.

Test technique

Organize your reasons for agreeing / disagreeing and add examples

☑ Read your supporting points again and make any changes or cuts you feel necessary.

☑ Then put your ideas into a suitable order, and add reasons / examples and connecting words.

☑ When writing notes, don't worry about making full sentences. Just make sure you have all the necessary information and it is in the correct order.

D Read notes 1–6 giving reasons agreeing and disagreeing with the decision in Opinion question 1 in A. Which ideas do you agree with?

Reasons for agreeing
1. It is wrong to endanger animals just to make money.
2. The factory could be built in another place.
3. It is important not to build in rural areas if possible.

Reasons for disagreeing
4. The factory will be good for the economy.
5. Many jobs might be lost.
6. Land is there to be used in whatever way necessary.

E Brainstorm three reasons either agreeing or disagreeing based on your thesis for Opinion question 2 in C.

F Read the outline below for agreeing with the decision in Opinion question 1. Look carefully at how the notes from D have been developed.

I strongly agree that they should stop construction of the new factory.

First of all,
Although the factory will be good for the economy,
it is wrong to endanger the animals just because of this.
I don't want to kill something to get money.

Next
It's true that many possible jobs might be lost.
However,
The factory could be built in another place.
There is free space on the west side of town that is almost as good.

Finally,
It's important not to build in rural areas if possible.
Although cities may be crowded and people don't want to live too close to a factory, there are usually old, unused places in cities where the factory could be located.

G Write an outline similar to the one in F, based on your thesis and reasons for Opinion question 2 in C and E.

Follow up: Explain your outline to your partner and compare your reasons.

B Tactic practice

For Opinion question 3, draft an outline by completing steps 1–4. After each step, compare answers with your partner.

1. Analyze the question and pick out the key points. Rephrase these points into a single sentence.
2. Write a thesis statement that answers the question.
3. Brainstorm reasons supporting your opinion.
4. Drop any weak points, and organize the rest into the order you think is best. Add as many reasons/examples as you can and add appropriate connecting words.

Opinion question 3

Some people enjoy jobs that include traveling a lot and meeting new people. Others like to work in a fixed location with the same group of coworkers. What is your preference? Explain why.

C Mini-test

Now apply the Test tactics at the actual test speed for Question 8.

Question 8:
Write an opinion
essay

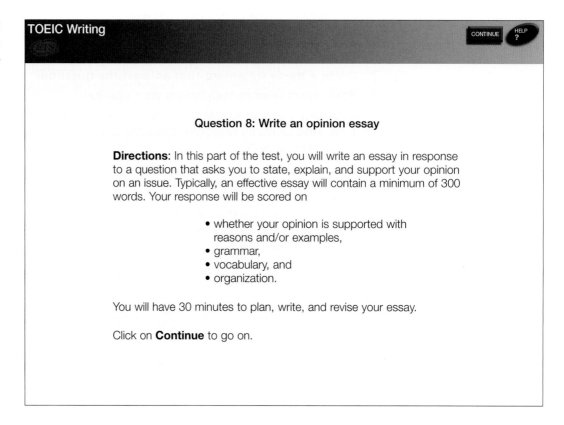

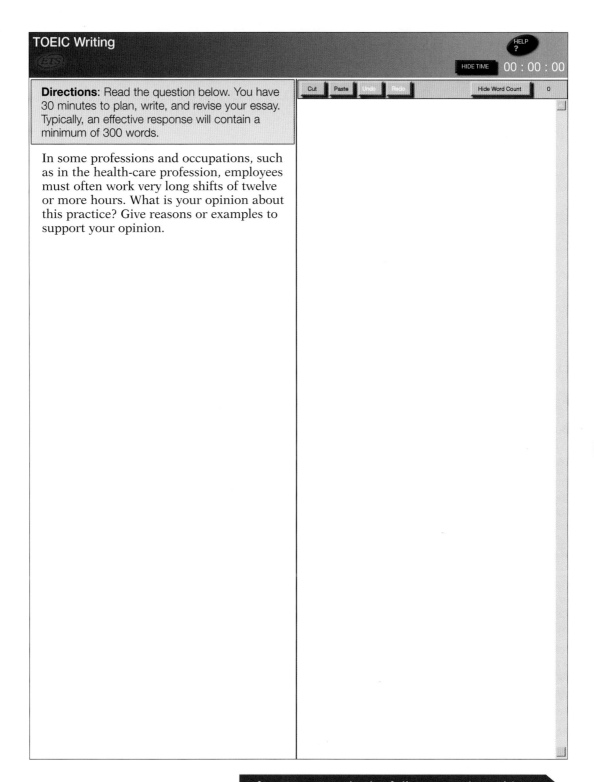

TOEIC Writing

Directions: Read the question below. You have 30 minutes to plan, write, and revise your essay. Typically, an effective response will contain a minimum of 300 words.

In some professions and occupations, such as in the health-care profession, employees must often work very long shifts of twelve or more hours. What is your opinion about this practice? Give reasons or examples to support your opinion.

HIDE TIME 00 : 00 : 00

Cut Paste Undo Redo   Hide Word Count 0

If you want to do the follow-up unit to this test item now, please go to Unit 20, page 217.

unit
17

A Focus: Using function words correctly

In the test

← **Sample test pp139–145**
← **Unit 13 p162**
Writing Test Questions 1–3

- In this part of the test, you will see a picture with two words or phrases under it.
- In Unit 13, we focused on the basic sentence structure of Subject/Verb/Object and looked at subjects / objects, verbs, modifiers, and prepositions.
- The types of words given in Writing Questions 1–3 may also include a function word (e.g. conjunction, non-spatial preposition, or intensifier).
- This unit will focus on function words.

1 Language building: Conjunctions, prepositions, and intensifiers

Conjunctions

Test tip

Become familiar with coordinating conjunctions

One of the words given may be a conjunction, so you will have to make a sentence with two ideas joined together. Become familiar with the use of **and**, **but**, **or** in order to join ideas of roughly equal importance.

A Sentences 1–4 show the use of conjunctions (in **bold**). Match them to their meanings a–d. Note the word **or** is used twice.

1. The woman is riding a bicycle **and** carrying a large bag. _____
2. He is trying to lift the box, **but** it is too heavy. _____
3. He can choose the red pen **or** the blue one. _____
4. They must take a cab, **or** they will miss their plane. _____

a. result – used to show the possible consequences if the people do (not) do the thing suggested in the first clause
b. alternative – used to link alternative things or ideas
c. addition – used to join two situations or things
d. contrast – used to give contrasting information

Test tip

Write only one sentence

Remember you must write only ONE sentence using both the words given.

B Match sentence beginnings 1–6 to the endings a–f. Then write in the conjunction that best joins them together.

1. He wants to see the show … _____ _____
2. The people are playing baseball … _____ _____
3. He must put on sunscreen … _____ _____
4. The woman is deciding whether to have chicken … _____ _____
5. He is wearing a raincoat … _____ _____
6. The people are waiting for a bus … _____ _____

a. it hasn't arrived yet.
b. he will get a bad sunburn.
c. flying kites in the park.
d. he doesn't have enough money.
e. fish for dinner.
f. carrying an umbrella.

C Complete sentences 1–3 using your own words.

1. My favorite foods are _____ and _____ .
2. I would like to buy a new car, but _____ .
3. I should study, or _____ .

Follow up: Compare answers with your partner.

Prepositions

unit 17

Test tip

Learn how to use a variety of prepositions

Not all prepositions are used for location. Become familiar with the meanings of prepositions for a variety of purposes.

D Read sentences 1–6. Write the correct preposition (in **bold**) next to the definitions a–f, that best match the way they are used in these sentences.

1. The man is traveling **by** bus.
2. We import lots of sugar **from** Thailand.
3. I've bought this present **for** my mother.
4. They said they would call back **during** the week.
5. This book is **about** a family who traveled to China.
6. She's having a meeting **with** him tomorrow.

a. _____ is used to say when something happens at some point within a period of time.

b. _____ means "related to" or "on the subject of".

c. _____ is used to show how or in what way something is done; e.g. how you travel.

d. _____ is used to indicate the origin of someone / something.

e. _____ means "together" or "in the company of someone".

f. _____ is used to show who is intended to use or have something.

E Use the prepositions in D to complete sentences 1–6.

1. The woman shares an apartment _____ her friend.
2. This book is _____ a girl growing up in China.
3. The man is sleeping _____ the movie.
4. He goes to work _____ bus.
5. Water is coming _____ the hole in the wall.
6. The girl has brought an apple _____ her teacher.

F Write six sentences using the words given below.

1. come here / by _____
2. I / from _____
3. present / for _____
4. go / during _____
5. book / about _____
6. go / with _____

Intensifiers

Test tip

Learn to use intensifiers appropriately

Intensifiers are used in front of adverbs and adjectives to give the idea of "degree" – to say "how much". Understanding the effect intensifiers have on the words around them and their position in a sentence will help you make well-formed sentences.

unit
17

G Read the information about intensifiers. Then choose the correct word in sentences 1–5.

Usually used in affirmative sentences:

a lot of + countable nouns   *She's carrying **a lot of** books.*

a lot of + uncountable nouns   *There's **a lot of** traffic today.*

Usually used in negatives and questions:

much + uncountable nouns   *I haven't got **much** free time today.*

many + countable nouns   *Were there **many** people at class today?*

very + adjective   *They look **very** happy.*

very + adverb   *He's working **very** hard.*

so + adjective   *That cake looks **so** delicious, I'd like to try some.*

so + adverb   *I've been working **so** hard, I'm feeling very tired.*

almost + noun   *It must be **almost** lunchtime, I feel hungry.*

almost + adjective   *Are you **almost** ready?*

almost + verb   *I've **almost** finished my homework.*

1. She looks **a lot of** / **very** happy today.
2. Have you got **many** / **much** CDs at home?
3. They've **almost** / **so** reached their destination.
4. The trees look **much** / **so** beautiful in the fall.
5. There are **much** / **a lot of** people downtown today.

H Write one sentence about each picture 1–4 using the words given.

1.

almost / cookies _____

2.

a lot of / road _____

3.

so / light _____

4.

food / very _____

Follow up: Compare answers with your partner.

2 Test tactic: Find where the function words fit in the picture and make sentences

Look at picture 1 on the next page, read steps 1–4 to make a sentence for picture 1. Then follow the steps again to write one sentence each for picture 2–6.

1. Look at the picture and the two words given. Identify the function word (intensifier, conjunction, or preposition), its meaning, and how it relates to the picture.
   Example (for picture 1): *almost* means "not quite": *almost full*.

2. Next, look at the other word and think of how it relates to the picture.

3. Then, write a short, simple sentence, using both words to describe what you see.

4. Check you have used both words in one sentence and that you have no grammatical errors. Then compare sentences with your partner.

Test tip	Test tip
Find where the function words fit in the picture	**Find where prepositions fit in the picture**
You will need to make ONE sentence that includes the two key words. Decide what the function word relates to and make a sentence that is relevant to the picture.	Prepositions often come before an object. You can choose a possible object (either the other word or something in the picture) and use your knowledge of the meaning of the preposition to make a sentence.

1.

glass / almost _____

2.

box / very _____

3.

through / airport _____

4.

drink / or _____

5.

travel / by _____

6.

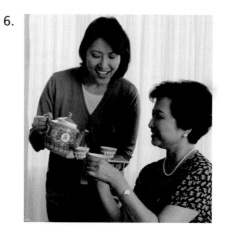

tea / for _____

Test tip

Remember! You may change the verb and noun forms. Use an appropriate tense and change nouns to plural according to the picture.

B Tactic practice

Use the Test tactics you have practiced to write a sentence for pictures 1–4. Begin by looking at the picture and the two words, then follow the steps in the Test technique. After each step, compare your answer with your partner's answer.

1.

friend / together _____

2.

read / with _____

3.

flower / and _____

4.

shout / for _____

Test technique

☑ Pick out the function word and note its type and meaning.

☑ Think of how the other word relates to the picture.

☑ Write a sentence that uses both the given words and clearly relates to the picture.

☑ Check that you have written one sentence with both words and correct any errors you see.

Test tip

Pace yourself

You have a total of eight minutes for this section. That gives you about 90 seconds for each of the five questions. Try to complete each stage within 10–20 seconds. This will leave you some time at the end for a final check.

C Mini-test

Now apply the Test tactics at the approximate test speed for Questions 1–3.

Important

In the test, Questions 1–5 appear together. You have 8 minutes to complete the questions. In this book, Questions 1–3 and 4 & 5 are covered in separate units. You have 3–4 minutes to complete Questions 1–3.

The TOEIC directions are printed in the book as if you were doing the test.

Questions 1–5: Write a sentence based on a picture

Questions 1–5: Write a sentence based on a picture

Directions: In this part of the test, you will write ONE sentence that is based on a picture. With each picture, you will be given TWO words or phrases that you must use in your sentence. You can change the form of the words and you can use the words in any order. Your sentences will be scored on

- the appropriate use of grammar and
- the relevance of the sentence to the picture.

In this part, you can move to the next question by clicking on **Next**. If you want to return to a previous question, click on **Back**. You will have 8 minutes to complete this part of the test.

Example	Sample response
	The man is writing in a notebook.
write / notebook	

Click on **Continue** to go on.

Question 1

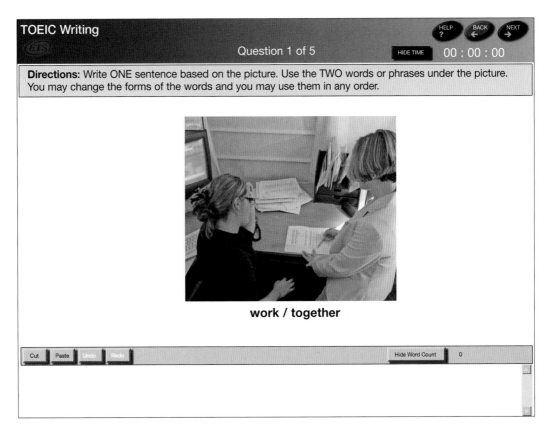

TOEIC Writing

Directions: Write ONE sentence based on the picture. Use the TWO words or phrases under the picture. You may change the forms of the words and you may use them in any order.

work / together

Question 2

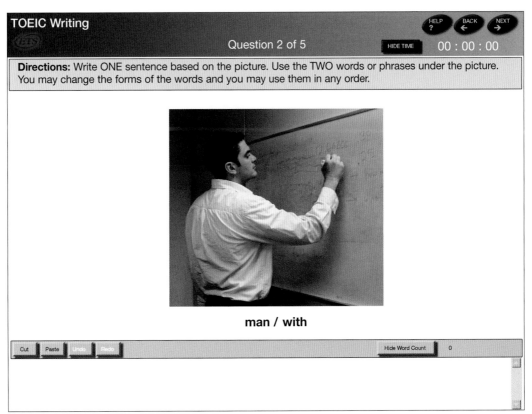

TOEIC Writing

Directions: Write ONE sentence based on the picture. Use the TWO words or phrases under the picture. You may change the forms of the words and you may use them in any order.

man / with

Question 3

Directions: Write ONE sentence based on the picture. Use the TWO words or phrases under the picture. You may change the forms of the words and you may use them in any order.

vegetable / very

Cut | Paste | Undo | Redo   Hide Word Count | 0

A Focus: Writing sentences with subordinate clauses

Important

In the test, Questions 1–5 appear together. In this book, Questions 1–3 and 4–5 are covered in separate units.

In the test

← **Sample test pp 139–145**
← **Unit 14 p171**
Writing Test Questions 4–5

- In this part of the test, you will see a picture with two words or phrases under it.
- One of the words given in Writing Questions 4–5 will be a noun, verb, adjective, adverb, or preposition directly related to the picture. The other word will be a subordinating conjunction (e.g. *because*, *so that*, *while*, *before*).
- In Unit 14, we focused on subordinating conjunctions of time / location and cause / effect.
- This unit will focus on making sentences using subordinating conjunctions of contrast (*in spite of*, *whereas*), similarity, and condition (e.g. *unless*, *only if*).

1 Language building: Subordinate clauses of contrast and condition

Contrast

Test tip

Learn ways of describing contrast

Sometimes, one of the words you are given will indicate a possible contrast of ideas. In this case, you will have to make a sentence describing this contrast.

A The subordinating conjunctions in **bold** in the sentences below are used to indicate contrasting ideas. Match sentence beginnings 1–5 with the endings a–e.

1. **Although** he is standing on a ladder, … _____
2. The people seem to be enjoying themselves, … _____
3. **Even though** it was raining heavily, … _____
4. The woman is dressed very formally, … _____
5. **In spite of** the fact that they lost the last game, … _____

a. they still went for a walk.
b. he still can't reach the book.
c. **though** the weather is terrible.
d. they still won the competition.
e. **whereas** the man's clothes are more casual.

B Complete sentences 1–5 using your own words.

1. Even though the computer is very small, _____

   _____

2. Although he has been driving a car for many years, _____

   _____

3. In spite of the fact that the team played well, _____

4. My friend has no interest in learning another language, whereas I

   _____

5. He looks a little unfriendly, though he is actually

   _____

Condition

C The subordinating conjunctions in **bold** are used to express a condition. Match sentence beginnings 1–5 with the most appropriate endings in a–e.

1. **If** you go out, … _____
2. They can't go in … _____
3. **As long as** you study hard, … _____
4. **Even if** it jumps high, … _____
5. The man can go on the boat … _____

a. the dog can't reach the bone.
b. I'm sure you'll pass the test.
c. could you lock the door?
d. **only if** he wears a lifejacket.
e. **unless** they buy tickets.

D Write sentences using the words under the pictures.

1.

although / work _____

2.

even though / bag _____

3.

unless / choose _____

4.

buy / if _____

Follow up: Compare answers with your partner.

2 Test tactic: Answering questions with a subordinating conjunction

unit

Test tip

Remember!

You must write ONE sentence that includes both key words. You may change the form of the words or the order they appear in.

Test tip

Remember!

You can use both words in the same clause. You may use words as any part of speech (e.g. *practice* can be a noun or a verb) or make them plural.

Look at picture 1 and read steps 1–4, then follow the same steps to write a sentence for pictures 2–4.

1. Look at the picture and the two words given. Identify the subordinating conjunction, its meaning (contrast or condition), and what effect it has on the other clause.
   Example: For picture 1, *unless* has a conditional meaning.

2. Next, look at the other word and think of how it relates to the picture. Then, think of a short, simple sentence, using the word, to describe what you see.
   Example: For picture 1, *The man is fixing the wires.*

3. Finally, think about how the subordinating conjunction relates to the picture and the sentence you made in step 2, and use this to make a single new sentence. You may have to change the words to make them fit grammatically in your sentence.
   Example: For picture 1, *Unless he fixes the wires, there will be no electricity.*

4. Check that you have used both words in one sentence and that you have no grammatical errors.

1.

unless / fix _____

2.

if / practice _____

3.

fast / even though _____

4.

although / meeting _____

B Tactic practice

- ☑ Use the conjunction to find the relationship between the clauses.

- ☑ Relate the other word to the picture and think of a short sentence.

- ☑ Write another clause with the proper relationship to the first clause, and join the two clauses with the conjunction.

- ☑ Check that you have one sentence with both words, and correct any errors you see.

unit
18

Use the Test tactics you have practiced to write a sentence for pictures 1–3. Begin by looking at the picture and the two words, then follow the steps in the Test technique. After each step, compare answers with your partner.

1.

whereas / modern

2.

student / if

3.

although / open

C Mini-test

Now apply the Test tactics at the approximate test speed for Questions 4 & 5.

Important

In the test, Questions 1–5 appear together. You have 8 minutes to complete the questions. In this book, Questions 1–3 and 4–5 are covered in separate units. You have 3–4 minutes to complete Questions 4–5.

The TOEIC directions are printed in the book as if you were doing the test.

Questions 1–5: Write a sentence based on a picture

TOEIC Writing

CONTINUE   HELP ?   BACK ←   NEXT →

HIDE TIME   00 : 00 : 00

Questions 1–5: Write a sentence based on a picture

Directions: In this part of the test, you will write ONE sentence that is based on a picture. With each picture, you will be given TWO words or phrases that you must use in your sentence. You can change the form of the words and you can use the words in any order. Your sentences will be scored on

- the appropriate use of grammar and
- the relevance of the sentence to the picture.

In this part, you can move to the next question by clicking on **Next**. If you want to return to a previous question, click on **Back**. You will have 8 minutes to complete this part of the test.

Example	Sample response
	The man is writing in a notebook.

write / notebook

Click on **Continue** to go on.

Question 4

Directions: Write ONE sentence based on the picture. Use the TWO words or phrases under the picture. You may change the forms of the words and you may use them in any order.

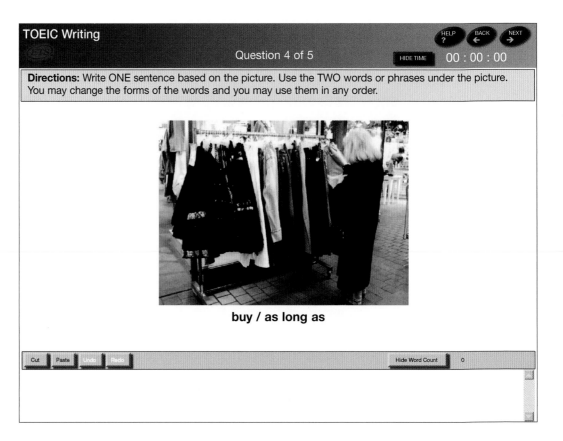

buy / as long as

Cut Paste Undo Redo   Hide Word Count 0

Question 5

Directions: Write ONE sentence based on the picture. Use the TWO words or phrases under the picture. You may change the forms of the words and you may use them in any order.

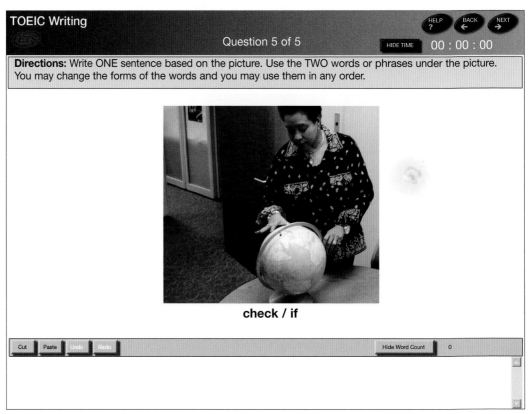

check / if

Cut Paste Undo Redo   Hide Word Count 0

unit
18

A Focus: Giving explanations, descriptions, directions, and opinions

> **In the test**
>
> ← **Sample test pp146–151**
> ← **Unit 15 p178**
> **Writing Test Questions 6–7**
>
> - In this part of the test, you will be given an e-mail to read and respond to.
> - In Unit 15, you practiced requesting goods, services, and information.
> - This unit will focus on giving explanations, descriptions of problems, and instructions.
> - You will also practice how to begin and organize your message.

1 Language building: Explaining, describing a situation, giving information and directions

unit
19

A Match the useful phrases (in **bold**) in sentences 1–4 to their uses in a–d below.

1. **The main reason** I am transferring my membership **is because of** the price change. _____

2. **I think the best way to solve the problem is** by discussing the situation with all concerned. _____

3. **The problem is that** we haven't received any of the last six deliveries on time. _____

4. **I'm pleased to let you know that** your order will reach you today. _____

a. Explaining a possible solution
b. Giving an explanation
c. Describing a problem
d. Giving information

B Write sentences based on the information in parentheses. Use the phrases in **bold** in A.

1. _____
   (inform employees that they will receive their annual bonuses next month)

2. _____
   (explain that the solution is for everyone to work harder for a while)

3. _____
   (say that the problem is that the part is unavailable at the moment)

4. _____
   (the reason for not attending the meeting is a very tight deadline)

Test Tip

Include clear reasons

You may be asked to explain why something can or can't happen. Use marker words (*because*/*due to*/*so that*) to signal your explanation.

C Read sentences 1–3 and match the conjunction in **bold** to its use, a or b.

1. I will not be able to come to class on Wednesday **because** I have to visit my mother in the hospital. _____

2. The extra expense in May is **due to** an increase in fuel prices. _____

3. I hired three new workers **so that** we can increase our production.

_____

a. giving a reason
b. explaining a purpose

D Choose the correct conjunction to join sentences 1–5.

1. We require two extra delivery trucks *because*/*due to*/*so that* we have fifteen new customers that we have to service in the Danforth area.
2. I left my last company *because*/*due to*/*so that* I got offered a better job.
3. The problem with attendance last month was *because*/*due to*/*so that* many people in the office catching a cold.
4. Our terrific sales in June were *because*/*due to*/*so that* the hiring of three new sales staff.
5. I quit my job *because*/*due to*/*so that* I could start my own company.

Test Tip

Introduce requests/ suggestions/ problems

Use marker words (*I'd like*/*I think you should*/*I'm sorry that*) to indicate what kind of information you are giving.

E Match the phrases in 1–6 to the uses a–c.

1. I think you/we should … _____
2. I'm afraid … _____
3. I believe … _____
4. I'm sorry, but … _____
5. In my opinion … _____
6. Why don't you … ? _____

a. giving an opinion
b. making a suggestion
c. introducing bad news

F Complete sentences 1–4 with one of the phrases in E.

1. _____ open a branch office in the Newton area so that we can increase our coverage in this area.

2. Due to an increase in costs, _____ we must increase your rent by $50 per month.

3. _____ that John deserves a bonus for the great job he did completing the project on time.

4. _____ that I won't be able to send a repair person to fix your plumbing until next week.

unit
19

2 Test tactics: Openings, connectors, and organization

Test tip

Use an appropriate opening sentence or reference

The opening sentence or reference of your message can explain why you are writing and sets an appropriate tone.

A Match opening sentences/references 1–5 to the appropriate descriptions a–e. Make a note of the useful phrases in **bold**. The first is done for you.

1. **Re:** Order No. 2354b   *e*
2. **Thank you for your** inquiry about our new machinery.   ____
3. **I am writing about / in regards to** the ad I saw in the Daily News.   ____
4. **I am writing to inquire about** …   ____
5. **I received your** invoice dated June 11.   ____

a. You wish to get information.
b. You are referring to some information you have received.
c. You are writing to someone for the first time based upon something you have seen in the newspaper, on the Internet, etc.
d. You are writing to a potential customer and want to be very polite.
e. The mail you are replying to included a reference or account number.

Test tip

Use connectors to organize your ideas

Use connecting words to clearly show the order of each part of your e-mail.

B Match connectors 1–10 to their uses in a–f (each use may apply to more than one connector).

1. First of all, …
2. I have a few questions about … (the job / the bill / etc.)
3. In response to your questions / inquiries, …
4. Best wishes,
5. Finally, …
6. I'm afraid that …
7. Next, …
8. Sincerely, …
9. To begin with, …
10. Also, …

a. Used when asking/answering questions.
b. Signals the first point you wish to make.
c. Signals a subsequent point you wish to make.
d. Signals the last point you wish to make.
e. Signals that you are going to end your message and is followed by your signature / name.
f. Used to introduce problems.

Test tip

Use appropriate salutations and closings

Make sure any salutation or closing (*Dear …, Sincerely yours*, etc.) in your response is appropriate. See page 262 for further information about salutations.

C Complete the e-mail using appropriate phrases from A and B.

Dear Mr. Gracy,

(1) _____ your ad in the newspaper for clerical staff.

(2) _____ , could you tell me when the position will begin? (3) _____ I would like to know if it is a full-time or part-time position.

(4) _____ I can't work on weekends or after 6:00. Will the job require much overtime?

(5) _____

Peter Barnett

B Tactic practice

Test technique

☑ Read the e-mail and directions and identify the three tasks.

☑ Note who you are writing to and who you are writing as.

☑ Brainstorm answers to the three tasks. Then write your ideas as sentences.

☑ Add an opening and closing sentence.

☑ Check your writing for errors.

unit **19**

Test tip

Leave time to edit your writing

Errors may reduce your score, especially if they make your writing hard to understand. Allow time to edit your work.

Test tip

Use salutations

If the e-mail ends using the person's full name, and if it's clear the writer is a man, you can open your response with, e.g. *Dear Mr. Smith*. If the writer is a woman, open your response with, e.g. *Dear Ms. Smith*. See page 262 for further information about Salutations.

For each e-mail 1 and 2, read the directions and the e-mail. Then write your reply following steps 1–5. After each step, compare answers with your partner.

1. Brainstorm and write response sentences for the three tasks as you learned in Unit 15, page 180.
2. Add an appropriate opening sentence and/or reference.
3. Add connecting words to organize your writing clearly.
4. Use a salutation and closing if appropriate.
5. Leave time to check your work before you finish.

1.

Directions: Read the e-mail.

> **FROM:** S. Banner, Industrial Cleaning, Customer Service Manager
>
> **TO:** J. Choi, Kenton Office Supplies
>
> **SUBJECT:** Renewal of your contract
>
> **SENT:** March 13, 10:40 A.M.
>
> Dear J. Choi,
>
> I have recently learned that your company is not renewing its contract with us to clean your office facilities. I would like to inquire why you have decided to make this change and see if there is anything we could do to keep your business.
>
> Sincerely,
> Steve Banner

Directions: Respond to the e-mail as if you are J. Choi, a manager at Kenton Supplies. In your e-mail, describe ONE problem and make TWO suggestions.

2.

Directions: Read the e-mail.

FROM:	K. Blascoe, Domcore Tools
TO:	S. Refo, Kipling Plant
SUBJECT:	Shipping delay
SENT:	May 5, 10:59 A.M.

Dear S. Refo,

We ordered some equipment from you on April 8, but we have not received it yet. Please could you investigate this matter and let me know what has happened to our order?

Sincerely,
Ken Blascoe
Shipping and Receiving Manager

Directions: Respond to the e-mail as if you are the warehouse supervisor at the Kipling Plant. In your e-mail, explain TWO problems and make ONE request.

unit
19

C Mini-test

Now apply the Test tactics at the actual test speed for Questions 6–7.

Important

In the test, it is a good strategy to write an opening and closing sentence in your response. Opening and closing sentences can improve the organizational logic of your answer. Look at the Sample test on pages 147–150 and the e-mails on pages 180–182 for examples of this.

Questions 6–7:
Respond to a
written request

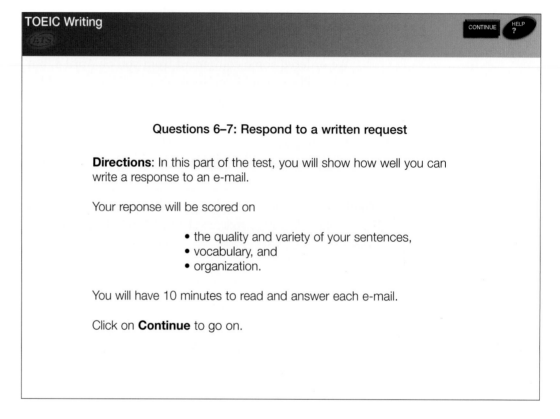

TOEIC Writing

CONTINUE   HELP ?

Questions 6–7: Respond to a written request

Directions: In this part of the test, you will show how well you can write a response to an e-mail.

Your reponse will be scored on

- the quality and variety of your sentences,
- vocabulary, and
- organization.

You will have 10 minutes to read and answer each e-mail.

Click on **Continue** to go on.

Question 6

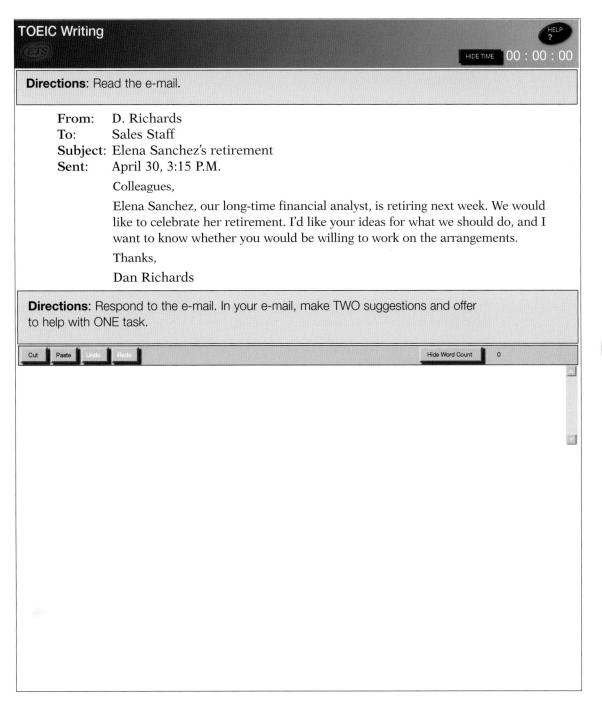

TOEIC Writing

HELP ?

HIDE TIME 00 : 00 : 00

Directions: Read the e-mail.

From: D. Richards
To: Sales Staff
Subject: Elena Sanchez's retirement
Sent: April 30, 3:15 P.M.

Colleagues,

Elena Sanchez, our long-time financial analyst, is retiring next week. We would like to celebrate her retirement. I'd like your ideas for what we should do, and I want to know whether you would be willing to work on the arrangements.

Thanks,

Dan Richards

Directions: Respond to the e-mail. In your e-mail, make TWO suggestions and offer to help with ONE task.

Cut | Paste | Undo | Redo   Hide Word Count | 0

unit
19

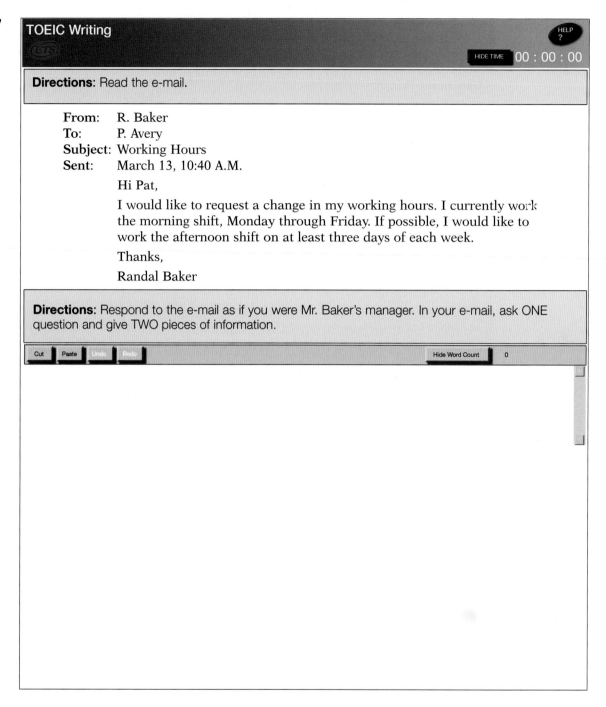

TOEIC Writing HELP ?

HIDE TIME 00 : 00 : 00

Directions: Read the e-mail.

From: R. Baker
To: P. Avery
Subject: Working Hours
Sent: March 13, 10:40 A.M.

Hi Pat,

I would like to request a change in my working hours. I currently work the morning shift, Monday through Friday. If possible, I would like to work the afternoon shift on at least three days of each week.

Thanks,

Randal Baker

Directions: Respond to the e-mail as if you were Mr. Baker's manager. In your e-mail, ask ONE question and give TWO pieces of information.

Cut   Paste   Undo   Redo   Hide Word Count   0

Writing Test
Question 8 — Write an opinion essay

A Focus: Completing an essay

> ### In the test
>
> ← **Sample test pp152–157**
> ← **Unit 16 p186**
> **Writing Test Question 8**
>
> • In this part of the test, you are asked to write an essay stating your opinion in response to the topic.
> • In Unit 16, you practiced understanding the question, brainstorming ideas, and writing a draft.
> • In this unit you will learn how to link your ideas and expand on the reasons and examples you give.
> • You will also practice editing your work for style and accuracy.

Test tip

Become familiar with phrases to show reasons / examples

All Opinion questions will ask you to give reasons or examples to support your answer. Become familiar with ways to introduce these key elements.

1 Language building: Language for giving reasons and examples

A Match beginnings 1–5 to the endings a–e. Note the common phrases for introducing examples in **bold**.

1. There are several disadvantages to working in a big city. **Some examples include** … _____

2. Spending money on research can have a great impact. **One clear example of this is** … _____

3. I think the most important factor is practical experience. **By this I mean** … _____

4. We could save money by reducing costs. **For example,** … _____

5. One example of the problems we faced was high material costs. **Another example was** … _____

a. Zentex's development of the first biochip in 2004.
b. a lack of understanding of the market.
c. we could stop giving free samples to all visitors.
d. expensive housing, heavy traffic, and a stressful lifestyle.
e. actual time spent working in the field.

B Look at each of the sentences in A and match the phrase in **bold** to the definition of how it is used below. The first one is done for you.

a. Used for providing a single and easily understood example.   2

b. Used to provide a second example of something.   _____

c. Used to clarify an example you have given.   _____

d. Used as a simple and common way to introduce an example.   _____

e. Used to introduce a list of example points to support your idea.   _____

C Use common phrases from A to write examples for the statements in 1–3.

1. Many countries in the world make cars.

    _____ .

2. People in my country get to work in many different ways.

    _____ .

3. After work, people like to relax.

    _____ .

unit
20

Test tip

Learn to use conditional sentences to show reasons

A common way to give support for your ideas is to show how a situation would be different in other circumstances.

Grammar note

Conditional sentences consist of two clauses. Generally, one clause uses *if* (or *unless*) and shows the situation or condition. The second clause shows the result.

An opinion essay may include a present condition, e.g. *If it rains, … .* Since you will probably be giving ideas about possible present or future results, you will generally use *will* or modal verb plus the infinitive, e.g. *… I will / may / could get wet.* Note that the order of the clauses can be switched, e.g. *I may get wet if it rains.*

D Complete conditional sentences 1–6 with the words and phrases a–f.

1. The _____ will melt if we don't do something to stop

    _____ .

2. If you study the _____ in school, you can get the _____ .

3. If employees are forced to do _____ , they will often do a

    _____ .

4. You should look for a _____ if you really don't like the

    _____ .

5. If we reduce _____ , we might be able to attract _____ .

6. Unless we change _____ , our _____ will stay very high.

a. prices / more customers
b. right subjects / job you want
c. suppliers / costs
d. ice caps / global warming
e. different job / working conditions
f. things they don't like / poor job

E Complete sentences 1–3.

1. Unless I finish my work, _____ .

2. If you are always polite to your coworkers,

    _____ .

3. If you don't get enough sleep, _____ .

Follow up: Compare answers with your partner and see if you agree with his or her ideas.

2 Test tactic: Completing and editing

Test tip

Start your introduction with a general statement

The purpose of this sentence is to show the reader the general focus of your essay and interest them in reading it. It should be clearly related to the main idea(s) in the question but need <u>not</u> give a specific answer (that is the job of your thesis statement).

A Read the Opinion essay title in 1. Then choose the more general introductory sentence to start your essay, a or b. This would appear just before the thesis statement, which states your opinion. Compare answers with a partner. Say why the other sentence is not appropriate. Repeat for questions 2 and 3.

1. **Do you agree or disagree with the following statement? Consulting with a group of people is the best way to make an important decision.**

   a. ☐ Making an important decision is not an easy thing to do, and there are different ways to do it.

   b. ☐ If you want to make an important decision, you should definitely always do it by yourself.

   (Thesis statement)
   Many people believe that getting the opinion of other people is the best way to make an important decision; however, I disagree with this approach.

2. **When traveling medium distances, some people prefer to fly. Others prefer to take express trains. Which do you prefer?**

   a. ☐ Trains and airplanes have both advantages and disadvantages.

   b. ☐ I don't really like flying because it is very expensive and I often get airsick.

   (Thesis statement)
   Although some people prefer to fly, I prefer to take the train.

3. **What would you consider the best type of job?**

   a. ☐ I really don't like my current job much and would like to find a new one soon.

   b. ☐ Choosing the best type of job involves considering many factors.

   (Thesis statement)
   I think the best type of job for me would be one that involves both sales and travel.

B In Unit 16, you looked at an example draft of the following essay question. Now write an introductory sentence following the examples in A above.

1. **Recently in your town, construction of a new factory that would employ thousands of workers has been halted because it would endanger animals living in the area.**

   _____

   _____

   (Thesis statement)
   I strongly agree that they should stop construction of the new factory.

unit
20

C   Now we will look at ways of expanding the draft you looked at in Unit 16. Study the Grammar note below.

> ## Grammar note
>
> Use conjunctions to join shorter sentences into longer, better-formed sentences.
>
> If the two sentences are of equal importance, use coordinating conjunctions (*and, but, or, so, not yet, for*): e.g. *I work hard,* **but** *I never work on weekends*. If one idea is more important than another, join them using subordinating conjunctions (*although, because, unless*): e.g. *I left my job because the pay was too low*.

D   Now use conjunctions to link the ideas together as shown in the Grammar note. Read the example question 1 then complete 2 and 3 in the same way. Compare answers with your partner after you have completed each one.

1.

(Draft)

First of all,
Although a factory will be good for the economy
wrong to endanger animals
building a factory in the area proposed – many animals would lose their home

(Expanded sentences)

First of all, although the factory may be very good for the economy, I think it is wrong to endanger animals. If we build the factory, many animals would lose their home. I definitely don't think we should risk killing animals in order to make money.

2.
(Draft)
Next
It's true that many possible jobs might be lost.
However,
factory could be built in another place
free space on the west side is almost as good

_____

_____

_____

Test tip

Write your conclusion

This should relate back to your introduction and summarize your main points (using other words).

3.

(Draft)
Finally,
Important not to build in rural areas if possible
Although cities crowded – usually places (old, unused) where the factory could be located

_____

_____

_____

E Read the example introductions and conclusions. In what way does the conclusion relate back to the introduction?

Introductory paragraph

Making an important decision is not an easy thing to do and there are different ways to do it. Some people believe that getting the opinion of other people is the best way to make an important decision; however, I disagree with this approach.

Concluding paragraph

In conclusion, although some people believe it is best to make important decisions by talking with other people, I think that important decisions are best made by a single knowledgeable person.

F Write a concluding paragraph to complete the opinion essay about building the factory or saving the animals (see page 190 and page 220).

Follow up: When you have finished, compare paragraphs with your partner.

B Tactic practice

Remember

☑ Analyze the question and form a clear thesis statement.

☑ Brainstorm and draft some notes for the body of your essay and add reasons / examples.

☑ Expand your draft and add a conclusion.

☑ In the last five minutes, edit your draft, and make any minor changes necessary.

Test tip

Leave time for final editing

You should aim to spend 5 minutes planning, 20 minutes writing, and the last 5 minutes editing your essay. It is important to read over your essay, correct any obvious mistakes, and make minor wording changes.

Complete steps 1–4 to write a complete essay using the outline you drafted for Opinion question 3 in Unit 16. After each step, compare answers with your partner.

1. Expand your introduction.
2. Expand the body, joining simple sentences into more complex ones, and supporting your ideas with reasons and examples.
3. Write a conclusion that reflects your introduction and summarizes the points you made (using different words).
4. Use the last few minutes to edit your work and look for obvious errors.

Opinion question 3

Some people enjoy jobs that include traveling a lot and meeting new people. Others like to work in a fixed location with the same group of coworkers. What is your preference? Explain why.

C Mini-test

Now apply the Test tactics at the actual test speed for Question 8.

Question 8: Write an opinion essay

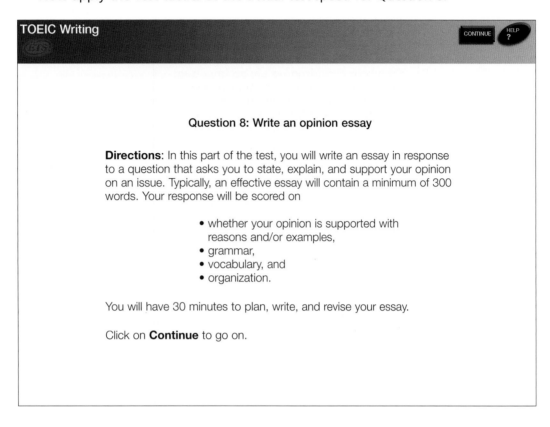

TOEIC Writing   CONTINUE   HELP ?

Question 8: Write an opinion essay

Directions: In this part of the test, you will write an essay in response to a question that asks you to state, explain, and support your opinion on an issue. Typically, an effective essay will contain a minimum of 300 words. Your response will be scored on

- whether your opinion is supported with reasons and/or examples,
- grammar,
- vocabulary, and
- organization.

You will have 30 minutes to plan, write, and revise your essay.

Click on **Continue** to go on.

unit
20

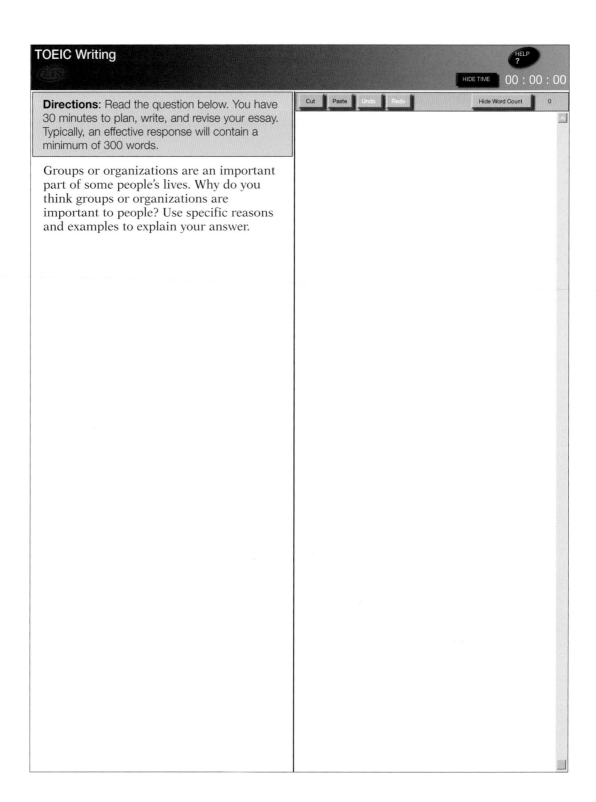

Directions: Read the question below. You have 30 minutes to plan, write, and revise your essay. Typically, an effective response will contain a minimum of 300 words.

Groups or organizations are an important part of some people's lives. Why do you think groups or organizations are important to people? Use specific reasons and examples to explain your answer.

unit
20

Activity Files

Activity File
Unit 6 p81

Student B

Take turns asking each other questions 1–3. When it is your turn to answer, give an opinion statement only.

Ask Student A these questions.

1. Do you think it's more important to spend years studying or to get experience working as soon as possible? Explain why.

2. Do you prefer holidays that are relaxed and luxurious or exciting and full of action? Give reasons to support your answer.

3. Do you think governments should spend more money on health care or protecting the environment? Explain why.

Activity File
Unit 9 p103

Student B

Take turns asking each other questions 1–3. The person answering the question must talk for as long as possible (maximum 30 seconds) without a silent pause of more then two seconds. If you need time to think, use hesitation devices.

Ask Student A these questions.

1. What country would you most like to live in for one year? Give reasons to support your answer.

2. What is the most unusual food you have ever eaten? In your answer, describe the food and explain why you like it.

3. What famous person would you most like to meet and why?

Activity File
Unit 12 p126

Student B

Take turns asking each other questions 1–3. The person answering the question must talk for 20 seconds without a silent pause of more then two seconds. If you need time to think, use hesitation devices.

Ask Student A these questions.

1. If you could either change your job or move house, which would you do? Explain why.

2. Would you rather have lots of money or lots of friends? Use specific reasons and examples to support your answer.

3. What is more important, having a job you enjoy or one that earns you a lot of money? Use specific reasons and examples to support your answer.

Pronunciation Tasks

Unit 1 page 39

1 s/ʃ practice

A 🎧 Listen to the pairs of words in 1–6 being read aloud and repeat them.

1. sign _____   shine _____
2. save _____   shave _____
3. seat _____   sheet _____
4. said _____   shed _____
5. cell _____   shell _____
6. gas _____   gash _____

B 🎧 Now listen to one of the words in each pair being read aloud. Mark (✔) the one you hear in each pair.

2 ɜː/ɔː practice

A 🎧 Listen to the pairs of words in 1–6 being read aloud and repeat them.

1. work _____   walk _____
2. burn _____   born _____
3. purr _____   poor _____
4. turn _____   torn _____
5. fur _____   four _____
6. sir _____   saw _____

B 🎧 Now listen to one of the words in each pair being read aloud. Mark (✔) the one you hear in each pair.

3 f/h practice

A 🎧 Listen to the pairs of words in 1–6 being read aloud and repeat them.

1. fill _____   hill _____
2. fair _____   hair _____
3. fall _____   hall _____
4. fanned _____   hand _____
5. farm _____   harm _____
6. fat _____   hat _____

B 🎧 Now listen to one of the words in each pair being read aloud. Mark (✔) the one you hear in each pair.

4 ɪ/iː practice

A 🎧 Listen to the pairs of words in 1–6 being read aloud and repeat them.

1. live _____   leave _____
2. thirty _____   thirteen _____
3. bin _____   bean _____
4. fit _____   feet _____
5. forty _____   fourteen _____
6. sit _____   seat _____

B 🎧 Now listen to one of the words in each pair being read aloud. Mark (✔) the one you hear in each pair.

5 h / no h practice

A 🎧 Listen to the pairs of words in 1–6 being read aloud and repeat them.

1. hair _____ air _____
2. hall _____ all _____
3. hand _____ and _____
4. harm _____ arm _____
5. hat _____ at _____
6. hill _____ ill _____

B 🎧 Now listen to one of the words in each pair being read aloud. Mark (✔) the one you hear in each pair.

6 tʃ / ʃ practice

A 🎧 Listen to the pairs of words in 1–6 being read aloud and repeat them.

1. chairs _____ shares _____
2. chips _____ ships _____
3. which _____ wish _____
4. watch _____ wash _____
5. much _____ mush _____
6. ditch _____ dish _____

B 🎧 Now listen to one of the words in each pair being read aloud. Mark (✔) the one you hear in each pair.

7 l / r practice

A 🎧 Listen to the pairs of words in 1–6 being read aloud and repeat them.

1. lights _____ rights _____
2. link _____ rink _____
3. bowling _____ boring _____
4. plank _____ prank _____
5. tally _____ tarry _____
6. long _____ wrong _____

B 🎧 Now listen to one of the words in each pair being read aloud. Mark (✔) the one you hear in each pair.

8 v / b practice

A 🎧 Listen to the pairs of words in 1–6 being read aloud and repeat them.

1. van _____ ban _____
2. vest _____ best _____
3. voter _____ boater _____
4. curve _____ curb _____
5. dove _____ dub _____
6. verve _____ verb _____

B 🎧 Now listen to one of the words in each pair being read aloud. Mark (✔) the one you hear in each pair.

9 θ or ð / s practice

A 🎧 Listen to the pairs of words in 1–6 being read aloud and repeat them.

1. thank _____ sank _____
2. clothing _____ closing _____
3. mouth _____ mouse _____
4. leather _____ lesser _____
5. bathe _____ base _____
6. that _____ sat _____

B 🎧 Now listen to one of the words in each pair being read aloud. Mark (✔) the one you hear in each pair.

Unit 1

accounting
(n) the activity or occupation of maintaining the financial records of a company or person
The lecture, "An introduction to accounting", has been canceled.
Give your travel expenses to the accounting department.

advice
(n) opinion about what to do, how to behave
Where else could you go for better advice?
She gave me some good advice on giving presentations.

apologize
(v) to say you are sorry for something
We would like to apologize for any inconvenience caused.
She apologized to the customer for the mistake in their order.

appropriately
(adv) done in a way suitable for a particular situation
Make sure your voice goes up and down appropriately.
He was dressed appropriately in a dark suit and tie for the wedding.

cancel
(v) to stop a previously scheduled event from happening
The lecture, "An introduction to accounting", has been canceled.
He had to cancel his golf game in order to visit an important client.

concern
(n) something you are interested in or which is important to you; anxiety.
The company's main concern is its profitability.
Today's stormy weather was causing him great concern.

consider
(v) to think carefully about something
Read through the paragraph and consider the following.
I am considering buying a new house.

contract
(n) an official written agreement
(v) to get smaller in size
I just heard they've renewed your contract.
Metals contract when the temperature changes.

convenient
(adj) suitable; handy; easy to get to / at; does not involve trouble or difficulty
Living in the city is very convenient for shopping.
Will 1:30 tomorrow be a more convenient time for you?

cooperation
(n) the act of working together to achieve a common goal
Thank you for your cooperation.
We will need a lot of cooperation to fix this problem.

destination
(n) the place to which someone or something is going
Destinations include Greece, Turkey and Egypt.
We'll arrive at our destination in one hour.

exotic
(adj) unusual, exciting and/or from a faraway place
This show will feature exotic animals from around the world.
The restaurant served exotic fruit from Asia.

experienced
(adj) having knowledge or skill gained by doing something for some time
Let our experienced staff attend to all your riding needs.
After 20 years, he is an extremely experienced worker.

export
(n) goods sent abroad
(v) to send goods abroad
Exports of car parts have decreased recently.
Mr. Longwood exports carpets to Europe.

inconvenience
(n) a lack of convenience; discomfort or trouble
We would like to apologize for any inconvenience caused.
Not having a car in the small town was a real inconvenience.

initial
(adj) coming first or at the start
I would like to summarize the initial response.
The initial problems were noticed a few days after the shop opened.

introduce
(v) to meet and become acquainted with another person
You will be introduced to the president.
When meeting someone for the first time, you should always introduce yourself.

lounge
(n) a room in a public building where people may sit and/or wait
The chairs in the lounge will be cleaned.
We waited for two hours in the departure lounge of the airport.

nevertheless
(adv) despite something; used to show contrast, similar to 'however'
Nevertheless, it has turned out to be very popular.
It was raining; nevertheless, we had a picnic.

originally
(adv) happening first or before
The lecture originally scheduled for this time has been canceled.
We were originally going to Mexico, but then we went to Europe instead.

personal
(adj) relating to someone's private life or possessions
All personal items should be removed from the floor.
This book is my personal property, not the company's.

premium
(n) additional money paid for a wage or service
This will help us cut our health premiums and bring us back to profitability.
If you wish to travel first-class, you'll have to pay a premium.

profitability
(n) ability to make a profit or get some benefit
The company's main concern is its profitability.
Profitability dropped when they lowered the prices.

proposal
(n) a (usually formal) idea or plan
I will summarize the initial response to our recent early retirement proposal.
I made a proposal to increase the advertising budget.

recently
(adv) not long ago; used to describe something that has happened a short time ago
Exports of car parts have decreased recently.
I recently bought a new computer because my old one broke last week.

record
(n) a (usually) written account of something
(v) to note something
I can't find any record of your order.
I have to record your name and number before you enter.

refund
(n) money that has been given back
(v) to return money to someone
I wanted to get a refund on the broken gift.
The store refused to refund the money.

retirement
(n) the act of leaving a job or career usually around age 60
I would like to summarize the initial response to our recent early retirement proposal.
After his retirement he started gardening.

selection
(n) the range of things from which you can choose
We have the city's largest selection of sport and cruising bikes.
The store has a huge selection of English books.

service
(n) work done by someone else or a public organization
Unfortunately, this service will be canceled until further notice.
Mail service was slowed during the storm.

summarize
(v) to make a shortened version of something said or written
I would like to summarize the initial response.
I summarize the main points of the meeting for my boss.

vat
(n) a large container for holding liquid
The vat was full of rainwater.
There was a huge vat of soup in the army kitchen.

volunteer
(v) to offer to do something of one's own free will
Who will volunteer?
He volunteered to help collect data for the research.

Quiz Unit 1

1 Complete the sentences with the following words.

> lounge cancel introduce
> destination inconvenience
> personal consider
> nevertheless originally

1 I don't have any _____ items at work.
2 The trains are delayed. We are sorry for any _____ .
3 The plane left at 10:30 and will arrive at its _____ at 3 o'clock.
4 If the project isn't finished this week, we will _____ the trip to Singapore.
5 Come with me and I'll _____ you to our managing director.

6 We will shortly be serving drinks in the visitors' _____ .
7 The managers would like you to _____ staying on at the company.
8 He _____ worked in sales. Now's he's in marketing.
9 Sales weren't good; _____ , we made a profit.

2 Read the definitions and write *true* or *false*.

1 *Convenient* means causing a lot of trouble.
2 A *premium* is additional money paid for an extra / special service.
3 *Accounting* is an occupation related to looking at financial records.
4 If something is done *appropriately*, it is done in a suitable way.
5 *Recently* means not long ago.
6 *To volunteer* is to work for money.
7 If you have a *concern*, you have a reason for worrying.
8 If something is *exotic*, it's unusual, exciting or from a faraway place.
9 *Initial* means coming last, or at the end.
10 *Service* is work done by someone else.
11 A *vat* is a kind of animal.
12 *Exports* are goods that are sent abroad.

3 Choose the correct answer.

1 We would like to _____ for any problems our customers have had.
(A) cancel
(B) apologize
(C) consider
(D) refund

2 The director would like to thank you for your _____ on this project.
(A) destination
(B) inconvenience
(C) cooperation
(D) profitability

3 Mr. Harrison gave me some good _____ on having interviews.
(A) advice
(B) premium
(C) selection
(D) service

4 Ben's _____ is to employ more sales staff.
(A) refund
(B) record
(C) premium
(D) proposal

5 When I joined the company they gave me a _____ for five years.
(A) contract
(B) proposal
(C) record
(D) selection

6 Mrs. Green is very _____ . She's worked here for twenty years.
(A) experienced
(B) convenient
(C) appropriate
(D) personal

7 _____ has increased since we've had a new marketing director.
(A) Premium
(B) Profitability
(C) Destination
(D) Record

8 I'm sorry, but I can't find a(n) _____ of your hotel booking.
(A) record
(B) refund
(C) proposal
(D) export

9 I'd like a _____ on this CD player, please. It's broken.
(A) volunteer
(B) refund
(C) vat
(D) profitability

10 After my _____ , I'm going to travel more.
(A) advice
(B) lounge
(C) concern
(D) retirement

11 The store has a large _____ of computers.
(A) export
(B) service
(C) selection
(D) premium

12 At the end of the meeting, I'll _____ the main points again.
(A) initial
(B) contract
(C) cancel
(D) summarize

Unit 2

brainstorm
(v) to think up creative ideas spontaneously
Brainstorm as many words as you can for each category.
The team brainstormed new ideas for their project.

café
(n) a small casual restaurant which serves drinks and often light meals
This picture shows a café.
Let's go for a tea in the café.

category
(n) a group of things, or people classified together because of their similarities
Brainstorm as many words as you can for each category.
I don't think these should be in the same category – they're not the same.

customer
(n) a person or a company, who buys goods or services
We can see a waiter and some customers.
This store has many customers because of its low prices.

diagram
(n) a simple drawing showing the basic layout, shape, or workings of some kind
They are looking closely at the diagram.
I showed him the diagram of the building.

entertainment
(n) activities that give people pleasure
The picture may show eating... entertainment, or street scenes.
Entertainment at the party was provided by the Blue Jays string quartet.

household
(adj) connected with looking after the house or the people in it
The focus of the picture may be health, household tasks, shopping ...
That company produces household goods.

introductory
(adj) related to something written or said at the beginning of something that describes what follows
Plan introductory sentences that answer where, who, what, why?
In Ms. Lans introductory statement she gave an overview of the project.

landscape
(n) a painting, drawing, or photograph of a view of the countryside
She is painting a landscape picture.
The hills and trees in the landscape are well done.

lie
(v) to stretch out on a slanted or horizontal surface
The dog is lying on the grass.
For this exercise, participants are asked to lie on their backs.

location
(n) the place or position of something or someone
Describe their location in the picture.
The store is in a convenient location.

paintbrush

(n) a brush for painting pictures or other things
She has a paintbrush in her right hand.
He used a large paintbrush to paint his house.

quietly

(adv) making no noise or only a small amount of noise
The children waited quietly while their mother was talking.
You must talk quietly in the library.

railing

(n) a barrier consisting of rails used to provide a fence or support in walking or climbing
He is leaning against the railing.
The old man used the railing to climb the stairs.

recommended

(adj) spoken favorably of; endorsed as fit, worthy or competent
Now draft an outline using the recommended test timing.
That product was highly recommended by my friend.

response

(n) something said or written that replies to a statement or question said before
You will have 30 seconds to prepare your response.
The man's response did not fully address the argument.

saltshaker

(n) a small container with holes in the top used for sprinkling salt on food
The restaurant has saltshakers on every table.
Table 12 has no salt – I must refill the empty saltshaker.

scene

(n) a place at which an event or action happens
Describe the scene and the people, and plan your response.
There was no evidence left at the crime scene.

skateboard

(n) a short narrow board with wheels attached underneath, used to move or perform jumps and stunts
The boy is holding his skateboard.
The man showed us tricks on his skateboard.

vendor

(n) a person or company that sells something
The vendor is at the stand.
Give your money to the vendor at the counter.

Quiz Unit 2

1 Choose the correct word.

1   He painted a beautiful _____ picture of mountains and lakes.
(A) diagram
(B) landscape
(C) location
(D) paintbrush

2   The _____ are waiting to be served in the restaurant.
(A) households
(B) saltshakers
(C) cafés
(D) customers

3   You can read about concerts, theaters, and other forms of _____ in the tourist guide.
(A) response
(B) entertainment
(C) category
(D) scene

4   Let's have a coffee in the _____ on the corner.
(A) café
(B) household
(C) customer
(D) landscape

5   Their _____ bills are usually paid once a month.
(A) railing
(B) response
(C) household
(D) location

6   I'd like to see a _____ of the machine.
(A) railing
(B) response
(C) scene
(D) diagram

7   My boss said this hotel is highly _____.
(A) brainstormed
(B) recommended
(C) delivered
(D) entertained

8   The man is _____ on the sofa, watching TV.
(A) lying
(B) brainstorming
(C) recommending
(D) introducing

9   She leaned against the _____ in the park.
(A) paintbrush
(B) diagram
(C) household
(D) railing

10   The boy is riding his _____ on the sidewalk.
(A) skateboard
(B) scene
(C) response
(D) diagram

2 Read the definitions and write the words.

1   you use it for sprinkling salt on your food (*rhaskeltas*) s_____

2   a group of similar things or people (*grcoaety*) c_____

3   to think up creative ideas (*mobarnistr*) b_____

4   making a little or no noise (*lyuiteq*) q_____

5   the place or position of something (*caltooin*) l_____

6   an artist uses it for painting (*ubpanhtirs*) p_____

7   the place where something happens (*ensec*) s_____

8   explaining a little about what is coming next (*oyinrtodcutr*) i_____

9   something that replies to something said or done (*poesrnes*) r_____

10   a person or company that sells something (*revdon*) v_____

Unit 3

advantage
(n) something useful or helpful
What are some of the advantages of living in a big city?
There are a number of advantages to working at home.

appropriately
(adv) done in a way suitable for a particular situation
You will receive marks for answering the question appropriately.
You must dress appropriately for the meeting.

celebrate
(v) to mark a special time or day with ceremonies or festivities
Where would you like to go to celebrate your birthday?
Everyone in my family celebrated Christmas at my house this year.

current
(adj) existing or happening in the present
How long have you been living in your current home?
I didn't find my previous job rewarding, but I enjoy my current job very much.

deal
(v) to handle or take care of something
In this unit we will look at dealing with common question types.
How are you going to deal with this problem?

employment
(n) paid work that someone does
People usually go to the government employment office.
After being fired, he had to find new employment.

entertainment facilities
(n) places where people can go to be entertained
What entertainment facilities are there near where you live?
The boys played video games at the entertainment facility.

familiar
(adj) well known, common and easily recognized
The questions are about familiar topics related to your personal experience.
After a month-long trip, he missed the familiar faces of his friends.

fireworks
(n) devices designed to make a loud and visual explosion when lit
I love the fireworks!
Let's go see the fireworks tonight at the festival.

firm
(n) a group of people in a commercial organization that sells goods or services
Imagine that a US marketing firm is doing research in your country.
I am planning to start a law firm.

function
(n) the role or purpose for someone or something
Questions can have a number of different functions.
My new cell phone has many useful functions.

government
(n) a group of people who have the power to put laws into effect
In my country people usually go to the government employment office.
Governments try to help all the citizens.

imagine
(v) to create an image or idea of something in the mind
Imagine that you are taking part in a telephone interview.
I can't imagine what she will say when she opens my gift!

improve
(v) to make something better
Why do you want to improve your English?
He started jogging everyday to improve his health.

interview
(n) a conversation during which someone is asked questions
You have agreed to participate in a telephone interview ...
The actor's interview brought him more fans.

participate
(v) to take part in a particular event or activity
You have agreed to participate in a telephone interview about vacations.
They can participate in the meeting.

prefer
(v) to want or like something more than something else
Many of the questions will ask about things you prefer.
Would you prefer to go home or go shopping now?

relevant
(adj) having a reasonable or logical connection with something else
You will receive marks for using relevant vocabulary appropriately.
Please support your argument with relevant details and examples.

vacation
(n) a period of time used for rest, travel, or take part in recreation
Where do you think is the best place for a summer vacation?
During his two-week vacation, he went to the U.S.A.

Quiz Unit 3

1 Complete the sentences with the following words.

employment   celebrate
appropriately   vacation
fireworks   firm
entertainment facilities   current

1   People must dress _____ for the work dinner tonight.
2   He lost his job and now he needs new _____ .
3   There's a new financial _____ in the city.
4   The town has many _____ in the center.
5   We're going to a Greek restaurant to _____ my new job.
6   I've been doing my _____ job for three years now.
7   The _____ at the festival were loud and colourful.
8   I'm looking forward to our two-week _____ in the U.S.A.

2 Use the definitions to find the words to complete the puzzle.

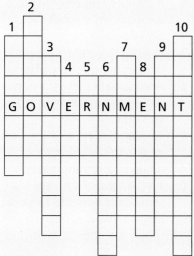

Clues

1 to create an idea in your mind
2 to make something better
3 a better position in relation to something or someone else
4 to take care of something
5 to want or like something more than something else
6 a meeting when somebody is asked questions
7 well known
8 having a connection with something else
9 the role or purpose of something or someone
10 to take part

Unit 4

accurate
(adj) correct and free from errors
You will be scored on giving accurate information.
All the data I have collected is accurate.

accurately
(adv) precisely and correctly
Answer each question as fully and as accurately as you can.
He was able to answer each of the questions accurately.

agenda
(n) a formal list of things to be done or discussed in a specific order
You will be given 30 seconds to read a written agenda or schedule.
The next item on the agenda is finalizing the floor plan of the new building.

appropriate
(adj) suitable for a particular situation
Use appropriate phrases to introduce bad news.
That was a very appropriate speech for the wedding.

arrival
(n) the reaching of a place after traveling from somewhere else
OK, first, I need to know their arrival time, and the flight number.
Her late arrival caused us to miss our flight.

autograph
(n) the signature of a famous person
You will meet the fans and have an autograph-signing session.
The man stood in line to get an autograph from his favorite actor.

avoid
(v) to not go near or to prevent something from happening
Learn phrases to give you time and to avoid a long pause.
After our argument, he has been avoiding me all day.

cafeteria
(n) a self-service restaurant or coffee shop
Cafeteria services will not be available due to renovations.
Let's go eat lunch at the cafeteria.

campaign
(n) a planned series of actions aimed at achieving a goal
Do you have any idea who is going to give the overview of the ad campaign?
Everyone needs to come up with a few new ideas for the campaign.

confirm
(v) to check that something is correct
I wanted to confirm that the food should be delivered to the cafeteria.
Mr. Lee called the hotel to confirm his reservation.

feature
(v) to include something or somebody as an important part of something
The visit will feature a guided tour around the building.
That movie features my favorite actress.

form
(n) the structure or appearance of something
Questions in the test and in real life rarely appear in the simple interrogative form.
The boy shaped a piece of clay to take on the form of a dog.

guided tour
(n) a trip that is led by someone
The visit will feature a guided tour around the building.
A guided tour is a great way to see a new place.

introductory
(adj) related to something written or said at the beginning of something that describes what follows
For 'no' answers use appropriate introductory phrases.
In Ms. Lans introductory statement, she gave an overview of the project.

itinerary
(n) a plan or a list of places to visit in order
I want to check some points before you send over the itinerary.
Looking at the itinerary, I note he is visiting Egypt on the 5th.

likely
(adj) in all probability
Would you be able to tell me when the meeting is likely to end?
You must take an umbrella because it's likely to rain today.

limousine
(n) a large vehicle for transporting passengers to and from the airport
There will be a limousine waiting to take you back to the hotel.
Whenever I fly to the U.S, I take a limousine to my hotel.

orchestra
(n) a large classical musical group
Were you able to reserve orchestra seats as I requested?
If I get better at playing the violin, I hope to join the orchestra.

politely
(adv) done in a way showing good manners or common courtesy
If the answer to the question is no, then you must politely say so.
I politely excused myself and left the party.

proposal
(n) an idea, suggestion or plan, usually a formal or official one
They were planning on voting on the proposal.
He sent in his proposal for the creation of a new band.

rarely
(adv) happening almost never or not very often
Questions in the test and in real life rarely appear in the simple interrogative form.
He is rarely late to work and always meets his deadlines.

recognize
(v) to identify someone or something that has been seen before
Learn to recognize the different forms that questions can take.
I could not recognize the man because he had grown a beard.

relevant
(adj) having some reasonable or logical connection with something else
You will be scored on using relevant vocabulary.
Please support your argument with relevant details and examples.

renovation
(n) the act of bringing something back to good condition
Cafeteria services will not be available due to renovations.
Because of the renovations, the store is now modern, bright, and airy.

rephrase
(v) to rewrite or restate something using different words
Rephrase the language used in the question to make your answer.
He needs to rephrase the sentence to make it clearer.

representative
(n) someone who speaks for other people
I will be taking the European representatives to the theater.
The representative from the company is waiting outside.

reservation
(n) an advance booking or arrangement made beforehand
Did you manage to get reservations for them at the Grand Hotel?
He made a reservation for our anniversary at a famous restaurant.

schedule
(n) a series of activities to be done in a certain order and time
You will be given 30 seconds to read a written schedule.
I am on a tight schedule for finishing this project.

skim
(v) to read something very quickly to get an idea of what it is about
Quickly skim the agenda in A and find the answer.
Just skim through the pages to get the general idea of the article.

specific
(adj) particular and detailed, relating to a definite thing
When answering a specific question, you will need to find the answer in your agenda.
My mother asked me to go get her a specific brand of milk.

tour
(n) a trip usually stopping off to see or visit places
The visit will feature a guided tour around the building.
The tour included all of the main galleries of the museum.

trainee
(n) someone training to do a job
Trainees are free to use this time as they like.
The trainee is learning so fast that she will be able to participate fully in our work in no time at all.

Quiz Unit 4

1 Choose the correct word.

1 An *autograph / agenda* is a signature of a famous person.
2 A *renovation / reservation* is an advance booking.
3 A *tour / proposal* is a trip or a journey.
4 *Accurate / Appropriate* means precise and correct.
5 A *schedule / guided tour* is a visit to somewhere which someone leads.
6 A *trainee / representative* is someone who speaks for other people.
7 *Rarely / Accurately* means happening not very often.
8 *Appropriate / Likely* means fitting the occasion or situation.
9 To *rephrase / recognize* means to say something again in a different way.
10 A(n) *itinerary / schedule* is a series of activities to be done.

2 Choose the correct word.

1 I'd like to _____ that the date for the meeting is the 15th.
(A) avoid
(B) guide
(C) confirm
(D) recognize
2 According to the _____ , we will be in Paris next week.
(A) arrival
(B) itinerary
(C) campaign
(D) renovation
3 I'm meeting a colleague for lunch in the _____ today.
(A) orchestra
(B) cafeteria
(C) limousine
(D) autograph
4 The tour will _____ a trip to the national gallery.
(A) form
(B) rephrase
(C) skim
(D) feature
5 Could you prepare a(n) _____ for the meeting, please?
(A) orchestra
(B) agenda
(C) arrival
(D) specific

6 Their _____ time is 3:00 P.M, so you need to be at the airport just before then.
(A) arrival
(B) agenda
(C) itinerary
(D) guide

7 Do you know when the talk is _____ to end?
(A) accurately
(B) rarely
(C) likely
(D) politely

8 The foreman showed the _____ around the factory.
(A) trainee
(B) arrival
(C) proposal
(D) agenda

9 Some new and exciting _____ were made at the meeting today.
(A) forms
(B) renovations
(C) autographs
(D) proposals

10 Some of the information in the report wasn't _____ to the project.
(A) introductory
(B) likely
(C) accurate
(D) relevant

3 Match the words with the definitions.

> orchestra accurately renovation politely recognize campaign specific limousine introductory skim avoid form

1 correct and free from errors
2 a large classical musical group
3 a large vehicle for transporting passengers to and from the airport
4 to read something quickly to get an idea of what it's about
5 showing good manners
6 to prevent something from happening
7 a planned and organized series of actions to achieve a goal
8 the structure or appearance of something
9 used to describe something at the beginning that tells us what will come next
10 particular and detailed
11 the result of bringing something back to good condition
12 to identify something or something that's been seen before

Unit 5

apologize
(v) to say you are sorry for something
We'd like to apologize for the defective product you bought in our store.
The student apologized for her unacceptable behaviour.

appreciate
(v) to be grateful for something
I'd appreciate it if you could call me back.
I really appreciate your coming all this way to see me.

cancel
(v) to stop a contract or previously arranged event from happening
You know, I feel like canceling my subscription to your newspaper.
He had to cancel the picnic because it was raining.

claim
(v) to say or maintain that something is true
The customer claims that a salesperson was very rude.
He claims that we've already met, but I believe he's mistaken.

clue
(n) something that helps to solve a problem, mystery, or crime
You will hear clues in the telephone message.
Detectives look for clues to help them catch the criminal.

compensate
(v) to pay someone for damages, expenses, or costs
To compensate you for your inconvenience …
My boss compensated me for my business travel costs.

compensation
(n) money paid for damages, expenses, or costs
We should offer some compensation to keep them happy.
She received compensation when her refrigerator broke the day after she bought it.

complainant
(n) an organization or a person who expresses dissatisfaction or displeasure with something
Name of complainant.
The complainant demanded to be taken straight to the hotel manager.

complaint
(n) the act of expressing dissatisfaction or displeasure with something
The caller will make either a request or a complaint.
Please make your complaints to the manager on duty.

condition
(n) a state of being; circumstances
You must pick out any special conditions that need to be dealt with.
We cannot renew your contract under these conditions.

confirm
(v) to check that something is correct
You will be able to confirm the name when it is repeated.
Please confirm your seat reservation the day before, as flights tend to be overbooked in the summer.

confusion
(n) uncertainty, misunderstanding of a situation or the facts
There was some confusion over the tools your team required.
He apologized for creating confusion among his crew.

damage
(v) to cause harm or injury to
A truck driver with your company damaged a customer's car.
The rain damaged my book.

defective

(adj) broken or not working properly

We'd like to apologize for the defective product you bought.

This radio doesn't work. I think it's defective.

definitely

(adv) certainly, without a doubt

It was definitely on the request I submitted and I really need it.

I definitely need to talk to the manager today.

disappointed

(adj) unsatisfied and unhappy because something was not as expected

I'm really disappointed that I've been paying extra for delivery.

I was very disappointed when I found out that our trip was canceled.

explanation

(n) a statement which gives the reasons for or the details of something

Generally, it's a good idea to include an explanation of the problem and its cause.

He gave me a full explanation of how this machine worked.

generally

(adv) usually, in most cases

Generally, it's a good idea to include an explanation of the problem and its cause.

Generally, proposals are requested as early as possible.

impression

(n) an effect, opinion, or an image of something that stays in someone's mind

We have a lot of customers and we want to make a good impression.

Be early for the job interview so you won't make a bad impression.

inconvenience

(n) discomfort or trouble

Once again, I am very sorry for any inconvenience this has caused.

I hope this matter was not an inconvenience for you.

misspell

(v) to spell something incorrectly

You misspelled a customer's name on a bill.

I accidentally misspelled the company's name.

necessary

(adj) required, needed, or essential to be done, achieved, or available

Your solution (and financial benefit if necessary).

It is absolutely necessary for humans to have food and water.

polite

(adj) showing good manners and courtesy

Polite complaint responses usually follow a set pattern.

The man was very polite and thanked me for returning his wallet.

projector

(n) a piece of equipment that displays an image on a screen

I'm giving a presentation in room 11, but I need a projector.

He used a projector to show his slides and pictures.

request

(n) the act of asking politely or formally for something or some favor

The caller will make either a request or a complaint.

I called the radio station and requested a song.

role

(n) the usual or expected purpose of something or someone

You will hear clues as to the role you are to play in your response.

Money plays an important role in our society today.

rude

(adj) disagreeable or unpleasant in manner or action

The customer claims that the sales person was very rude.

The rude man slammed the door in my face.

similar

(adj) things that are alike or share some qualities

Try to remember similar situations that you have experienced.

That suit looks very similar to mine.

sincerely

(adv) in a straightforward, honest and genuine way

We sincerely hope you will accept our apologies for this situation.

He promised sincerely that he would try to stop his bad habit.

situation

(n) the condition or circumstance in which someone finds themselves

We sincerely hope you will accept our apologies for this situation.

After understanding what kind of situation he was in, I forgave him.

solution

(n) the answer to a problem or difficulty

Brainstorm possible causes of the problem, and your solution.

We must come up with a solution before the problem gets worse.

strike

(n) the act of refusing to work as a collective protest against an employer

The parts were delayed due to the airline strike in Europe.

The strike in the factory caused a decrease in production.

submit

(v) to present or hand in for consideration, approval, or judgment

It was definitely on the request that I submitted and I really need it.

All reports must be submitted by 5:00 P.M.

suitable

(adj) right or appropriate for a particular purpose or occasion

You will be scored on dealing with the task in a suitable way.

That suit looks very suitable for the interview.

supposed to

(v) to be required or expected to do something that was arranged before

You will hear clues as to the role you are supposed to play in your response.

Were you not supposed to be on the plane by now?

typical

(adj) usual, common

Read steps 1–6 explaining how to organize a typical response.

It was a typical, dark, mid-sized car.

warehouse

(n) a large building for storing goods, supplies or raw materials

Due to a mistake in the warehouse the wrong color chair was shipped.

He had the goods sent back to the warehouse this morning.

1 Find ten words in the puzzle. Match them with their meanings.

N	A	D	W	A	R	E	H	O	U	S	E	S
S	L	T	E	R	J	U	O	F	E	R	A	D
D	T	K	M	I	E	P	C	L	D	E	N	A
A	G	R	B	E	G	U	O	M	C	Q	A	M
P	I	L	I	O	A	R	W	K	L	U	R	A
O	N	U	S	K	V	C	E	T	U	E	B	G
L	C	M	A	Y	E	I	H	O	E	S	Q	E
O	P	E	D	U	K	Z	R	A	X	T	T	N
G	N	T	A	S	P	M	E	G	O	F	I	S
Y	C	O	M	P	E	N	S	A	T	I	O	N
I	F	T	S	H	L	E	V	O	N	A	J	K
R	E	Q	P	R	O	J	E	C	T	O	R	D
F	M	K	G	E	C	U	L	N	A	T	O	P
A	N	I	S	O	L	U	T	I	O	N	M	R

1 a large building for storing goods and other materials
2 the act of refusing to work as a protest against an employer
3 a statement which admits to and regrets mistakes and offences
4 the usual or expected purpose of something or someone
5 money paid to cover loss
6 to physically cause harm to someone or something
7 a piece of equipment that displays an image on a screen
8 the answer to a problem or difficulty
9 a hint or something that helps to solve a problem, mystery or crime
10 the act of asking politely or formally for something

2 Read the definitions and write *true* or *false.*

1 *Appreciate* means recognize the value and feel grateful for something.
2 *Claim* means to say that something is true.
3 If you make a *complaint,* you express your pleasure.
4 A *condition* is a state of being; circumstances.
5 *Typical* means not very common.
6 *Rude* people speak kindly to others.
7 If you *confirm* something you want to make sure of the truth.
8 *Definitely* means unsure.
9 If something is *necessary,* it's needed.
10 If you are *disappointed,* you are unhappy about something.
11 If you *submit* something, you don't show it to anyone.
12 *Generally* means usually.
13 *Misspell* means to write a word correctly.
14 If you are *supposed to* do something, you should try to do it.

3 Complete the sentences with the following words.

cancel defective complainant
suitable inconvenience
situation confusion polite
impression similar explanation
sincerely compensate

1 They're going to _____ the game because of the bad weather.
2 We are sorry for any _____ caused to passengers by the delay.
3 The firm isn't in a good _____ after losing a lot of money.
4 The _____ has asked for his money back.
5 The employee had to give a full _____ of why he hadn't finished the project.
6 The company would like to make a good _____ on its new client.
7 It's important to be _____ to all of our customers.
8 We will be playing sport, so please wear _____ clothes.
9 There was _____ about the time of the meeting, so some people were late.
10 The men look _____ ; they both have brown hair and brown eyes.
11 We both _____ promised never to be late for work again.
12 We'd like to _____ you for all the problems.
13 I think my new cell phone is _____ – it won't work properly.

Unit 6

ban
(v) to make it illegal for something to be done, used, seen or read
Some people believe private cars should be banned from city centers.
The use of the poisonous substance was banned.

competition
(n) a situation in which people or organizations do something to try to beat someone and/or win something
Competition is a fact of life, and children should learn to be competitive when they are young.
Several companies are in competition for the contract.

cruise
(n) a journey by sea in a ship for pleasure
You have just won a contest, and for your prize you can choose either a small car or a luxury cruise.
Would you like to join me in a cruise around the Caribbean this summer?

develop
(v) to create or produce over time; to improve by a process of growth
We will practice how to express and develop an opinion.
It is interesting to see how the human brain develops over the ages.

express
(v) to reveal your thoughts and feelings about something
We will practice how to express your ideas.
Children may use drawings as a way to express their feelings.

financial
(adj) relating to money or finance
The actual cost for a repair is usually only in time and effort and not really of any financial cost to you.
After losing his job, he has had many financial problems.

individual
(adj) single, separate, something done by oneself
Would you rather play an individual sport or a team sport?
Have you got any individual rooms?

intelligent
(adj) having the ability to demonstrate knowledge and skills
When hiring a new employee, would you choose someone who is very intelligent?
The famous scientist is a very intelligent man.

link
(v) to connect, join or associate something or someone with another
We will practice how to link your ideas.
They linked the falling sales to the recent increase in prices.

opinion
(n) the view a person has about a certain issue
In this question, you will be asked to give your opinion on a topic.
I strongly disagree with her opinion on this subject.

professional
(n) a person who has a paid job especially one involving training and a formal qualification
Professionals do a better job fixing things.
The footballer has played in the league for many years – he's a real professional.

rather
(adv) showing preference of one thing over another
Would you rather play an individual sport or a team sport?
I think I would rather go home now.

reliable
(adj) dependable and able to be trusted to do what is expected
When hiring a new employee would you choose someone who is very reliable?
My secretary is a very reliable person and is never late for work.

repair
(v) to fix or mend something
Why don't you usually pay others to repair things for you?
I need to have my car tire repaired.

sequence
(n) a series of things arranged in a particular order and connected in some way
Join the ideas together using the sequence words.
You must try to recall the sequence of events.

vary
(v) to be different or to give variety to something
The focus of the question will vary, but will be familiar in context.
The reasons for traveling generally vary among different people.

Quiz Unit 6

1 Choose the correct word.

1 A *competition / cruise* is a journey by sea in a ship for pleasure.
2 *Professional / Financial* means someone who has a paid job especially one involving training and a formal qualification.
3 *Intelligent / Individual* means having the ability to gain and apply knowledge and skills.
4 If you *express / ban* something you make it illegal.
5 To *repair / develop* something is to fix or mend it.

6 To *vary / link* means to be different.
7 A *sequence / opinion* is a series of things arranged in a particular order.

2 Read the definitions and write the words.

1 showing preference for one thing over another *(rehatr)* r_____
2 a situation in which people do something to try to win *(iincmopetto)* c_____
3 involving or connected with money *(nacaifnli)* f_____
4 something done by oneself *(vidiidulna)* i_____
5 a person's views about an issue *(nopiion)* o_____
6 to reveal your thoughts and feelings *(ssxpere)* e_____
7 dependable and able to be trusted *(iabelrle)* r_____
8 to connect something or someone with another *(knil)* l_____
9 to create or produce over time; to improve by a process of growth *(podvele)* d_____

Unit 7

apologize
(v) to say you are sorry for something
We apologize for any inconvenience.
She apologized to the customer for the mistake in their order.

cancel
(v) to call off, usually without expectation of conducting or performing at a later time
He thinks the project will be canceled.
The game was canceled because of the rain.

coach

(v) to train someone in sports or some other type of performance
He coached our winning softball team.
The tennis star was coached by her father.

colonial

(adj) relating to a colony (a country ruled by another country)
We have a special display of colonial era items.
The colonial era ended when my country became independent.

complex

(adj) complicated; hard to separate, analyze, or solve
Complex sentences are divided up into shorter chunks.
The professor's speech was very complex and difficult to understand.

delay

(v) to put something off or make it late
The train has been delayed for thirty minutes.
I was delayed because of the heavy traffic.

disposal

(n) the process of getting rid of something you don't want
Please come up and take care of my garbage disposal.
We called a disposal company to pick up the broken stove.

essential

(adj) of the very highest importance
We will be doing essential work on the server.
It is essential that you pay these bills by Friday.

facilities

(n) something that is built, installed, or established to serve a particular purpose
We have luxurious spa facilities that other clubs can't match.
The facilities include a pool, a weight room and showers.

fireworks

(n) devices designed to make a loud and visual explosion when lit
The fireworks are on Sunday evening.
Let's go see the fireworks tonight at the festival.

guarantee

(v) to make a (usually formal) promise of quality
We guarantee we'll make you a happy customer.
The MP3 player was guaranteed for three years after purchase.

inconvenience

(n) discomfort or trouble
We apologize for any inconvenience.
Having to go to another building to take a shower was a very big inconvenience.

indicate

(v) to point out or show something
The marks indicate when the reader pauses.
The flashing light indicates the temperature is too high.

leak

(n) the accidental escape of liquid or gas
The builder couldn't fix the leak in the roof.
Water was leaking out of a hole in the bath.

orientation

(n) a meeting in which introductory information is given
You will be attending an orientation session.
My first morning at the job was mainly a long orientation.

refreshments

(n) things to eat, usually light food or snacks
You will have about 20 minutes to buy soft drinks and other refreshments.
After the meeting, there will be free refreshments outside.

refurbishment

(n) the act of restoring something to a cleaner and better state
The museum is closed for refurbishment at the moment.
The old dirty office is really in need of refurbishment.

session

(n) a period of time spent doing something
You will be attending an orientation session.
I had to go to a training session on the new software.

spa

(n) a health resort featuring mineral baths
We have luxurious spa facilities that other clubs can't match.
Visiting a health spa can be the perfect way to reenergize one's body and mind.

terrace

(n) a flat outdoor area used for sitting or eating
Take in the view from our roof-top terrace.
It was sunny, so we had lunch on the terrace.

terrific

(adj) very good, inspiring enthusiasm
The Thornburg summer festival got off to a terrific start today.
The food in the restaurant was terrific!

Quiz Unit 7

1 Complete the sentences with the correct word.

cancel guarantee terrific
facilities leak refreshments
colonial indicate orientation
essential delayed

1   If the project isn't finished this week, we will _____ the trip to Singapore.

2   The plane has been _____ by three hours.

3   We _____ you will be happy with all of our products.

4   The country wasn't independent during the _____ era.

5   Higher profits are _____ for the success of the company.

6 I'll _____ when its time for you to begin your speech.

7 We need a plumber. There's a _____ in the bathroom.

8 We stayed in a _____ 5-star hotel in the Caribbean. It was wonderful.

9 I met my new colleagues at the _____ meeting on my first day.

10 _____ are available in the café on the ground floor.

11 The party was _____ . Everybody really enjoyed themselves.

2 Match the words with the definitions.

> inconvenience session coach
> complex refurbishment
> apologize spa terrace
> fireworks disposal

1 devices designed to make a loud and visual explosion when lit
2 to say you are sorry for something
3 a health resort that has mineral baths
4 discomfort or trouble
5 restoring something to a better and cleaner state
6 an area where you can sit outside a building
7 to train someone in sports or another type of performance
8 complicated; having many parts
9 the process of getting rid of something you don't want
10 a period of time spent doing something

Unit 8

appear
(v) to seem likely or seem to be the case
He appears to be writing a report.
This looks like the kitchen and they appear to be cooking something.

background
(n) the setting and surroundings behind something
Take turns to speculate about the background.
The photographer always used a black background.

coworker
(n) someone who works with other people in the same place
I think the people in the picture are coworkers.
Yesterday I had an argument with one of my coworkers.

character
(n) a person in a book, movie, story or other scene
… begin to speculate about the characters.
The characters in the novel are very interesting.

demonstrate
(v) to show or prove the existence of some thing or ability
In order to score well, you must demonstrate as fully as possible what you can say.
The soccer player demonstrated his amazing skills in front of the fans.

dentist
(n) a doctor who treats conditions involving the teeth and gums
He looks like a dentist or a doctor maybe.
Most people get their teeth checked by a dentist every six months.

emotional (state)
(adj) connected with a person's current mental situation, feelings and emotions
What is her emotional state?
He was in a very happy and excited emotional state after he won.

expand
(v) to make or become larger or greater in number or amount
Expand your description to talk about things that may be about to happen.
Most metals expand when heated.

fashionable
(adj) following a style that is popular at a particular time
This restaurant looks really fashionable.
The movie star was seen in the fashionable new club.

fit
(adj) strong and healthy because of regular exercise
She's probably an athlete because she looks fit.
He jogs 5 miles a day to keep fit.

lean
(v) to rest against something for support
They look like they are leaning against a car.
The tired child was leaning on his mother's arm.

refund
(n) a sum of money given back to someone
He might be asking for a refund.
Because the shirt I bought was too small, I was given a refund.

report
(n) a written document that gives information about something
He appears to be writing a report.
I have to write a report on the new sales campaign.

speculate
(v) to guess something without firm evidence
Focus on how to speculate and talk about details in the picture you are not sure about.
Speculating can sometimes lead to incorrect conclusions.

unsure
(adj) doubtful, uncertain about, or lacking confidence in someone or something
Talk about details in the picture that you are unsure about.
I was unsure of how to start the unfamiliar computer program.

1 Choose the correct word.

1 If you are *fit / unsure*, you are healthy and exercise regularly.

2 If something *speculates / appears* to happen, it seems to be likely.

3 A *background / report* is a written document giving information about something.

4 Your *emotional state / character* is your current mental situation and feelings.

5 *Dentists / Coworkers* are people who work in the same place.

6 A *fashionable / fit* person is someone who follows current fashions.

7 *Characters / Coworkers* are people in a book or movie.

2 Read the definitions and write *true* or *false*.

1 *Lean* means to rest against something for support.

2 A *dentist* is someone who looks after the condition of your feet.

3 You give someone a *refund* if you are returning money to them.

4 The *background* is the setting behind someone or something.

5 To *speculate* means to know something is definitely true.

6 If something *expands* it becomes smaller.

7 If you are *unsure,* you are certain about something.

8 To *demonstrate* means to show or prove the existence of some thing.

Unit 9

activity
(n) something that a person does or takes part in
Describe a summer activity that is popular in your community.
I have prepared many interesting activities for my students to enjoy.

additional
(adj) more than was first mentioned or expected
To add additional supporting sentences ...
For a small additional charge, the man brought me an extra large coffee.

alternative
(adj) different (from the usual) that can be used instead of something else
Use cell phones as an alternative way to tell the time and date.
An alternative decision would be to reduce our costs.

argument
(n) a reason used to support a point of view or opinion
We will look at how to introduce opposing arguments.
His main argument was that the cost of the program was too high.

community
(n) a group of people living together in the same area
Describe a summer activity that is popular in your community.
The elementary school in our community is one of the best in the state.

conclusion
(n) the decision or a final part of the argument made after comparing the facts
If you added an opposing point, add a final conclusion sentence.
After studying the report his conclusion was that the product was too expensive.

device
(n) a way of doing something or a machine that performs a certain task
If you need time to think, use English hesitation devices.
A device which allows you to take pictures is called a camera.

education
(n) a process of gaining knowledge and information through teaching and learning
How do you think English education could be improved in your community?
Her education included four years at a university in Europe.

exercise
(n) physical activity or movement
My favourite sport is ice hockey because it is good exercise.
Due to lack of exercise, I gained 10 kg.

facility
(n) buildings, services, or equipment designed to provide a function, or to fulfill a need
What type of entertainment facility would you like to see opened in your community?
This hotel has a large number of facilities including a pool and a gym.

hesitation
(n) the act of pausing to think
If you need time to think, use English hesitation devices.
During the interview, she was able to answer all my questions without any hesitation.

improve
(v) to make better than before
How do you think English education could be improved in your community?
He started jogging everyday to improve his health.

model
(n) an example that should be imitated
Follow an appropriate organization model for the question.
As I have never done this before, I would appreciate a model to follow.

opposing
(adj) very different to or actively against something else
If you include opposing points, you should finish with a sentence that restates your opinion.
The opposing side in the debate made a lot of good points.

physical
(adj) related to the body
How important is it for children to take part in physical education in school?
Running a marathon is an amazing physical feat.

popular
(adj) attractive to or appreciated by a wide range of people
Describe a summer activity that is popular in your community.
I wish I could be more popular and have lots of friends.

regular
(adj) having a fixed or equal space or time between events
How important do you think it is for children to do regular physical exercise?
I practice English on a regular basis.

research
(n) an organized study or investigation on a subject to discover facts
Imagine that you are taking part in a market research telephone interview.
Research on car accidents shows wearing a seatbelt increases survival chances.

restate
(v) to say the same thing again, usually to clarify or summarize what has been said already

If you include opposing points, you should finish with a sentence that restates your opinion.
Could you please restate your goals?

signal
(v) to make a gesture or sign to communicate a message
You should signal your conclusion after you give an opposing point.
A red light signals that you must not cross the street.

skill
(n) the ability to do something well; expertise
How important is if for people to have computer skills, and why?
His greatest skill is getting people to work together.

stylish
(adj) having good taste and looking sophisticated and fashionable
I think watches look very stylish and professional.
He always dresses in a stylish and expensive fashion.

Quiz Unit 9

1 Use the words to complete the crossword.

> model signal additional improve education community facility argument device exercise

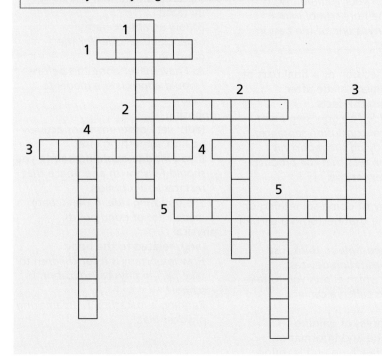

Clues

Across →
1 an example that should be imitated
2 a reason used to support a point of view or opinion
3 something designed to provide a function or service
4 equipment or place to perform a certain function or task
5 something extra or added on to something else

Down ↓
1 gaining knowledge and information through teaching and learning
2 physical activity or movement
3 an action, gesture or sign used for communications
4 a group of people living together in the same area
5 to make something better than it was before

2 Complete the sentences with the following words.

> popular conclusion hesitation opposing activity physical alternative research stylish restate skills regular

1 If you aren't sure what to say during a speech, use a _____ device.
2 I like my boss, but we often have _____ views.
3 I would like to _____ that my opinion about wages has not changed.
4 Every year, the company offers a new _____ for its employees to take part in.
5 If your idea isn't working, try to think of an _____ .
6 It's important to eat meals at _____ times.
7 I used to work for a market _____ company.

8 The new secretary has excellent computer _____ .

9 My boss wears expensive clothes and always looks _____ .

10 When you write an essay you always need to finish with a _____ .

11 Doing _____ exercise three times a week is good for your health.

12 Baseball and American football are very _____ in the US.

Unit 10

acknowledge
(v) to give a response that shows that something has been noticed or received
Start by acknowledging the person's request.
The letter acknowledges that they have received our complaint.

adjourn
(v) to stop or postpone something
At four o'clock, the meeting will be adjourned.
The vice president suggested we adjourn the meeting until tomorrow.

agenda
(n) a list of items to be discussed at a meeting
The information found on an agenda is usually in note form.
The second point on our agenda is this year's budget.

awkward
(adj) inappropriate and/or uncomfortable for the situation
Use phrases to avoid creating awkward silence.
He was very awkward the first time he met the new manager.

book
(v) to make a reservation of something for a specific time
The bluebird restaurant was fully booked.
If you want tickets to that show, you should book well in advance.

campaign
(n) a planned series of actions aimed at achieving a goal
In the meeting the president discussed the advertising campaign.
The recent sales campaign was very successful.

conference
(n) a long meeting or series of meetings to discuss important matters of common interest
On May the 23rd there will be a graphic design conference.
I've been asked to be a guest speaker at the national conference.

confirm
(v) to check or state that something is correct or definite
Please confirm attendance by phone or e-mail.
Mr. Smith confirmed that he will be arriving at nine o'clock.

limousine
(n) a large vehicle for transporting passengers to and from the airport
The limousine will pick you up and take you to head office.
We'll take a limousine to the hotel.

maintain
(v) to make something continue without major change
At 11:15 there is a presentation on maintaining consistent color.
The machine operators watch carefully to maintain a constant temperature.

performance
(n) the manner or effectiveness of the way something or somebody functions
The second presentation is on maximizing sales performance.
Our new training procedures aim to improve staff performance.

performer
(n) a person who does artistic work such as music
Miss Rhodes was a very popular performer at last year's show.
She can sing like an angel and is a very talented performer.

plenary
(adj) attended by every member
There will be a plenary discussion starting at two o'clock.
The delegates held a plenary meeting to discuss the problem.

prior
(adj) earlier in time, before
Please confirm attendance, one week prior to the meeting.
You should call the airline prior to the date of your flight.

raffle
(n) a kind of lottery to raise money, often for an organization or charity
The prize raffle will take place at 10 o'clock.
I won a trip to Hawaii in the club raffle.

sample
(n) a small amount or single example of something used to demonstrate its qualities
I need to deliver some samples for the demonstration.
They were giving out sample copies of the new book at the conference.

schedule
(n) a plan that lists all the things you need to do and at what particular time
What do we have on the schedule after the managers' meeting finishes?
The meeting is scheduled for four o'clock.

stationery
(n) things used in writing such as paper, pens, envelopes, etc.
At three o'clock there's a presentation on customizing business stationery.
The company used expensive beige stationery for all letters.

summarize
(v) to make or give a shortened version of something that has been said or written
Summarizing multiple pieces of information …
Can you summarize the main points of the article for me?

trend
(n) a current tendency or fashion
You will be meeting to discuss recent sales trends.
There is a recent trend to invest in overseas companies.

vendor
(n) a company or person who sells something
You can visit the vendor exhibits all day long in the main hall.
I bought my lunch from a food vendor outside the main building.

1 Choose the correct word.

1 The pens are in the _____ cupboard.
(A) sample
(B) vendor
(C) stationery
(D) performance

2 It's getting late, so the meeting will be _____ until tomorrow.
(A) summarized
(B) adjourned
(C) booked
(D) confirmed

3 The new ad _____ has been very successful so far.
(A) performance
(B) conference
(C) campaign
(D) limousine

4 We're going to a sales _____ in March.
(A) vendor
(B) stationery
(C) campaign
(D) conference

5 I _____ a table at the new Italian restaurant.
(A) booked
(B) sampled
(C) maintained
(D) adjourned

6 The school will raise money by having a _____ .
(A) raffle
(B) sample
(C) performance
(D) stationery

7 We have decided to change our _____ for tomorrow and begin at 9:00 a.m.
(A) vendor
(B) schedule
(C) sample
(D) stationery

8 Unfortunately recent sales _____ haven't been good.
(A) performers
(B) samples
(C) plenaries
(D) trends

9 The singer at this year's office party was an excellent _____ .
(A) sample
(B) campaign
(C) conference
(D) performer

10 There were several _____ silences during our first business meeting.
(A) summarize
(B) awkward
(C) parallel
(D) maintain

2 Choose the correct word.

1 A *performance / campaign* is the effectiveness of how something or somebody functions.

2 *Acknowledge / Adjourn* means to give a response that shows something has been noticed.

3 A *performance / limousine* is a large vehicle for transporting passengers to and from the airport.

4 A *vendor / stationery* is a company or person that sells something.

5 *Plenary / Prior* means attended by every member.

6 To *summarize / confirm* is to make or give a shortened version of something.

7 If you *confirm / book* something, you check the truth of it.

8 To *summarize / maintain* is to keep something working continuously without major change.

9 *Prior / Trend* means earlier in time.

10 A *sample / raffle* is a small amount of something.

11 The last point on the *stationery / agenda* is usually "any other business".

Unit 11

appreciate
(v) to be grateful for something
I'd appreciate if you could call me back.
I really appreciated the card you sent me in hospital.

bother
(v) to annoy, disturb
I really hate to bother you like this.
Those noisy children upstairs really bother me when I'm trying to work.

charge
(n) a fee or cost for buying or doing something
If you pay an extra charge, we can put extra workers on the project.
There's an extra $25 service charge on weekends.

client
(n) a customer or organization you provide goods or services to
I have an all-day meeting with some important clients.
This client has made some very large orders in the past year.

complaint
(n) the act of expressing dissatisfaction or displeasure with something
The caller will make either a request or a complaint.
We have had many complaints about late deliveries.

confirm
(v) to check or state that something is correct or definite
I will call you (tomorrow) to confirm this.
Can you confirm that Mr. Jones will be attending the meeting on Tuesday?

consideration
(n) long and careful thinking
Thanks for your consideration.
After much consideration, he decided not to accept the job offer.

contractor

(n) an individual or company, who does a specific job on a contract

I'm a contractor that builds houses in the valley.

I hired a contractor to fix the pipes in the building.

custom

(adj) made to a special order or for a special purpose

It usually takes three weeks to make custom furniture.

Charlie uses a custom-made set of golf clubs.

day care center

(n) a place where children are cared for and supervised for part of the day

This is Marge from the Little Angel Day Care Center on the 11th floor.

Many parents leave their children in day care centers.

desperate

(adj) in an extremely difficult, serious or dangerous situation

I'm really desperate.

The order didn't arrive, so there was a desperate shortage.

emergency

(n) an unexpected problem or sudden event that must be dealt with quickly

However, as this is an emergency …

We have an emergency on the 10th floor. There's been a fire.

engagement

(n) a fixed or already scheduled arrangement

He can't come because he has another engagement this evening.

Sorry, I've got a prior engagement and can't make it.

grant

(v) to comply with a request or allow something as a favor

Give an explanation of why the request is difficult to grant.

The government minister refused to grant an interview.

imagination

(n) the creative part of your mind that forms images and ideas

You must use your imagination to think of possible reasons.

John has a great imagination and can tell really funny stories.

immediately

(adv) as soon as possible, without delay

Please call me immediately and we can get started.

I jumped on the train and it immediately left the station.

operator

(n) someone who owns or runs a business

Please contact the tour operator and ask them to send a brochure.

The operator of the bus line has said the service will continue tomorrow.

possibility

(n) something that is possible

In this question, you may have to talk about possibilities.

There is a very small possibility that we might get this contract.

reasonably

(adv) to a degree that is fairly good, but not very good

You can build a complete response of small, reasonably simple parts.

It wasn't a great meal, but it was reasonably tasty.

recognize

(v) to identify someone or something you've seen before

You must show you recognize the problem.

I didn't recognize the man whom I had worked with five years before.

request

(n) the act of asking somebody to do something, or give something

The caller will make either a request or a complaint.

I made a request to my boss for some paid holidays.

requestor

(n) the person who makes a request

Write the name of the requestor in the space provided.

Using the requestor's name makes a message more personal.

spare

(v) to give up something to another person without great cost to oneself

I could spare you about a half an hour at lunch time.

Can you spare $10? I left my wallet at home.

suitable

(adj) the right person or thing for a particular purpose or job

Think of a suitable explanation and solution for the problem.

I think the most suitable response is to offer a free replacement item.

translator

(n) someone who translates from one language to another in speech or writing

I'm looking for a translator to come with me on a business trip.

My brother works as a translator from English to Japanese.

Yellow Pages™

(n) a telephone directory printed on yellow paper that contains the names and addresses of local businesses

I saw your ad in the Yellow Pages.

Looking in the Yellow Pages is a popular way to find a business or service.

Quiz Unit 11

1 Use the definitions to find the words to complete the puzzle.

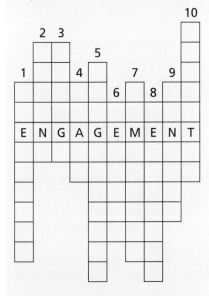

Clues

1 an unexpected problem or sudden event that must be dealt with quickly

2 a customer or organization you provide goods or services to

3 a fee or cost for buying or doing something

4 to comply with a request or allow something as a favour

5 the ability to use the creative part of your mind to form images and ideas

6 to ask somebody to do something

7 a statement that you're unhappy with something

8 to identify someone or something you've seen before

9 to check that something is correct

10 someone who owns or runs a business

2 Complete the sentences with the following words.

appreciate custom translator requestor immediately Yellow Pages desperate consideration possibilities day care center

1 I got to work and _____ went to see the director.

2 If you could write this report as soon as possible I would really _____ it.

3 This report is written in French so I need to find a _____ .

4 There are several _____ for the location of our new offices.

5 If people want _____ furniture they have to wait longer.

6 The company provides an excellent _____ for small children.

7 Who is the _____ for these machines?

8 I'm getting a bit _____ here, I really don't understand these figures.

9 I found your service advertised in the _____ .

10 It's clear he's given a lot of _____ to this very detailed report.

3 Match the words with the definitions.

bother suitable contractor reasonably spare

1 to annoy, disturb or give extra work to someone

2 an individual or company who does a specific job

3 to give up something to another person without great cost to yourself

4 to a degree that is fairly good, but not very good

5 the right person or thing for a particular purpose or job.

Unit 12

argument
(n) the reason used to support a point of view
In this unit, we will focus on opposing arguments.
His main argument was that the cost of the program was too high.

commute
(n) the journey to and from work
The longer day may not be suitable for people who have a long commute to work.
I have only a short commute to work.

conclusion
(n) the decision or final part of an argument made after comparing all the facts
… before giving your final conclusion.
After studying the report, his conclusion was that the product was too expensive.

consider
(v) to think about something carefully in order to make an opinion
All things considered, I would …
She considered her options carefully.

express
(v) to state your thoughts and feelings about something
We practiced how to express and develop opinions.
John is a very good speaker and is able to express his ideas clearly.

issue
(n) the topic of discussion or main subject
Decide your opinion on the issue.
The key issue was whether to close the Toronto plant or not.

opposing
(adj) actively against something
In this unit, we will focus on opposing arguments.
The opposing side in the debate made a lot of good points.

rough
(adj) generally correct, but not exact or detailed, approximate
Use the following rough guide to time your essay.
As a rough estimate, it should take about 20 minutes to get there.

sequence
(v) to do things or arrange things in a set order
Use language for introducing, presenting and sequencing your ideas.
We must sequence the training, so the easier activities come first.

summarize
(v) to make a shortened oral or written version of something
Follow the steps summarized in the Test techniques.
For your homework, summarize what happens in Chapter 4.

superhighway
(n) a highway with several lanes in each direction designed for high-speed travel
I oppose the plan to build a new superhighway near where I live.
Superhighways are very noisy and create a lot of pollution.

supporting
(adj) used to describe people, things, or ideas in a secondary or assisting role
Brainstorm two or three supporting reasons.
His supporting arguments were very strong.

1 Read the definitions and write *true* or *false*.

1 To *summarize* is to make something longer.

2 *Consider* means to think about something carefully.

3 The *superhighway* is a highway that's designed for high speed travel.

4 To have a long *commute* means to have known someone for a long time.

5 The *conclusion* is the beginning of an argument.

6 An *argument* is the reason used to support a point of view.

7 *Supporting* ideas are secondary to the main ideas.

8 To *express* is to listen to somebody's ideas.

9 If you are *opposing,* you agree with somebody's ideas.

10 An *issue* is the topic of discussion or main subject.

11 A *rough* guide is an approximate guide.

12 To *sequence* is to do things in a set order.

Unit 13

accurate
(adj) correct and free from errors
The sentence must relate to the picture and must be grammatically accurate.
The news story was an accurate report of what happened.

appropriate
(adj) suitable for a particular situation
The present continuous is often the most appropriate tense if you are describing an action.
A dark suit and tie is appropriate clothing for a wedding.

combination
(n) a mixture of different things
The types of words given in the question may be a combination of a noun, verb, etc.
The meal was a combination of various meat and fish dishes.

compare
(v) to look for things that are the same or different between two or more things
Compare the words you have chosen.
Look in different shops and compare prices when buying expensive things.

construction
(n) a group of words with a particular grammatical structure
Be familiar with SVO constructions.
The text gives many examples of past tense constructions.

dessert
(n) sweet food usually eaten at the end of a meal
The chefs are finishing the desserts.
My favorite dessert is chocolate cake.

neat
(adj) clean and well ordered
The man has a neat desk.
The boy's room was very neat after he spent an hour cleaning and organizing it.

obvious
(adj) easy to see or understand
Check you haven't made any obvious grammatical mistakes.
Is the mark on my shirt really obvious?

relate
(v) to connect two or more things together
Choose ones that relate to the picture.
How does your story relate to the problem?

relevance
(n) the logical connection between one thing and another
Your sentences will be scored on the relevance of the sentence to the picture.
The comments he made had no relevance to the situation.

technique
(n) the special ability or way in which you do something
He wanted to learn techniques to improve his test score.
The star hockey player had an excellent skating technique.

uniform
(n) a set of clothes with a particular look used to identify a particular job, team or group
The chefs are wearing uniforms.
All of the workers wore dark blue uniforms.

1 Choose the correct word.

1 Always read through your work and look for _____ mistakes.
(A) accurate
(B) neat
(C) obvious
(D) compare

2 We didn't employ him because his experience had no _____ to the job.
(A) dessert
(B) construction
(C) technique
(D) relevance

3 Students should study the _____ of different sentences.
(A) obvious
(B) constructions
(C) techniques
(D) uniform

4 His comments were not _____ for the situation – he shouldn't have said that.
(A) construction
(B) obvious
(C) appropriate
(D) relevance

5 Could you _____ these two reports and e-mail your comments to me?
(A) compare
(B) relate
(C) combination
(D) decorate

6 I've checked the summary and it's a(n) _____ account of the matter.
(A) relevance
(B) uniform
(C) neat
(D) accurate

2 Read the definitions and write the words.

1 sweet food usually eaten at the end of a meal *(ssertde)* d_____

2 clean and well-ordered *(taen)* n_____

3 a mixture of things *(ntonicmbaoi)* c_____

4 a set of clothes used to identify a particular job, team or group *(oruinfm)* u_____

5 to have a connection with something else *(atreel)* r_____

6 the special ability or way in which you do something *(chteniqeu)* t_____

Unit 14

accounting
(n) the activity or job of checking and maintaining business records
She is reading the book so that she can learn about accounting.
They wanted someone with accounting experience to look after the company payroll.

affect
(v) to change or have an effect on something or someone
Note that the order of the clauses can be switched without affecting the meaning.
The change in weather affected the farmer's plans greatly.

approximate
(adj) close in number or similarity, but not exactly the same
Now apply the Test tactics at the approximate test speed.
He was asked to give the approximate cost of the repairs.

attract
(v) to make people want to go somewhere
So they can attract more customers, they have reduced prices.
If we advertise well, we will attract people from all over the country.

combine
(v) to join or mix something or things together
Sentences 1–5 combine a main clause and a subordinate clause.
Some diets mean not combining certain food groups.

independent
(adj) not dependent, or reliant, on someone or something
"We ate in the garden" is an independent clause.
I became independent when I left home and got a job.

indicate
(v) to point out or show something
The conjunction indicates the purpose/goal of the main clause.
The sign indicated that the road was closed.

melt
(v) to change from a solid (e.g. ice) to a liquid (e.g. water)
Most of the snow has melted.
If you don't eat your ice cream quickly it will melt.

obvious
(adj) easy to see or understand
Check and correct any obvious mistakes.
Is the mark on my shirt really obvious?

reduce
(v) to make something smaller in size or number
So they can attract more customers, they have reduced prices.
We have reduced our sales staff from 5 to 3 people.

relationship
(n) a connection or bond between two or more things
Use the conjunction to find the relationship between the two clauses.
The two companies had a strong business relationship.

separate
(adj) not together or in the same place
The words given do not have to be placed in separate clauses.
The couple had a fight and they left in separate taxis.

stretch
(n) an exercise to loosen parts of the body
The players are doing some stretches before they play football.
Stretches can help you relax after a long journey.

1 Find seven words in the puzzle. Match them with their meanings.

G	P	A	T	T	R	A	C	T	D	R	R	I
C	S	T	R	E	T	C	H	J	E	V	E	P
L	F	U	C	A	Y	H	I	B	G	A	L	U
I	R	N	G	U	C	O	R	W	C	X	A	S
D	W	O	J	T	K	F	P	C	A	E	T	O
H	I	S	U	S	I	U	U	L	H	N	I	G
D	K	R	H	E	K	L	E	N	S	T	O	B
T	C	B	A	C	E	C	L	O	L	I	N	H
A	J	M	R	C	Z	U	A	E	F	U	S	C
Q	G	F	U	O	P	I	M	R	I	P	H	A
U	A	D	I	H	A	S	C	P	M	K	I	R
O	E	P	K	E	S	N	J	K	G	O	P	I
R	V	I	N	D	E	P	E	N	D	E	N	T
A	C	C	O	U	N	T	I	N	G	A	F	E

1 to change from a solid to a liquid

2 a connection or similarity between two or more things

3 not dependent, or reliant on someone or something

4 an exercise to loosen parts of the body

5 the activity or job of checking and maintaining business records

6 to make people want to go somewhere

7 to make something smaller in size or number

2 Match the words with the definitions.

> affect approximate separate obvious combine indicate

1 to join or mix something or things together

2 to point out or show something

3 not together or in the same place

4 easy to see or understand

5   to change or have an effect on something or someone
6   close in number or similarity but not exactly the same

Unit 15

appreciate
(v) to be grateful for something
I would appreciate it if you could have your delivery staff use the back entrance.
Mr. Smith really appreciated his retirement gift.

catalog
(n) a booklet that lists goods for sale, usually with pictures and prices
Order one product from a catalog.
They have a very beautiful color catalog of all this year's cars.

convenient
(adj) something that does not involve much effort or trouble
Could you tell us a time convenient for you?
Living next to a large shopping mall is very convenient if you need something.

facility
(n) a place with a clear purpose that provides a service or fulfills a need
You can get a 30% discount at our fully-equipped facility.
The center has all the facilities we need, including meeting rooms, and computer services.

formality
(n) the degree to which something is formal; an official part of a procedure
Match the salutations to the appropriate level of formality.
You must complete all the formalities before you may receive a visa.

human resources
(n) the department in a company that deals with recruiting and managing employees
If you want a transfer, you must apply to human resources.
I have a meeting with human resources to discuss the new job.

opportunity
(n) a chance to do or achieve something positive
What training opportunities are offered by your company?
I quit my job because I had the opportunity to go on a world trip.

postpone
(v) to delay something until a later date or time
Would you mind postponing our meeting until the end of May?
I will have to postpone the trip. I am too busy in July.

regarding
(prep) about, or on the subject or topic of something
Thank you for your e-mail regarding the replacement of my computer.
I would like to talk to you regarding the change in advertising.

representative
(n) somebody who speaks on behalf of someone else
He is the representative of an auto association.
The sales representative has come to show us some books.

respond
(v) to reply to something, often in spoken or written form
You will be given an e-mail to read and respond to.
I responded to the problem with a written complaint.

salutation
(n) the opening (usually) greeting phrase of a letter or speech, e.g. "Dear John", "Hi Joe"
Use salutations at the beginning of your e-mail.
I thought his e-mail salutation of "Hi Mary" was very casual, as we have never met.

superintendent
(n) a type of manager of something (often maintenance), e.g. a system, or building
I told the superintendent of my apartment about the broken window.
To make those changes you will have to speak to the department superintendent.

Quiz Unit 15

1 Choose the correct word.

1   A *catalog / facility* is a booklet that lists goods for sale.
2   A *superintendent / representative* is a type of manager.
3   To *require / respond* is to reply to something.
4   A *salutation / respond* is the opening greeting phrase of a letter or speech.
5   To *postpone / appreciate* means to feel grateful for something.
6   A(n) *opportunity / formality* is a chance to do something positive.

2 Complete the sentences with the following words.

representative regarding
facility   convenient postpone
formality   human resources

1   The center has an excellent sports _____ .
2   A _____ from the marketing department is going to talk to us this afternoon.
3   Is Thursday a _____ day for a meeting?
4   I'm going to _____ our meeting until after my vacation.
5   You need to talk to _____ if you want to work in one of our offices abroad.
6   Remember to wear something to match the _____ of the occasion.
7   Did you receive my e-mail _____ our plans for a new project?

Unit 16

advantage
(n) a good thing that makes something better or more attractive
There are a number of advantages to working longer hours.
The first advantage is the extra rest you get from working a four-day week.

Quiz Unit 16

1 Use the words to complete the crossword.

> express train benefits draft population current shift
> leisure time introduction conclusion advantage

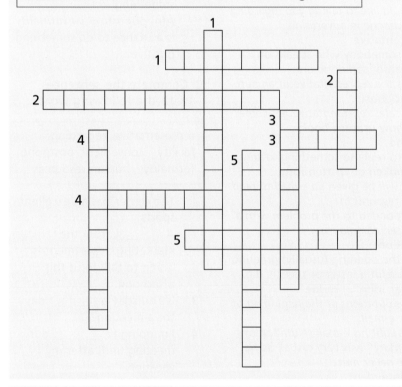

Clues

Across →

1   the positive aspects of something
2   a train or coach that goes from one place to another without making many stops
3   to write a first or rough version of a letter or report
4   happening now, being done or being used at the present
5   all the people or creatures that inhabit an area

Down ↓

1   the first part of an essay, speech, etc
2   a fixed period of working time that can include night work
3   something that gives a positive benefit
4   the final part of an essay, speech, etc
5   free time to enjoy as you wish

benefits
(n) the positive aspects of something
For me the benefits far outweigh the drawbacks.
There are several benefits this kind of therapy can bring.

concentrate
(v) to focus all of your thoughts on one subject or activity
If people were more relaxed, they would probably concentrate better.
Most people can only concentrate for about 40 minutes at a time.

conclusion
(n) the final part of an essay, speech, etc. that summarizes and reinforces the main points; a decision made after all the information has been thought through
A good conclusion should make it very clear what your opinion is.
His conclusion was that we should close the Boston office.

current
(adj) happening now, being done or being used at the present
What do you like most about your current job?
Our current financial situation is much better than last year.

disadvantage
(n) a bad thing that makes something worse or less attractive
There are a number of disadvantages to working longer hours.
His lack of experience was a major disadvantage.

draft
(v) to write a first or rough version of a letter or report
Drafting an essay should always be your first step.
You should always draft your ideas, then revise them later.

express train
(n) a train or coach that goes from one place to another without making many stops
Some people prefer to take express trains.
I'm going to wait to take the express train; this is the slow coach which stops in all the small towns.

expression
(n) a word or phrase that communicates an idea or feeling
Some expressions can make it clear that you have strong opinions.
The expression he used let me know he was very angry!

introduction
(n) the first part of an essay, speech, etc. that introduces the topic and main points
Use your introduction to show clearly what you are writing about.
The introduction to his speech got everyone very interested in the talk.

leisure time

(n) free time to enjoy as you wish
Having an extra day of leisure time would make people more relaxed.
In my leisure time I enjoy reading and playing golf.

outweigh

(v) to be more important than something else
In my opinion, the advantages outweigh the disadvantages.
The problems with this idea outweigh any benefits I can see.

population

(n) all of the people or creatures that inhabit an area
Do you agree that health care should be free for the whole population?
China is the country with the largest population in the world.

reference

(n) something spoken or written that mentions somebody or something else
Your essay should make a clear reference to the question.
At the start of his letter he made a reference to the mistake in last month's bill.

revise

(v) to change something in order to make it better or more correct
You have 30 minutes to plan, write, and revise your essay.
Revising your work can help you find many obvious mistakes.

shift

(n) a fixed period of working time that can include night work
In some occupations, employees must work very long shifts.
I usually work an eight-hour shift, from 11:00 p.m. to 7:00 a.m.

typically

(adv) in the usual or expected way; in most cases
Typically, an effective essay will contain a minimum of 300 words.
It is very unusual for him to be late. Typically, he is at least 30 minutes early.

2 Read the definitions and write *true* or *false*.

1 A *disadvantage* makes things better.

2 To *concentrate* is to focus all your thoughts on something.

3 A *reference* is something spoken or written about somebody else.

4 *Typically* means unexpected.

5 An *expression* is a word or phrase that communicates an idea.

6 To *revise* something is to make it better or more correct.

7 To *outweigh* is to be less important than something else.

Unit 17

alternative

(adj) different (from the usual) that can be used instead of something else
"Or" is used to link alternative things or ideas.
An alternative decision would be to reduce our costs.

cab

(n) a taxi
They must take a cab, or they will miss their plane.
We've got so much shopping, it'll be simpler if we take a cab.

contrasting

(adj) very different (in style, color or attitude) compared with something else
It is used to give contrasting information or show 'why not'.
First class seats and economy seats have greatly contrasting prices.

degree

(n) the relative amount or level of something
Intensifiers are used to give the idea of degree.
When children reach a certain age, you should allow them a degree of independence.

destination

(n) a place to which someone or something is going or being sent
They've almost reached their destination.
We will arrive at our final destination in approximately one hour.

intend

(v) to have a purpose or plan for something
The word "for" shows who is intended to use or have something.
I intended to buy a present for her, but I forgot.

intensifier

(n) a word (adjective/adverb) that makes the meaning of another word stronger
Learn to use intensifiers appropriately.
The words "much" and "very" are intensifiers.

origin

(n) the place where someone or something comes from
The word "from" is used to indicate the origin of someone or something.
No one knew the origin of the statue they found in the temple.

related to

(v) to be connected with someone or something
"about" means "related to".
She's related to my mother.

relevant

(adj) having a logical connection to something else
Make a sentence that is relevant to the picture.
The problem of training is very relevant to this decision.

sunburn

(n) skin which is burnt after being too long in the sun
He will get a bad sunburn.
Be careful you don't get a sunburn today, the sun is very strong.

sunscreen

(n) a cream or lotion used to protect the skin from getting burnt
He must put on sunscreen or he will get a bad sunburn.
I went to the beach and forgot to put on sunscreen.

1 Read the definitions and write the words.

1   having painful skin after spending too long in the sun *(ursbnun)* s_____
2   a place to which someone or something is going or being sent *(sineaitdtno)* d_____
3   the relative amount or level of something *(eerdge)* d_____
4   a word that makes the meaning of another word stronger *(tenifiesirn)* i_____
5   a cream or lotion used to protect the skin from getting burnt *(nenusrecs)* s_____
6   to be connected with someone or something *(latrede ot)* r_____ t_____
7   to have a purpose or plan *(ndntie)* i_____
8   the place where something comes from *(nigori)* o_____
9   having a logical connection to something else *(eealvtnr)* r_____
10 a taxi *(bac)* c_____
11 something that is different compared with something else *(angrocnitst)* c _____
12 something that can be substituted for something else *(veletiraant)* a _____

Unit 18

conditional
(adj) expressing something that will happen only if another thing is done
For picture 1, "unless" has a conditional meaning.
They signed a conditional deal, saying he would buy the house if he got the loan.

contrast
(n) the noticeable differences between two or more things
You will have to make a sentence describing this contrast.
He noticed a great contrast between first class and economy class when he flew.

electricity
(n) a common form of energy used to power lights and all sorts of electric equipment
Unless he fixes the wires, there will be no electricity.
He couldn't watch TV, because there was no electricity in the old house.

indicate
(v) to point out, show or be a sign of something
One word will indicate a contrast.
A red sky indicates fine weather.

ladder
(n) a piece of equipment for climbing up and down
Although he is standing on a ladder, he still can't reach the book.

lifejacket
(n) a safety device you wear to protect from drowning in water
The man can go on the boat only if he wears a lifejacket.
On an airplane, you can find a lifejacket under the seat.

modern
(adj) new, advanced, relating to the present
The new office building was very modern.
Modern airplanes are very safe.

1 Complete the sentences with the following words.

> conditional modern electricity contrast lifejackets indicate ladder

1   We didn't go in the boat because there weren't any _____ .
2   He climbed a _____ to change a light bulb.
3   The deal is _____ ; it will only happen if the directors agree.
4   The _____ between this job and my last job is great.
5   The wires have been accidentally cut which means there's no _____ .
6   I don't like old houses, I prefer _____ buildings.
7   Dark clouds _____ rain.

Unit 19

analyst
(n) somebody with specialist knowledge or skill who studies or examines something
Our long-time financial analyst is retiring next week.
We should hire an analyst to study our problems and make recommendations for the company.

attendance
(n) the number of people who are present, e.g. at an event
The problem with attendance last month was due to many people in the office catching a cold.
There will be about 50 people in attendance.

clerical
(adj) relating to office work or administration
I saw your ad in the newspaper for clerical staff.
We need to advertise for more people to do clerical work.

contract

(n) a legal agreement between people or companies

I have recently learned that your company is not renewing its contract with us.

They signed a contract to buy 100 cases of stationery equipment.

coverage

(n) the amount or percentage of potential customers that can be dealt with in a given area

We can increase our coverage in this area.

Our coverage in Asia is very limited unfortunately.

deadline

(n) the time by which something must be completed

He couldn't attend the meeting because he had a very tight deadline.

We were given a one-month deadline to complete the job.

deserve

(v) to earn or be worthy of something

John deserves a bonus for the great job he did completing the project on time.

She has worked really hard, so she deserves a raise.

expense

(n) the cost spent in order to buy or do something

The extra expense in May is due to an increase in fuel prices.

I want to take a holiday, but I couldn't afford the expense.

explanation

(n) the reasons or details of something

Use marker words (because, due to, so that) to signal your explanation.

They want an explanation of why the shipment is late.

indicate

(v) to point out, show or be a sign of something

Use marker words that indicate what kind of information you are giving.

The message indicated he would be arriving on the next flight.

inquiry

(n) a request for information

Thank you for your inquiry about our new machinery.

He made an inquiry about our price changes.

opinion

(n) a person's personal views or judgments

His opinion was that the plan was a good one.

In my opinion, I think the price is too low.

organize

(v) to arrange something in order to make it more effective or efficient

Use connectors to organize your ideas.

He always organized his work and completed it on time.

overtime

(n) extra time worked beyond the usual hours of your job

Will the job require much overtime?

I have worked 30 hours of overtime this month.

plumbing

(n) the pipes and equipment that carry water or gas in a building

I won't be able to send a repair person to fix your plumbing until next week.

There's a problem with our plumbing. We have no water.

position

(n) a person's job in an organization or company

Could you tell me when the position will begin?

What kind of position would you be looking for in our company?

refer

(v) to say or write something in order to remind you about someone or something else

You are referring to some information you have received.

I'm afraid we no longer sell the product you referred to.

renew

(v) to re-sign something, e.g. a contract, so that it will last for a longer period

I have recently learned that your company is not renewing its contract with us.

I plan to renew my membership at the gym for another three months.

retirement

(n) the act of leaving a job or career, usually around age 60

We would like to celebrate her retirement.

After my retirement, I plan to sail a boat around the world.

solution

(n) the way of successfully dealing with a problem

The solution is for everyone to work harder for a while.

One solution to the problem is to order the parts directly from Spain.

subsequent

(adj) happening or following after something else

Clearly link subsequent points you wish to make.

His first point was very good, but I disagree with his subsequent points.

terrific

(adj) wonderful, amazing

Our terrific sales in June were due to the hiring of three new sales staff.

The new diet is terrific. I have lost 5 kg.

tone

(n) the way in which something is said or written that indicates the attitude of the speaker

Your message should have an appropriate tone.

I thought the tone of his message was very rude.

1 Use the definitions to find the words to complete the puzzle.

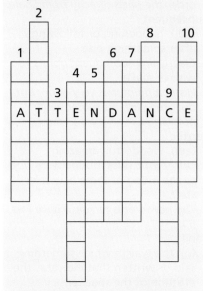

A T T E N D A N C E

Clues

1 somebody with specialist knowledge who studies or examines something
2 extra time worked beyond the usual hours of your job
3 the way in which something is said or written
4 the act of leaving a job or career, usually around age 60
5 a request for information
6 to point out, show or be a sign of something
7 the time by which something must be completed
8 a person's personal views or judgments
9 a legal agreement
10 the cost spent in order to buy or do something

2 Match the words with the definitions.

> clerical organize subsequent
> renew coverage deserve
> explanation

1 the reasons or details of something
2 relating to office work
3 the amount of potential customers that can be dealt with in a given area
4 to earn or be worthy of something
5 to arrange something to make it more effective
6 something happening or following after something else
7 to re-sign something so it will last for a longer period

3 Complete the sentences with the following words.

> plumbing position refer
> solution terrific

1 I want to apply for the _____ of secretary.
2 Please finish the report as I'd like to _____ to it in the meeting.
3 Profits this year have been _____ thanks to your hard work.
4 The _____ needs repairing as we haven't got any hot water.
5 The company will close as there is no _____ to their financial problems.

Unit 20

clarify
(v) to make something clear, by explaining it in detail
It is important to clarify the examples you have given.
Can you clarify the payment details in the last paragraph of this document?

decision
(n) the process of coming to a conclusion about something
Consulting with a group of people is the best way to make a decision.
We need a decision on this problem by next week.

element
(n) a separate part or small amount of something
Become familiar with ways to introduce these key elements.
The contract was very complex so we had to discuss each element.

endanger
(v) to put someone or something in danger
Building the factory would endanger animals living in the area.
The new tax will seriously endanger our profits for next year.

expand
(v) to cause something to become larger in size or number
Expand your introduction.
We have expanded the number of our offices in Europe to fifteen.

ice cap
(n) the thick permanent layers of ice at the North and South poles
The ice caps will melt if we don't stop global warming.
The survey team is investigating changes to the ice caps.

impact
(n) an effect that something or someone has on something or someone else
Spending money on research can have a great impact.
The discount had a huge impact on sales.

lifestyle
(n) the work, leisure, and eating habits that make a person's way of life
One disadvantage to working in a big city is the stressful lifestyle.
To improve my health, the doctor says I must change my lifestyle.

obvious
(adj) easy to see or understand
Edit your work and look for obvious errors.
The misspelled word in the title was very obvious.

polite
(adj) showing good manners and courtesy
You should always be polite to your coworkers.
The receptionist was polite and professional to all the guests.

practical

(adj) concerned with actual facts and experience, rather than theory
The most important factor is practical experience.
His engineering background gives him a very practical approach to problem solving.

stressful

(adj) causing or involving mental or physical stress
Living in a big city can mean heavy traffic and a stressful lifestyle.
Working in the stock market can be very stressful.

supplier

(n) a company that provides things that others need
Unless we change suppliers our costs will stay very high.
Our new supplier will give us a 20% discount on large orders.

support

(v) to provide further evidence of something, to be in favor of something and wish to see it succeed
Use conditional sentences to give support for your ideas.
The increase in sales supports our decision to hire more sales staff.

thesis

(n) the main idea or position someone has with regards to an essay topic
An introductory sentence should appear just before your thesis statement.
Having a clear thesis is the starting point of producing a good paper.

Quiz Unit 20

1 Choose the correct word.

1 When I'm busy, my job can be very _____ .
(A) practical
(B) stressful
(C) obvious
(D) polite

2 Pollution from factories can _____ wild animals.
(A) expand
(B) endanger
(C) clarify
(D) support

3 We need to make a(n) _____ about the possible contract in Singapore.
(A) lifestyle
(B) decision
(C) supplier
(D) element

4 Improving conditions will have a positive _____ on staff performance.
(A) lifestyle
(B) element
(C) thesis
(D) impact

5 We're looking for a new _____ of office furniture who will give us a better discount.
(A) supplier
(B) element
(C) lifestyle
(D) decision

6 We want all our staff to be _____ and well-mannered towards customers.
(A) stressful
(B) obvious
(C) polite
(D) element

2 Read the definitions and write *true* or *false*.

1 The *thesis* is the main idea of an essay.
2 If you *support* your ideas you don't provide evidence.
3 *Clarify* means to make something clear.
4 An *element* is the biggest part of something.
5 *Obvious* means difficult to understand.
6 If you *expand* something you make it smaller.
7 *Ice caps* are thick layers of ice at the North and South poles.
8 A person's *lifestyle* includes their work, leisure, and eating habits.
9 A *practical* person is concerned with theory.

Unit 1

1

1 personal   2 inconvenience
3 destination   4 cancel
5 introduce   6 lounge
7 consider   8 originally
9 nevertheless

2

1 false   2 true   3 true
4 true   5 true   6 false
7 true   8 true   9 false
10 true   11 false   12 true

3

1 B   2 C   3 A   4 D   5 A
6 A   7 B   8 A   9 B   10 D
11 C   12 D

Unit 2

1

1 B   2 D   3 B   4 A   5 C
6 D   7 B   8 A   9 D   10 A

2

1 saltshaker   2 category
3 brainstorm   4 quietly
5 location   6 paintbrush
7 scene   8 introductory
9 response   10 vendor

Unit 3

1

1 appropriately
2 employment   3 firm
4 entertainment facilities
5 celebrate   6 current
7 fireworks   8 vacation

2

1 imagine   2 improve
3 advantage   4 deal   5 prefer
6 interview   7 familiar
8 relevant   9 function
10 participate

Unit 4

1

1 autograph   2 reservation
3 tour   4 Accurate
5 guided tour   6 representative
7 Rarely   8 Appropriate
9 rephrase   10 schedule

2

1 C   2 B   3 B   4 D   5 B
6 A   7 C   8 A   9 D   10 D

3

1 accurately   2 orchestra
3 limousine   4 skim
5 politely   6 avoid
7 campaign   8 form
9 introductory   10 specific
11 renovation   12 recognize

Unit 5

1

N	A	D	W	A	R	E	H	O	U	S	E	S
S	L	T	E	R	J	U	O	F	E	R	A	D
D	T	K	M	I	E	P	C	L	D	E	N	A
A	G	R	B	E	G	U	O	M	C	Q	A	M
P	I	L	I	O	A	R	W	K	L	U	R	A
O	N	U	S	K	V	C	E	T	U	E	B	G
L	C	M	A	Y	E	I	H	O	E	S	Q	E
O	P	E	D	U	K	Z	R	A	X	T	T	N
G	N	T	A	S	P	M	E	G	O	F	I	S
Y	C	O	M	P	E	N	S	A	T	I	O	N
I	F	T	S	H	L	E	V	O	N	A	J	K
R	E	Q	P	R	O	J	E	C	T	O	R	D
F	M	K	G	E	C	U	L	N	A	T	O	P
A	N	I	S	O	L	U	T	I	O	N	M	R

1 warehouse   2 strike
3 apology   4 role
5 compensation   6 damage
7 projector   8 solution
9 clue   10 request

2

1 true   2 true   3 false
4 true   5 false   6 false
7 true   8 false   9 true
10 true   11 false   12 true
13 false   14 true

3

1 cancel   2 inconvenience
3 situation   4 complainant
5 explanation   6 impression
7 polite   8 suitable
9 confusion   10 similar
11 sincerely   12 compensate
13 defective

Unit 6

1

1 cruise   2 Professional
3 Intelligent   4 ban   5 repair
6 vary   7 sequence

2

1 rather   2 competition
3 financial   4 individual
5 opinion   6 express
7 reliable   8 link   9 develop

Unit 7

1

1 cancel 2 delayed
3 guarantee 4 colonial
5 essential 6 facilities
7 indicate 8 leak
9 orientation 10 Refreshments
11 terrific

2

1 fireworks 2 apologize
3 spa 4 inconvenience
5 refurbishment 6 terrace
7 coach 8 complex
9 disposal 10 session

Unit 8

1

1 fit 2 appears
3 report 4 emotional state
5 Coworkers 6 fashionable
7 Characters

2

1 true 2 false 3 true
4 true 5 false 6 false
7 false 8 true

Unit 9

1

Across
1 model 2 argument 3 facility
4 device 5 additional
Down
1 education 2 exercise
3 signal 4 community
5 improve

2

1 hesitation 2 opposing
3 restate 4 activity
5 alternative 6 regular
7 research 8 skills 9 stylish
10 conclusion 11 physical
12 popular

Unit 10

1

1 C 2 B 3 C 4 D 5 A
6 A 7 B 8 D 9 D 10 B

2

1 performance
2 Acknowledge 3 limousine
4 vendor 5 Plenary
6 summarize 7 confirm
8 maintain 9 Prior
10 sample 11 agenda

Unit 11

1

1 emergency 2 client
3 charge 4 grant
5 imagination 6 request
7 complaint 8 recognize
9 confirm 10 operator

2

1 immediately 2 appreciate
3 translator 4 possibilities
5 custom 6 day care center
7 requestor 8 desperate
9 Yellow Pages
10 consideration

3

1 bother 2 contractor
3 spare 4 reasonably
5 suitable

Unit 12

1

1 false 2 true 3 true
4 false 5 false 6 true
7 true 8 false 9 false
10 true 11 true 12 true

Unit 13

1

1 C 2 D 3 B 4 C
5 A 6 D

2

1 dessert 2 neat
3 combination 4 uniform
5 relate 6 technique

Unit 14

1

1 melt 2 relationship
3 independent 4 stretch
5 accounting 6 attract
7 reduce

2

1 combine 2 indicate
3 separate 4 obvious
5 affect 6 approximate

Unit 15

1

1 catalog 2 superintendent
3 respond 4 salutation
5 appreciate 6 opportunity

2

1 facility 2 representative
3 convenient 4 postpone
5 human resources
6 formality 7 regarding

Unit 16

1

Across
1 benefits 2 express train
3 draft 4 current
5 population
Down
1 introduction 2 shift
3 advantage 4 conclusion
5 leisure time

2

1 false 2 true 3 true
4 false 5 true 6 true
7 false

Unit 17

1

1 sunburn 2 destination
3 degree 4 intensifier
5 sunscreen 6 relate to
7 intend 8 origin
9 relevant 10 cab
11 contrasting 12 alternative

Unit 18

1

1 lifejackets 2 ladder
3 conditional 4 contrast
5 electricity 6 modern
7 indicate

Unit 19

1

1 analyst 2 overtime
3 tone 4 retirement
5 inquiry 6 indicate
7 deadline 8 opinion
9 contract 10 expense

2

1 explanation 2 clerical
3 coverage 4 deserve
5 organize 6 subsequent
7 renew

3

1 position 2 refer 3 terrific
4 plumbing 5 solution

Unit 20

1

1 B 2 B 3 B 4 D 5 A
6 C

2

1 true 2 false 3 true
4 false 5 false 6 false
7 true 8 true 9 false

General Glossary of Terms

Terms used in instructions

brainstorm (v)	To think of many ideas on a topic quickly and creatively
focus (n)	The main or most important thing or things
key words (n)	The most important words in terms of meaning, usually nouns, verbs, adjectives and adverbs
related (adj)	Connected in some way to an idea
scan (v)	To read quickly in order to pick out specific information (e.g. looking for a name in a phone book)
similar (adj)	Having some things in common but not completely identical (e.g. African elephants are very similar to Indian elephants)
skim (v)	To read quickly in order to get a general idea of the contents (e.g. quickly going over a movie review to see if it is worth watching)
tactic (n)	A method or technique used to achieve an immediate goal. The Test tactics in this book will help you to answer the questions more effectively and efficiently.
well-formed (adj)	Following the rules of grammar and to a high standard

Grammar terms

adjective (adj)	A word that describes a noun or pronoun (e.g. *big*, *happy*), or gives extra information about them
adverb (adv)	A word that adds more information about place, time, manner, cause, or degree to a verb, an adjective, a phrase or another adverb (e.g. *look carefully, incredibly fast*)
clause	A group of words that contains a subject and a verb and expresses an idea
conditional sentence	A sentence made of two clauses. One is called the "*if* clause" (e.g. *If it starts raining ...*) and the other is called the "result clause" (e.g. *... we will get wet.*) It can have a variety of verb tenses with real (e.g. *If I drop the glass, it will break.*) or hypothetical meanings (e.g. *If I hadn't been born in Canada, I might not speak English.*)
coordinating conjunction	A word used to join two clauses of equal weight (e.g. *and*, *but*, *or*)
indefinite pronoun	A pronoun that doesn't refer to any specific person or thing (e.g. *something, anything*)
intensifier / diminisher	A word used to make the meaning of another word stronger (e.g. *very, extremely, absolutely*) or weaker (e.g. *slightly, a little*)

modal	A grammatical word that is a type of auxiliary verb used to express possibility, intention, obligation and necessity (e.g. *can, could, would, might,* etc)
noun (n)	A word which is used as the name of a person, place or thing (e.g. *John, Canada, pencil*)
object (o)	A grammatical word describing the noun or noun phrase that is being acted upon or affected by the verb in a sentence (e.g. *Cats eat fish* – "fish" is the object)
object pronoun	A word that takes the place of an object noun (e.g. *him, us*)
preposition (prep)	A word which is used to indicate position, or movement in time or space (e.g. *The ball is in the box, It finishes at 9:00, He is going into the store.*)
pronoun (pron)	A word that takes the place of a noun (e.g. *I, you, it*)
subject (s)	A grammatical word describing the noun or noun phrase that performs the action in a sentence (e.g. *Cats eat fish* – "Cats" is the subject). Or in a passive sentence, the noun that is affected by the action of the verb (e.g. *The tree was blown over by the strong wind.*)
subject pronoun	A word that takes the place of a subject noun (e.g. *he, they*)
subordinating conjunctions	A word used to join clauses where one is more important and cannot exist by itself , (e.g. *because, although, when*) (For a more complete list, see page 260)
verb (v)	A word that is used to show an action, or state (e.g. *run, is*)

Phonology

intonation	A rise and fall in sound pitch that carries meaning, e.g. "*It is a dog*", if said with a falling intonation at the end, (↘) it is a statement. If said with a rising intonation (↗) at the end, it is a question.
sentence stress	The emphasis on individual words in a sentence or phrase. In general, only functions words (nouns, verbs, adjectives, adverbs) are stressed. Stressing words can also alter the meaning, e.g. "*She ordered the **fish**"* suggests the woman didn't receive the fish, whereas "***She** ordered the fish*" suggests another person received the woman's fish.
thought groups	The shorter chunk of a complex sentence that contains a separate idea.
word stress	The emphasis on individual syllables in a word (e.g. ré·cord makes the word a noun, recórd makes it a verb)

Useful Language

Language for describing schedules and agendas

Most useful in:

- Speaking Q7–9: Respond to questions using information provided

Time markers	Extra information markers	Choice markers
after (dinner, arriving ...) and then ... then, after that ... at 7:30 ... finally ...	... and ... (there is) also ... ... and also ... in addition ...	You have two choices/options ... You can choose (either X or Y) Also, at the same time, there is ... You have to choose one of these ...

Subordinating conjunctions

Most useful in:

- Writing Q4–5: Write a sentence based on a picture (difficult level)

Questions 4–5 may include one of these words, along with a function word.

Time (When?)	Location (Where?)	Cause + effect (Why?)	Conditional (Under what condition?)	Exemplification (Like what?)	Opposition/ Contrast
until after before when while since by the time as soon as whenever as long as	wherever where	because now that so (that) in order that/to as so (X) that such (an X) that ... in as much as	if unless provided (that) as/so long as even if in case only if whether (or not) providing that	as if like as though	even though although though whereas in spite of the (fact that) while where as much as

Phrases to introduce agenda responses

Most useful in:

- Speaking Q7–9: Responding to questions using information provided

Used when:

- Answering questions, especially over the phone

> **Let me see now** ... . It starts at 7:30 p.m. and finishes at 10:00 p.m.
> **Let me just check the agenda** ... . The event is taking place at the National Theater.
> **Looking at the agenda, it shows** the meeting starts at 12:00 p.m.
> **I'm really sorry, but I'm afraid** you'll have to get from the station to the hotel on your own.
> **I'm sorry, but** we won't be voting on the proposal as planned, as it isn't ready yet.

Dealing with complaints and requests

Most useful in:
- Speaking Q 10: Propose a solution
- Writing Q 6–7: Respond to a written request

Used when:
- Making or responding to complaints/requests or explaining situations

Complaints

Phrases for apologies

less formal	I'm/We're sorry about .... I'm really/very sorry for...
more formal	I/We'd like to apologize for (the mistake with) ... Please accept my/our apologies for this ...

Explanations of the problem

> **It seems there was some kind of problem with** our computer records so ...
> **I believe there was some confusion over** the tools your team ordered ...
> **I'm afraid that** the wrong delivery date was put on your order which ...
> **There appears to have been a problem at** the factory ...

Offering a solution

> **We're going to arrange for someone to** (fix the problem this afternoon).
> **We'd like to send** (the missing parts) **by courier to** (your office this evening).
> **I'd like to offer you a** (new one/a replacement this week).
> **We have** (fixed the problem/replaced the system, etc) **now, so this problem will never happen again.**
> **Because this is our mistake, we would like to** (offer you a 20% discount/something free, etc.).

Requests

Explaining complications in granting requests

> **I'm afraid that** (doing X) **by** (tomorrow) is ...
> **I'm afraid the** (Wednesday class is fully booked), **so ...**
> **... however, I'm afraid** (all of our rooms are ...)
> **As it says in the** (ad/brochure, etc) **we aren't** (open on Sundays) ...
> **As you can see from the notice** (I don't work on Saturdays) ...

Explaining possible solutions

> **On the other hand, we do also offer** an individual lesson schedule which ...
> **The only thing I can suggest is** I could spare you about a half an hour from ...
> **... but what I can do is** contact one of our other suppliers who might be able to get you the material. Then you get it made up yourself.
> **However, if you could** come by our office, then I could arrange for you ...
> **However, as this is an emergency, if you can** bring your cat in now ...
> **... but I'll tell you what, if you** (come in) we may be able to arrange ...

Making polite requests

> Please send …
> Could you tell me …
> Would it be possible to …
> I was wondering if it would be possible to …
> I would appreciate it if you could …
> Would you mind …

Starting and ending a letter or e-mail – Salutations

Most useful in:

• Writing Q 6–7: Respond to a written request

Used when:

• Beginning / ending a letter or e-mail

Opening salutation	Audience
Dear David / Mary, Dear Mr. Abbott / Ms. Jones, To whom it may concern, Dear Sir / Madam,	To a person you know well (*casual*) When you don't know the person very well (*formal*) When you don't know the name of the person (*formal*)
Closing salutation	**Audience**
Talk to you later! All the best, Sincerely,	To a friend or some one you talk to often (*very casual*) To a person you know well (*casual*) When you don't know the person very well (*formal*)

Giving opinions

Most useful in:

• Speaking Q11: Express an opinion
• Writing Q8: Write an opinion essay

Used when:

• Stating and organizing and supporting opinions

I (strongly / firmly) believe … I'm completely in favor of …	Positive opinion (strong)
It's a difficult choice, but I think I would prefer to … If I had to choose, I would pick / say … In my opinion … I would prefer to …	Positive opinion (neutral or weak)
I'm totally opposed to … I really don't agree with …	Negative opinion

Language for giving reasons and examples

We could save money by reducing costs. **For example** …	Used as a simple and common way to introduce an example.
Spending money on research can have a great impact. **One clear example of this is** …	Used for providing a single and easily understood and certain example.
One example of the problems we faced was high materials cost. **Another example was** …	Used to provide another example of something.
There are several disadvantages to working in a big city. **Some examples include** …	Used to introduce a list of example points to support your idea.
I think the most important factor is practical experience. **By this I mean** …	Used to clarify an example you have given.

Phrases for organizing ideas

First of all … My first point is …	To note your first supporting point
The reason I say this is that … … because … One reason for this is … Another reason is …	To give reasons supporting an opinion
Another thing … Also … Another point is … In addition … I also think that …	To add additional supporting sentences
On the other hand … However … Although … Whereas …	To introduce an opposing point
Overall … In spite of that … … though … In conclusion …	To signal your conclusion after you have stated an opposing point

Explaining, describing, giving information

I am pleased to let you know that as from next week we will have new equipment.	Giving information
The main reason why I am transferring my membership **is because of** the price change.	Giving an explanation
The problem is that we haven't received any of the last six deliveries on time	Describing a problem
I think the best way to solve the problem is by discussing the situation with all concerned.	Explaining a solution

OXFORD
UNIVERSITY PRESS

Great Clarendon Street, Oxford OX2 6DP

Oxford University Press is a department of the University of Oxford.
It furthers the University's objective of excellence in research, scholarship,
and education by publishing worldwide in

Oxford New York

Auckland Cape Town Dar es Salaam Hong Kong Karachi
Kuala Lumpur Madrid Melbourne Mexico City Nairobi
New Delhi Shanghai Taipei Toronto

With offices in

Argentina Austria Brazil Chile Czech Republic France Greece
Guatemala Hungary Italy Japan Poland Portugal Singapore
South Korea Switzerland Thailand Turkey Ukraine Vietnam

OXFORD and OXFORD ENGLISH are registered trade marks of
Oxford University Press in the UK and in certain other countries

ISBN: 978 0 19 452950 1
ISBN: 978 0 19 452952 5 PACK

Printed in China

This book is printed on paper from certified and well-managed sources.

ACKNOWLEDGEMENTS

Alamy pp52br (Chad Ehlers), 52t (Nic Cleave Photography), 95 (Iain
Masterton); Corbis UK Ltd. pp1l, 49t (Paul Barton), 96bl (Claudia Kunin),
96br, 96tr (Setboun), 198br (Paul Barton), 198cr, 198tr (David H. Wells), 205c;
Getty Images pp97tl (Saeed Khan/AFP), 197br (Yoshikazu Tsuno/AFP); Grant
Trew p198 (glass on table); OUP pp47 (woman painting with dog/Photodisc),
47 (teen boys on the porch/Photodisc), 47 (couple looking at
salad/Photodisc), 47 (women buying vegetables at vegetable
market/Photodisc), 49 (looking at plans/Photodisc), 50 (teenagers in a café),
50 (hailing a taxi/Stockbyte), 50 (kitchen in restaurant/Photodisc), 50
(helping customer with tie/Photodisc), 51 (Eiffel Tower, Paris,
France/Imagesource), 51 (meeting in hotel room/Photodisc), 52 (trying on
athletic shoes/Photodisc), 52 (carnival barbecue/Photodisc), 52 (produce
worker and customer/Photodisc), 93 (family planning the route/Photodisc),
93 (women cooking thanksgiving gravy/Photodisc), 93 (doctor reading a
medical chart/Photodisc), 93 (children playing a drawing game/Photodisc),
96 (businesswoman giving a presentation/Photodisc), 97 (couple in bakery
section/Photodisc), 97 (kids feeding chickens/Photodisc), 97 (business people
at a computer/Photodisc), 162 (man on telephone/Photodisc), 162 (making
desserts at culinary school/Photodisc), 164 (newsstand in Italy/Photodisc),
164 (line for fast food/Photodisc), 165 (woman reading/Photodisc), 166 (man
harvesting limes/Photodisc), 166 (shaking hands/Stockbyte), 167 (restaurant
tables/Photodisc), 167 (woman smelling roses/Photodisc), 167 (city square in
Bulgaria/Photodisc), 174 (business presentation/Image 100), 174
(cafe/Photodisc), 174 (men repairing furniture/Photodisc), 175
(businesswoman entering taxi/Photodisc), 175 (girl winning prize/Photodisc),
175 (man and woman with trolley/Stockbyte), 175 (florist/Photodisc), 175
(drawing with granddad/Photodisc), 196 (boy reaching for cookies on
counter/Photodisc), 196 (heavy traffic/Digital Vision), 197 (Tokyo by
night/Photodisc), 197 (person cooking sukiyaki/Photodisc), 198 (people in
airport/Photodisc), 198 (train station/Photodisc), 198 (friends at coffee
shop/Photodisc), 199 (mother teaching daughter to read/Photodisc), 199
(garden vegetables/Photodisc), 204 (businessman coming home from
work/Photodisc), 204 (woman with shopping/Photodisc), 204 (pointing to
salmon/Photodisc), 204 (checking sticker price/Photodisc), 205 (piano
teacher/Photodisc), 205 (driving in the rain/Photodisc), 205
(electrician/Photodisc), 205 (uncertain businessman/Photodisc), 206
(architecture/Photodisc), 206 (French restaurant/Photodisc; Photolibrary
Group pp1r (Banana Stock), 49br (Index Stock Imagery).

Cover: left: Corbis UK Ltd. right: Banana Stock/Photolibrary Group

All remaining images courtesy of ETS